# HOCKEY'S
## GREATEST TEAMS

TEAMS, PLAYERS, AND PLAYS THAT CHANGED THE GAME

PENGUIN
STUDIO

AN
OTHERWISE INC.
EDITION

*Hockey's Greatest Teams* was produced by Otherwise Inc. Editions

**Editorial direction and art direction** Sara Borins
**Design and Typesetting** 52 Pick-up Inc., Toronto
**Editors** Karen Alliston, Rick Archbold
**Assistant editor** Tom Berkhout
**Editorial assistance** Sarah Webster

Otherwise Inc. Editions offers special thanks to Bruce Bennett, Derek Berkhout, Cynthia Good, Kevin Hanson, Bruce Jessop, Jackie Kaiser, Susan McIntee, Nick Monteleone, Phil Norton, Ian Rapsey, Michael Schellenberg

**PENGUIN STUDIO**
**Published by the Penguin Group**
Penguin Books Canada Ltd, 10 Alcorn Avenue, Toronto, Ontario, Canada M4V 3B2
Penguin Books Ltd, 27 Wrights Lane, London W8 5TZ, England
Penguin Putnam Inc., 375 Hudson Street, New York, New York 10014, U.S.A.
Penguin Books Australia Ltd, Ringwood, Victoria, Australia
Penguin Books (NZ) Ltd, cnr Rosedale and Airborne Roads, Albany, Auckland 1310, New Zealand

Penguin Books Ltd, Registered Offices: Harmondsworth, Middlesex, England

First published 2000

10 9 8 7 6 5 4 3 2 1

Printed and bound in Canada on acid free paper

**Canadian Cataloguing in Publication Data**
Podnieks, Andrew
Hockey's greatest teams
ISBN 0-670-89309-9

1. Hockey teams – Canada – History. 2. Hockey teams – United States – History.
I. Title.

GV848.4.C3P64 2000          796.962'0971          C00-931054-1

Visit Penguin Canada's web site at **www.penguin.ca**

**Produced by**
Otherwise Inc. Editions
356A Queen Street West
Toronto ON M5V 2A2

# TABLE OF CONTENTS

# HOCKEY'S GREATEST TEAMS

# INTRODUCTION

TEAMS, PLAYERS, AND PLAYS THAT CHANGED THE GAME

Most readers will open this book with challenge in mind. "Hockey's greatest teams, eh? We'll see about that." Many will examine the Contents page before they strike off into the book's interior: "Is the author nuts?" they will surely ask. "He didn't include a chapter on the New York Islanders that won four Stanley Cups in the early 1980s, but he did include one on the Edmonton Mercurys? Nothing on the Americans' 1980 Miracle on Ice team or the vaunted Soviets of the late 1960s or late 1970s but chapters on the Preston Rivulettes and the Toronto Granites?"

**Many of these teams did more than just win; they changed the way the game was played on ice and how it was perceived off it. Some also influenced the way we put the game into a social context, and their accomplishments have endured to this day.**

By its very nature, any list of the greatest this or the top 10 that is confrontational. That's part of the purpose of this book – to stir debate. But controversy is not the motivating force behind the work. Foremost is the simple fact that no such chronicle exists. Many a hockey tome has celebrated one particular team, usually soon after some memorable accomplishment. There have been books on NHL dynasties and on famous players, and compilations of famous moments, but no book has considered the greatest teams, amateur and pro, NHL and international, past and present, all under one title.

Selecting the 15 greatest teams has not been an arbitrary process. Because great teams have existed outside the professional NHL, some great pro teams were necessarily eliminated. If there were room to discuss 30 great teams, the 1983 New York Islanders would be found in these pages, likely the Pittsburgh Penguins of the early 1990s, and Eddie Shore's Boston Bruins of the 1930s, and many others. Nonetheless, the 15 teams included in this book collectively represent hockey's finest and shed much light on the history of the game.

By the late 1880s something resembling the modern game of hockey was being played, although organized competition was still rare. When the Right Honourable Sir Frederick Arthur Stanley, Canada's then governor general, witnessed his first hockey game at the Montreal Winter Carnival in February of 1888, only Montreal and Ottawa could boast anything resembling leagues and teams playing a fixed schedule with consistent rules in front of paying fans. By 1893, when Lord Stanley donated his now-famous Cup, he was able to write, "I have

The Montreal AAA won the first Stanley Cup in 1893, defeating Victoria in the deciding game *(AN ADVERTISEMENT FOR THE GAME IS PICTURED ABOVE)*. An avid outdoorsman, Lord Stanley *(OPPOSITE)* did not confine his Canadian interests to hockey.

for some time been thinking it would be a good idea if there were a challenge cup which could be held from year to year by the leading hockey team in Canada…. Considering the interest that hockey matches now elicit and the importance of having games fairly played under generally recognized rules, I am willing to give a cup that shall be annually held by the winning club." The first challenge cup was won by the amateur Montreal AAA in 1893. It continued as a challenge cup until 1914, and was first won by a National Hockey League team in 1918, the first year of NHL play. In 1927, it became a trophy only NHL teams could win. Thus by the 1920s, when the first team profiled in this book came to the fore, the Stanley Cup was a strictly professional trophy, but amateur hockey was often as good or better than professional play.

Although I haven't adopted a decade-by-decade approach, each decade from the 1920s on is, by coincidence, represented by at least one team. Often, a great team defined its era of play. In every case, it won at the highest level – the Stanley Cup, Olympic gold, or, as is the case with the only women's team in the book, the Lady Bessborough Cup. But many of these teams did more than just win; they changed the way the game was played on ice and how it was perceived off it. Some also influenced the way we put the game into a social context, and their accomplishments have endured to this day. So, the Oilers of 1988, for instance, took precedence over the Islanders of 1983 because that Edmonton team irrefutably defined hockey for its era. The Islanders didn't.

Goals and assists and trophies are important, but greatness can't be measured in statistics alone. Take, for example, the Preston Rivulettes, the most important women's team of the 1930s. Little is known about the team today, save the

remarkable abilities of its star player, Hilda Ranscombe. But because her career flourished many decades ago in an unsophisticated league, even she has been rejected as a candidate for entry into the Hockey Hall of Fame, though she was in many ways the Wayne Gretzky of her day. For the modern fan, it's far easier to accept Hayley Wickenheiser or Cammi Granato as the Great One of women's hockey, but the very existence of a women's team in the 1930s – let alone one as powerful as the Rivs – had enormous social relevance. And, without Ranscombe, the modern women's game might never have evolved as it did. A forgotten team? Yes. One of the greatest? Absolutely.

On ice, a great team had to prove itself to be absolutely the best. Such a criterion may seem understood, but it automatically eliminates a number of almost-great teams. Those dreaded, beautiful Soviets of the late '60s and early '70s, for instance, fall just short of true greatness. An almost unbeatable team in international competition, they won gold at the World Championships every year from 1963 to 1975 with one exception, a loss to the Czechs in 1972. But when CCCP faced the best in the world – at the Summit Series of September 1972 – and led Team Canada 3-1-1 with three games to play and all of them in Moscow, the Soviets lost three in a row. Great players on that team? Without question. Great team? One can't be so certain.

How, then, can I eliminate those mighty Soviets when I've included the fleeting success story that was the 1952 Edmonton Mercurys? Wouldn't Tretiak and Kharlamov and the rest of the team have demolished Billy Dawe and the Mercs? To resort to such cross-era comparisons is to miss the point. Would the Team Canada that won the 1972 Summit Series have been able to keep up with the Team Canada that won the 1987 Canada Cup? Wayne Gretzky, Mario Lemieux, Paul Coffey, Dale Hawerchuk, the greatest skaters of all time in their prime with Grant Fuhr in goal? I'd say Esposito, Clarke, and Henderson would have more than met their match. The important truth is that no amateur team could beat the Mercs in the early '50s, just as no women's team could beat the Rivs in the '30s, and almost no one could so much as score a goal on the Toronto Granites in 1924. Those Granites were so superior to the teams they played that some critics might want them eliminated because they suffered from lack of competition. After all, how can we possibly comprehend or rate Harry Watson's 13 goals in one game? The same way we can now look back more recently and try to put into perspective Wayne Gretzky's 92 goals and 215 points in one season – with awe, admiration, and wonder.

Some of the near-great teams are considered in the pages that follow. The Blackhawks of the 1960s, for instance, that looked so great on paper and in the regular season, year after year lost to the Leafs or Habs or the Red Wings. One of the more talented teams in NHL history? Definitely. But for all their talent, they have just one Stanley Cup to show. Not good enough. Why no NHL teams before the 1948 Leafs? Two companion reasons. For one, no great pro dynasty emerged prior to those Leafs, with the possible exception of the Ottawa Silver Seven, holders of the Stanley Cup from 1903 to 1906. For another, this lack of dynastic success indicates, I think, how great amateur hockey was during the NHL's early years. Over the course of the 20th century, as the NHL increased in quality, size, scope, and popularity, the serious amateur ranks have gone in the other direction. The Allan Cup, once as important as the Stanley Cup – no joke! – is now all but forgotten, and Olympic gold meant progressively little until NHLers began participating.

Each of the teams in this book also has a certain something, a team chemistry, a unique and intangible element that goes beyond wins and losses. The Toronto Granites evolved out of a posh curling and social club in post-World War I Toronto; the 1948 Leafs, created by Conn Smythe and made a national symbol by the radio voice of Foster Hewitt, became an indelible piece of the Canadian fabric; the Red Wings of the early 1950s invented the angled shoot-in and changed the game forever; the Habs of the late '50s were, simply, unbeatable; the Leafs' Over-the-Hill Gang won the 1967 Cup with a group of players every other team thought was well beyond their prime; Bobby Orr's flying Cup-winning goal in the 1970 finals symbolized a team and a hockey legend; the Canadiens of the late 1970s not only won four Cups but then almost to a man pursued careers in the coaching and managerial ranks of the modern NHL; the 1988 Edmonton Oilers scored and skated with unheard-of ease; Team USA's World Cup victory confirmed the arrival of a new hockey power; and the Red Wings of the 1990s were the first in history to deliberately build a team with European content into an unbeatable force.

Sometimes great teams win when they aren't supposed to. Other times they win despite expectations, an often equally tough accomplishment. In all, the stories of these 15 teams tell the modern history of hockey. They narrate the development of plays, spotlight the careers of many of the game's greatest players, chronicle the shift in dominance from amateur to pro, from international to NHL, from Canada to the world.

This book's Table of Contents shouldn't be too offputting. The stories that follow should convince the reader of the impact of each team and its contribution to hockey's history. When Lord Stanley introduced the Stanley Cup in 1893 he began the process that led to the formation of leagues and schedules and formal competitions so that players could make a living at their sport and compete for a prize emblematic of supremacy. Hockey is the fastest sport in the world. It is the only contact sport played in an enclosed area, and the most demanding. These 15 teams show clearly why it is also the most entertaining and compelling of sports.

# CHAPTER 1

# THE FIRST GREAT AMATEURS

1924 TORONTO GRANITES

No group of players ever dominated an era more than the 1924 Toronto Granites, a team comprised almost entirely of veterans of the Great War living in Toronto. All were members of the "Church Street Curling Team," as sportswriters dubbed the Granite Club, the upscale social and curling club located just north of Wellesley Street in what was then the city's midtown. The Granite Club was a meeting place for many of Toronto's leading citizens and home to some of the country's finest curlers and hockey players. From the time the Granites hockey team began competing in 1919 – in the senior Ontario Hockey Association (OHA) – to the time they disbanded – after the 1924 Olympics – they were all but unbeatable. Although they could not play professional teams without compromising their amateur status, many of the players were regarded as the best outside the professional NHL, which had been founded in 1917. So overpowering was their premier player, Harry Watson, that he could single-handedly win many games. Twice the Granites won the Allan Cup, symbol of Canadian amateur hockey supremacy. And, because Olympic participation was limited strictly to amateur athletes, the Granites were given the right to represent Canada at the first-ever Olympic Winter Games. They were hockey's first truly great international team.

THE GRANITE CLUB HAD NOT COMPETED IN HOCKEY SINCE 1896, but with men returning from war in great numbers, interest in re-establishing a team grew. In 1919, a number of the servicemen returning to civilian life who gravitated toward the club decided to form the Granites. Among the original players were three men who would become the most dominant line in amateur hockey: left-winger Harry "Moose" Watson, right-winger Bert McCaffery, and centre Hooley Smith. All three had taken their hockey seriously before the war, and all three were excellent bets to turn professional if and when they so desired, above all Watson, who had earned his nickname because of his size and skill. They alone could carry the Toronto Granites to victory most nights.

The Granites entered the Ontario Hockey Association in 1919 and won the OHA Senior championship the following spring. The 1920 Allan Cup was won by the Winnipeg Falcons, and it was that team that represented Canada at the 1920 Summer Olympics in Antwerp, Belgium, where hockey made its first Olympic appearance as a demonstration sport. The Falcons easily won the gold medal, outscoring their opponents by a combined 29-1 in three games. But by the time the first official Olympic Winter Games were in the offing, scheduled for February 1924, the Granites were the logical choice to represent Canada, having won two more OHA championships and two straight Allan Cups. In the 1922 finals they overpowered the western Canadian champion Regina Victorias, 6-2 and 7-0, in a two-game total-goals series played at the sold-out Arena Gardens in Toronto, home of the Toronto St. Pats (precursors of the Maple Leafs). The next spring the Granites annihilated the University of Saskatchewan by scores of 6-1 and 5-1, ensuring their selection as Canada's representatives for the Olympics to be held in Chamonix, France.

The core of the team that would go to Chamonix had been playing together for much of the last five years. However, three of the Granites' best-known players – Alex Romeril, Hugh Fox, and Eddie Rodden – did not make the trip. Such was the strength of amateur play in the country that two equally talented substitutes – Harold McMunn, from the Winnipeg Falcon Hockey Club of Manitoba, and Cyril "Sig" Slater from the Victorias Hockey Club of Montreal – were easily found. Once the final roster had been established in late 1923, the Granites played a series of exhibition games in southern Ontario as preparation for the Olympic tournament, all against non-professional teams. The Olympic eligibility code was so strict that for the Granites to have faced an opponent with even one man in its lineup who had played even one game professionally would have tainted the entire team's amateur status. The Granites won every game they played.

By the time the Granites left Toronto on January 6, 1924, they were a well-trained, fully prepared team. The two new forwards, McMunn and Slater, had worked in nicely. On January 11, when they boarded the SS *Montcalm* in Saint John, New Brunswick, they had been joined by Canadian champion figure skaters Melville Rogers and Miss Cecil Eustace Smith, who were entered in both singles and pairs competition, and

**The Granite Club had not competed in hockey since 1896, but with men returning from war in great numbers, interest in re-establishing a team grew. In 1919, a number of the servicemen returning to civilian life who gravitated toward the club decided to form the Granites.**

Charles Gorman, national speed skating champion, who was to race in the men's 500 metres. Canada's small Olympic team was now complete.

The week-long voyage to Liverpool, England, affected many an appetite but not the players' sense of humour. Harry Watson's diary-like dispatches to the *Toronto Telegram* revealed that "Hooley Smith had bet me $10 that he wouldn't be sea-sick, but about 11 p.m. was counted out by referee P.J. Mulqueen. Breakfast … was a very sad affair, as Jack Cameron, Ramsay, Rankin and myself were the only members to appear. This was the day of Dunc Munro's famous quotation: 'Why the – don't they hold the games at Oakville?' He was afraid he was going to die; the next day he was afraid he wasn't going to die." Watson was but one of the team's entourage, including secretary P.J. Mulqueen and coach Frank Rankin, to write newspaper reports of the team's progress.

During the voyage the players nonetheless combined fun with intense training. Team manager and Canadian Amateur Hockey Association (CAHA) registrar William Hewitt oversaw a shuffleboard competition, won by the pairing of Miss Edna Mulqueen (the referee's daughter) and Watson. A tennis tournament was captured by goalie Jack Cameron and Maude Smith (Miss Cecil Smith's sister). But Granites coach Frank Rankin worked the team hard with an intense dry-land training regimen: throwing a medicine ball, skipping rope, and jogging around the deck.

When the SS *Montcalm* docked at Liverpool, the Granites got their first taste of international celebrity when they were besieged by photographers from the *Daily Mail*. After stopping briefly in London the players travelled by train and boat to Paris, where they enjoyed a night of adult entertainment at the Folies Bergères. "A wonderful time was had by all," Watson wrote before adding as a small qualifier, "the best parts of which I will withhold until I hear from the censor." Finally, 11 days after leaving Toronto, the weary Canadians arrived in Chamonix, a village "about 5,000 feet above sea level, but set down in a beautiful valley surrounded by towering mountains which reach into the clouds," in the words of team manager Hewitt. The most spectacular peak was that of Mont Blanc, some 16,400 feet high.

*(LEFT)* A telegram from Moose Watson, notifying friends back home of the Granites' gold medal. *(OPPOSITE ABOVE)* The 1924 Toronto Granites: *(TOP ROW, LEFT TO RIGHT)* Harold McMunn, Bert McCaffery, Hooley Smith, Beattie Ramsay, Ernie Collett, Sig Slater, Jack Cameron; *(BOTTOM ROW, LEFT TO RIGHT)* Pete Campbell (trainer), Harry Watson, William Hewitt (manager), Dunc Munro (captain), Frank Rankin (coach). *(OPPOSITE BELOW, FROM LEFT TO RIGHT)* Four images of the Great War in which most of the Granites fought: a young flyer named Lester Pearson; flying ace Billy Bishop; battlefield ablutions performed by an unnamed soldier; a cockpit serves as a makeshift pulpit.

The Granites had six days to prepare for their first game of the Olympics, but the weather conditions made practice impossible. Either the sun was so warm that it almost melted the ice, or the rains were so heavy that skating couldn't be considered. On one occasion when the ice was suitable, the team made an attempt to skate but was quickly whisked off the rink by officials after complaints from the Norwegians, Swedes, Czechs, and Finns, all of whom claimed that Canada had not scheduled the practice. In order to stay in shape, the Granites spent several hours each day mountain-climbing. During their evening leisure hours the players supported the casino, but only until 10 p.m., the hour of coach Rankin's lights-out curfew. In the end, the Canadians didn't have a single practice to familiarize themselves with the rink.

## THE GAMES BEGIN

At the opening ceremonies on January 25, 1924, goalie Ernie Collett was the flag-bearer for Canada's 12-member Olympic team – nine hockey players, two figure skaters, and one speed skater. Three days later the preliminary round robin began for the eight competing nations (Britain, France, Sweden, Belgium, Switzerland, and Czechoslovakia), an utterly superfluous formality in determining the two best teams in the competition.

The games were played at the Stade Olympique du Mont Blanc, an outdoor, natural rink contained within the speed-skating oval. The rink measured 230 feet long and 105 feet wide, and dwarfed even the modern European rink of 210 by 100 feet. Its size was alien to the Canadians, who were used to the smaller confines of NHL rinks (200 by 85 feet), which created a faster and more physical game.

The rinkside boards were only about six inches high, preventing the Canadians from using them with their accustomed skill, particularly for hitting, passing, and balance. Netting was put up above the boards behind both goals, but after a missed shot, pucks routinely sailed over the netting and down the length of the speed-skating oval. As a result,

the Olympic committee placed volunteers around the rink to chase down pucks that went out of play.

The inconstant ice conditions caused the organizing committee to relocate the boards almost daily to ensure that the best possible patch of ice within the speed-skating oval was being used. Frequently, games started in bright afternoon daylight and finished in virtual darkness. Although the rink was illuminated by electric lights, they were so far from the hockey-playing area that the players often had trouble seeing the puck by game's end. The standard-size goal nets, installed using wood pegs and nails, regularly collapsed when a goalie leaned on them.

All games consisted of three 15-minute periods, except for the gold medal final which was an NHL-regulation 60 minutes. As had happened in Antwerp in 1920, William Hewitt brought a plentiful supply of Canadian pucks, and these, like the CAHA rules of play, became standard for the tournament and all future international competitions.

The Canadians did not allow a single goal during the round robin, winning by the extraordinary scores of 30-0, 22-0, and 33-0 over the Czechs, Swedes, and Swiss. The next best team, the Americans, routed their European opponents by 19-0, 22-0, and 11-0. In the semi-finals both North American teams again crushed their European opponents, setting up a predictable Canada-U.S. gold medal game two days later.

Indicative of the one-sided action leading up to the finals was this Canadian Press account of play during the Canada-Czechoslovakia match: "Hooley Smith stole the puck, and, dashing through the opponents' team, scored. Soon afterward Harry Watson added another goal by a magnificent long shot, and Smith again scored in a few seconds." And so it went, goal after goal scored with the greatest of ease. Of the Granites' 110 total goals scored in Chamonix, Harry Watson accounted for 36, including 11 against Czechoslovakia and 13 against Switzerland, records that will surely never be equalled. His size, stickhandling, and blazing shot were a wonder to all who watched him play, and the team's impenetrable defence made scoring a virtual impossibility.

Such was the strength of the Canadian team that goalers Jack Cameron and Ernie Collett were often idle from start to finish, seldom having to face a single shot. Legend has it that Cameron frequently skated to the low boards to chat up the young ladies who were in attendance, all of them awed by the Granites' superiority. To convey the team's extraordinary dominance, the renowned cartoonist A. Lerso of *Paris-Matin* sketched Cameron reading a copy of the *Montreal Gazette* while playing goal. Cameron played down his game-time socializing, but did offer one pleasant anecdote: "The only girl I remember," he recalled, "was a little blonde 11-year-old figure skater on the Norwegian team. When she wasn't competing, she sat on our bench. Her name was Sonja Henie and she was a great booster of the Granites." Henie finished dead last in competition that year, but at the 1928 Olympics in St. Moritz, Switzerland, she would dazzle the world with her performance, then go on to become both a professional skater and a wildly popular movie star.

## THE GOLD MEDAL GAME

Even before the puck was faced off to begin the gold medal game on February 3, there was animosity between the Canadians and Americans. The previous day, both William Hewitt and W.S. Haddock, managers of the Canadian and American teams respectively, rejected the official proposal for selecting the referee. (Remarkably, participating players also served as referees for all matches throughout these Olympics.) They argued that drawing from a hat containing only the names of officials from each of the Continental countries in the competition would likely leave the game in the hands of an inexperienced man. In the end, Hewitt proposed Paul Loicq of Belgium and Haddock selected Lacroix of France. Hewitt objected that perhaps this Frenchman Lacroix was in some way related to the American goalie of the same last name, but was overruled. A coin toss settled the question – Canadian heads prevailing over American tails – and Loicq was named the official.

Just before the start of play, the Americans protested the size of Cameron's goal pads. But upon measurement it was found that, while his were of legal width, Lacroix's pads were deemed too wide and had to be adjusted! Then referee Loicq arbitrarily awarded the choice of starting end to the team whose captain was older. U.S. captain Irving Small elected to defend the west end, meaning that Canada would have to play into the sun for the first and third periods. The game was further delayed while the two captains argued with Loicq over his interpretation of bodychecking, one of the key differences between the North American game, which permitted full contact anywhere on the ice, and the European game, which did not allow contact in the offensive end at all, a rule that prevailed, incredibly, until 1968.

The game finally began at 3 p.m. in perfect weather – clear and cold – that produced hard, fast ice. Thousands of fans crowded around the rink, many having taken special trains from Paris or London expressly to see this all-North American final. Local citizens stood precariously on nearby roofs and even chimneys to witness the action, and both teams were accorded tremendous welcoming ovations.

From the drop of the puck it was clear the Americans were ready to play to the death. Earlier in the tournament, Harry Watson had confidently remarked that Canada would beat the States by 10 or 12 to nothing in their inevitable gold medal meeting. Not surprisingly, Watson's words angered the Americans and stirred them to battle. Less than two minutes after the opening faceoff, Watson was knocked unconscious and was bleeding from the nose, down briefly but certainly not out. "Moose" got to his feet, remained in the game, and played with even greater determination. Moments later, American Willard Rice was kayoed by a retaliatory swing of Hooley Smith's stick, and the war was on. As defenceman Beattie Ramsay later explained, "The U.S. players evidently intended to stop our star forward [Watson], if possible, because they figured with his goal-scoring ability lessened their chances would be improved. But it only tended to make Watson play all the harder."

Indeed, Watson's bravery ignited the whole team. "There was blood in every player's eye after Watson resumed," read one Canadian account of the vicious beginning. He scored two goals in the first period to give Canada what would prove to be an insurmountable 2-0 lead. The Americans, however, continued to play violent hockey for the full 60 minutes.

The Canadians backchecked ferociously, and the American stars Herb Drury and Willard Rice were consistently checked off the puck each time they tried to break into the Canadian end. Although Drury scored late in the first to make it 2-1, Canada scored three more times in the second (including another by Watson) and once more in the third on their way to a penalty-filled 6-1 win that was as lopsided as the score indicated.

By the end of the game, "the Americans were physically exhausted and stumbling from fatigue," according to newspaper accounts, while the Canadians were weary but ebullient thanks to the heroic and skilful play of their star forward combination of Watson, Smith, and McCaffery. Taffy Abel, the behemoth 230-pound American defenceman, was penalized four times in a game that Loicq simply could not control. "The rough play had a lot to do with the small score," Ramsay opined. "Had

the U.S. team decided to play clean hockey and made it a game of real hockey, we would have beaten them … by 20 goals under equal conditions, with a referee who would have penalized for all infringements." Even still, the Granites won the gold medal easily.

The players received their medals on ice immediately after the victory as the Canadian ensign was raised to the top of the stadium and the band played "The Maple Leaf Forever." An Olympic official presented a second ensign to William Hewitt to acknowledge the team's gold medal. At a sumptuous banquet that night, Count Clary, chairman of the French Olympic Committee, wrote a note on the visiting card sent to his Canadian counterpart that read, "Le Comte Justinien Clary presents his compliments to Mr. Hewitt with all his admiration for your splendid hockey team and your brilliant final victory."

Mission accomplished, the Granites began their triumphal journey home. In Paris, they played a unique exhibition match against a team from Great Britain on a circular rink 120 feet in diameter and surrounded by tuxedoed banqueters dining formally at tables. As Hooley Smith confessed, however, the two-month European tour was beginning to take its toll and the players had little energy left: "Between the champagne parties, excursions to the Folies Bergères and the like, we were pooped out, and the only way we could get a rest during the exhibition game was to shoot the puck up among the champagne drinkers at the tables surrounding the rink. It was messy but effective." The Parisians were nonplussed by the crashes of pucks with glasses but delighted by the unparalleled skill displayed by the Granites in their 17-1 win.

The Granites had not only won Olympic gold, they had confirmed Canada's hockey supremacy and demonstrated to all of Europe a sophisticated knowledge and love of the game that laid the foundation for future international hockey success. Against even the U.S. team, the Granites had won with much the same ease as when they had captured their two Allan Cups. Although the Granites disbanded after the Chamonix Olympics, they had made an indelible mark on amateur hockey.

(TOP) Figure skater Sonja Henie. (OPPOSITE) Perhaps no hockey tournament has been played with such an idyllic backdrop as in Chamonix.

# WOMEN'S FINEST HOUR

*1930-39 PRESTON RIVULETTES*

"Nobody can dare me to do anything and get away with it," said pint-sized Nellie Ranscombe in the fall of 1930, little knowing that her fighting spirit would lead to the creation of the first great women's hockey team. Nellie was the catcher for the Preston Rivulettes, a women's baseball team in the quiet town of Preston, Ontario, on the banks of the Speed River an hour west of Toronto. She and a group of her teammates were sitting at the Lowther Street hockey rink bemoaning the advent of another winter without organized sporting activity for themselves. One of their number suggested forming a hockey team, but an interloper scoffed at the very suggestion: girls just did not play hockey, and certainly not girls from a baseball team. It was all Nellie Ranscombe needed. "That did it," she said, convinced that her teammates were up to the challenge. Her younger sister, 18-year-old Hilda, a natural athlete who had been skating with the boys on the frozen rivers of Preston for years, seconded Nellie's motion. Most of the other Rivs, as they were more commonly called, were less confident than the Ranscombes but were supportive nonetheless. Then one of them mentioned that Bobbie Rosenfeld and Alexandrine Gibb were in town. Why not ask their advice? They immediately decided to walk over to the Preston Springs Hotel, where the two women were staying.

ROSENFELD AND GIBB WERE TWO PIONEERING WOMEN from Toronto. Rosenfeld had been an Olympic champion sprinter and had played hockey for a women's team known as the Toronto Pals. After retiring just a few months earlier she began to write a column for the *Toronto Telegram* called "Feminine Sports Reel." Gibb was perhaps the first woman to write regularly on hockey, in her *Toronto Globe* column called "No Man's Land of Sport – News and Views of Feminine Activities." Such were their reputations that their very presence in town was public knowledge from the minute they stepped off the train.

The young women seized this opportunity both to meet Rosenfeld and Gibb and to gain valuable advice about forming a hockey team. Not surprisingly, Rosenfeld and Gibb endorsed the Rivs' ambitions wholeheartedly. The idea of forming a women's hockey team was hardly novel. But most female teams functioned at universities such as McGill, Queen's, and Toronto, which had all supported the women's game since the start of the century. Even at the university level competition was sporadic, and there was no formal league or schedule to speak of. Hockey was seen as a way of augmenting studies with some healthy exercise and was not intended in any way to show up the boys. By 1930, however, the Ladies' Ontario Hockey Association (LOHA), run entirely by women, oversaw what meagre formal competitions existed between women's teams.

Having secured Rosenfeld and Gibb's encouragement, the players next called on Herb Fach, the manager of the Preston arena, to ask about getting the ice for games and practices. Not only was Fach happy to oblige, he agreed to coach the team. He put the young women in touch with Marvin Dykeman, a local combinationman for Bell telephone, who became their manager. Dykeman's wife, Olive, agreed to act as the girls' chaperone whenever they travelled out of town. Now all the team needed was financial backing, a difficulty faced by far more prosperous operations during the Depression, let alone a fledgling women's hockey team. One of the players, Norma Hipel, petitioned her father, Norman, a former mayor of Preston and now Liberal member of parliament for Waterloo South. He agreed to sponsor the players for their first year. Thus the Preston Rivulettes hockey team was born.

At their first official tryouts, only nine players – most of them Rivulettes ballplayers, most of them teenagers – showed up: sisters Nellie and Hilda Ranscombe, sisters Marm and Helen Schmuck, Marg Gabitas, Myrtle Parr, Toddy Webb, Pat Marriott, and Helen Sault. In the ensuing weeks Norma Hipel, Gladys Hawkins, Violet Hall, Alvis Williams, Ruth Dargel, and Marie Beilstein joined, giving the team enough players to allow for injuries and illnesses.

The team's greatest challenge was finding time to practise. Most of these young women, having finished school at 16, worked weekdays until 5 p.m. and so couldn't practise until the early evening. Nellie had a job in a shoe factory; the Schmuck sisters worked at the Savage Shoe store in Preston; Helen Sault worked at a woollen factory in nearby Hespeler and

along with Gladys Hawkins and Ruth Dargel commuted by trolley; Marie worked at a rubber company in Berlin (later renamed Kitchener); and Violet, Alvis, and Norma were still students at the Preston Continuation School. Hilda, the youngest of the nine Ranscombe children, stayed at home and took care of her mother. Although the team was based in Preston, it was representative of a larger region that included Galt, Hespeler, and Berlin. But for all the difficulties and sacrifices of time and travel that they made to play, these young women made them happily and without any sense they were doing anything extraordinary.

The nearby Galt *Daily Reporter* described the tryouts for the Rivs with predictable condescension to the "fair race": "To 'make' the team, a girl has to be a good fast skater, and in the present line-up all the girls are agile young women with the power to coordinate their skating and stick-handling." Finding teams to play against was an equal challenge, for there was no formal league or schedule. Fach organized games, and teams from other cities contacted him for games, but in their early days the Rivulettes played more or less ad hoc.

The Rivs played their home games at the Lowther Arena; for trips to other cities they relied on Fach, Dykeman, and friends to drive them. One such friend was Don Pitcher, who met Gladys Hawkins between periods of a game and subsequently volunteered to help drive the players to away games so that he could spend time with "Gladdie." (The couple eventually married.) Pitcher's commitment looked commendable even in the name of love, given that road trips would often see the team return at dawn after driving all night following a game. (To keep expenses to a minimum, the team stayed in hotels only as a last resort.)

The Rivs usually practised twice a week after work, and these were highly structured on-ice sessions during which they worked on passing, stickhandling, and skating. They scrimmaged primarily against themselves because there was no equivalent team close by, though sometimes a Senior A team in Preston gave them a workout. The Rivs were far superior to almost any women's team they played. Their skating was stronger, their teamwork seamless, and their stickhandling virtually impossible to defend. They played according to traditional men's rules – three periods of 20 minutes – and subs came on only to give the regular five skaters a chance to catch their breath. While NHLers often drank water or tea between periods, the women preferred Bovril to fortify themselves. They wore only the most basic equipment: small gloves, a red and white sweater, hockey pants, shin pads, elbow pads.

Although the Rivs' first year of play was informal and makeshift, in 1930-31 they played teams from Grimsby, Port Dover, and London, the early glimmerings of a small but quickly expanding hockey community that emerged primarily in southern Ontario during the early 1930s. The Rivs' efforts soon brought about a growing interest among young women of the area in forming a ladies' league of sorts.

**DOMINION FINALS**
**LADIES' HOCKEY**
(For Lady Bessborough Trophy)
**WINNIPEG "EATONS" vs.**
**PRESTON "RIVULETTES"**
GALT ARENA —— SECOND GAME
**WEDNESDAY**
MARCH 27, at 8.30
General Admission 25c. Reserves 40c and 50c. Reserved boxes 75c. Plan now open at Star Electric, Preston; Smith's Studio, Galt; W. J. Marriott's, Hespeler. Plan closes Wednesday at 6 p.m. reopens at arena at 7 o'clock.

(LEFT) Newspaper ad promoting a Bessborough Cup match at the Galt Arena. (OPPOSITE) The Rivulettes baseball team was as good as, if not better than, its hockey namesake.

## A LEAGUE OF THEIR OWN

From the start, Bobbie Rosenfeld covered the team for the *Toronto Telegram* with fanatical devotion. During the Rivs' first season she gave this glowing account of the younger Ranscombe's play: "Hilda knows every trick of the trade, has dazzling speed, and looks invincible with puck and stick. She has all the equipment for stardom and has really gone places in every hockey contest played. She is an instinctive performer. In home competition or on foreign ice she is the same and natural gifted player. We have seen her in gruelling struggles, and she has come through with flying colours, where other performers might crack wide open. We have seen other athletes who seemed to know what to do under ordinary circumstances, but when the battle generated a fighting situation, they were a bit helpless. These situations have only tended to make Hilda dig in deeper and play harder."

A dedicated fair player and scorer without compare, the right-winger in the number five sweater was the class of the team from its earliest days, head and shoulders above everyone else the Rivs faced. Her exploits soon helped make the Rivulettes famous, but she got along well with her teammates because she was a humble star who delighted in sharing the glory. She continued to live at home, just a couple of blocks from the Speed River, where she spent every free moment skating and stickhandling by herself.

By the Rivulettes' second season they had become the centrepiece of the newly formed Ladies' Intercounty Hockey League, which played under the auspices of the LOHA. As well as the Rivulettes and their first-year opponents, the young league included the London Silverwoods, the Stratford Maids, the Toronto Pals, the Guelph Maple Leafs, and the Port Dover Sailorettes. In the spring of 1932, the top team in the Intercounty league was crowned Ontario champions and presented the newly minted Bobbie Rosenfeld Trophy, named in honour of the association's new president. Not surprisingly, the Rivs took home the first cup.

By the fall of 1931 and the start of league play, the Rivs were playing some of their games in the Shade Street arena in nearby Galt because that rink had artificial ice and could hold greater crowds. (The Lowther Arena was made of natural ice and had only a few rows of seats behind only three sides of the boards.) For important matches it was common for 3,000 or more fans to jam into the building. It was also at Galt that Hilda's exploits took on mythic proportions. One day the Rivs arrived at the arena for practice only to find the Junior Red Wings, farm team of NHL's Detroit, already on the ice and unwilling to cede the hour. The juniors challenged the Rivs to a game of shinny, during which Hilda made a great end-to-end rush and scored, much to the delight of everyone present.

The team featured two dominating lines. The top threesome included Hilda on right wing, with Marm Schmuck at centre and Gladys Hawkins on the left. The second threesome, known as the "Kid Line," comprised Ruth Dargel, Violet Hall, and Alvis Williams, aged 14, 15, and 16, a trio that displayed speed and great passing. Coach Fach stressed the importance of teamwork, passing from defence to forward, for instance, over the individual rushes favoured by the other teams that lacked the Rivs' talent player for player. In goal, Nellie Ranscombe was the tiniest wisp of a creature but also the most competitive and tenacious netminder. She applied her catching abilities from baseball to goaltending, the mirror position between the two sports. No puck was going to get by her without a fight.

The other teams in the Intercounty league soon grew tired of losing to the Rivs, and animosity on ice was not uncommon. Indeed, the women's game was hardly effete: "Miss Smith was enlivening the tail-end of an LOHA game at Preston by raining blows of her fair fists upon the person of Hilda Ranscombe, one of Preston Rivulettes' stars," according to one game report. "The despatch from the rinkside, or ringside, indicates that the Port Dover girl knocked Miss Ranscombe to the ice and then and there pummelled her until Referee Gordon Wright pulled the aggressor off by main force. The official penalised Miss Smith for the balance of the game, which Preston won 3-1." After another game, one sportswriter reported that "Nellie Jones, pretty Maroons centre player, is in the Western hospital following an emergency operation to her nose which was broken in Saturday's game. With but eight minutes to play, she got in the way of a hard shot off Gladys Hawkins' stick and skated off the ice leaving a trail of crimson."

team together during the darkest days of the Depression, to make it to practice after working eight hours, to endure the taunts and attacks of inferior teams. That girls dared to play shinny on ponds and lakes with the boys was itself a sign of cultural rebellion. This same spirit of independence helped them get to their games. While not exactly a hand-to-mouth organization, the Rivs relied on donations and gate receipts to cover expenses. They were amateur women athletes who played because they loved the game.

## THE BESSBOROUGH CUP

By the second year of operation of the Ladies' Intercounty Hockey League, the Ontario playdown had become part of a national championship. Myrtle Cook, like Rosenfeld a gold medallist on Canada's 1928 Olympic track team and a strong voice in support of the female athletic cause – her

During one Ontario finals game in Port Dover, it took a late goal by Helen Schmuck to give the Rivulettes a slim 1-0 win over the "local lassies," a rare close game for the Prestonians. Port Dover fans were so enraged by the loss that they ran en masse at the Rivulettes as they left the ice. The Rivs scrambled back to their dressing room and had to be escorted by police out to their cars. The win, however, was sweet revenge for the team. During an earlier game, the Port Dover coach had questioned Helen Schmuck's gender to game officials, forcing a humiliated Schmuck to undress to prove she was a woman.

The Rivs not only quickly developed into an almost unbeatable hockey team, they formed a group of remarkable women for their place and time. Marie Beilstein became famous with the team after the summer that she and a friend hitchhiked to the Maritimes and back, something no proper lady would ever have thought of doing. It was this kind of determination that enabled these young women to put the

Hilda Ranscombe *(OPPOSITE)* was without doubt the finest women's hockey player of the pre-war era. *(ABOVE LEFT, LEFT TO RIGHT)* Hilda, sister Nellie, and Helen Schmuck hoist Helen's sister Marm on their shoulders. Bobbie Rosenfeld *(ABOVE RIGHT, LEFT TO RIGHT)* Myrtle Cook, Grace Conacher, and Rosa Gross, a relay team in Toronto.

columns appeared in the *Montreal Gazette* – became president of the Canadian Women's Hockey Association (WHA), under whose auspices the various provincial leagues operated. Under Cook's leadership, the WHA oversaw the regional and national tournaments.

At the end of the 1932-33 season, after winning the second Rosenfeld Trophy, the Rivulettes advanced to the Eastern finals, where they competed for the Romeo Doust Cup. The winner of this game would play the Western champions for the national Lady Bessborough Cup, named in honour of Vere Brabazon Ponsonby, the wife of Canada's then-Governor General, the Earl of Bessborough. But first the Rivs had to find a way to pay for their trip to Prince Edward Island, where they were scheduled to play the Eastern champions, the Summerside Crystal Sisters.

Coach Herb Fach took out a mortgage on his house, a sum he hoped to recoup through ticket sales. But only 542 souls showed up for the first game in Summerside, won 6-1 by the Rivs, and even fewer attended the second, also won by the women from Preston. With the Romeo Doust Cup secured but Fach now out of pocket a goodly sum, the trip to Alberta to play the Edmonton Rustlers for the Bessborough Cup appeared out of the question.

Incredibly, the Rivulettes' opponents came to the rescue. The Rustlers shouldered part of the $1,000 travel costs themselves and solicited donations from the people of Edmonton to cover the rest. After a gruelling two and a half day train ride, the Rivs arrived in town only a few hours before game time, all of them exhausted and several too ill to play. Only seven of the Rivulettes dressed for the first game.

Before some 2,500 fans, the largest crowd ever to attend a women's game in that city, the Rivs went down to defeat, 3-2, on a disputed last-minute goal. After the game the referee, an Edmonton native by the name of Gordon Williams, came into the Rivs' dressing room to apologize for the biased whistle that had cost them the first game. "I'm sorry, girls," Williams told them, "I couldn't let you win." At this, one of the Schmuck sisters jumped on him and had to be pulled off by her teammates. The next game was equally well attended and equally close, a 1-0 loss by the still-ailing Prestonians. The Edmonton Rustlers had captured the inaugural Bessborough Cup and, for the first time in their three-year existence, the Preston Rivulettes had been beaten.

During the next two years the Rivs won successive Bessborough Cups with overpowering ease. In 1934 they avenged their loss to Edmonton and in 1935 they played the Winnipeg Olympics in Galt before 3,126 fans, a record turnout for a women's game any time, anywhere. On that occasion, the Rivs appeared on the ice wearing their softball sweaters emblazoned on the back with a commercial sponsor's name, but the Dominion league president ordered the name removed before play began. The game was covered for the *Toronto Globe* by Alexandrine Gibb, was featured prominently in newspapers throughout Ontario, and was even broadcast by radio. The local heroes lived up to their advance billing, winning 7-3. As usual, Hilda Ranscombe stole the show, scoring three goals and backchecking with characteristic tenacity.

After the victory the city of Preston honoured the team with a banquet and presented every member with an engraved wristwatch. From the gate receipts the visiting Winnipeg team received $740 to cover their expenses and the Galt arena $500 as hosts – leaving the Rivs with a mere $100!

## WITHOUT COMPARE

By the mid-1930s the Prestonians were so successful and popular that many local politicians and hockey fans lobbied to send them to the 1936 Olympic Winter Games, a trip to be preceded by an exhibition tour through England to finance their journey. However, the suggestion never gained momentum and the trip never occurred. Alexandrine Gibb, who frequently travelled with the team, did some soliciting of her own, trying to convince Toronto to host the Rivs for

a more meaningful game than the city had previously experienced: "While paying a second visit to Foster Hewitt's gondola up in the rafters in the Maple Leaf Gardens Saturday night, Mr. Hewitt – always polite – asked how the girls' hockey teams were coming on," Gibb wrote in one of her columns. "That gave me an idea – that and the fact that Myrtle Cook had written from Montreal and asked how the Gardens patrons would like to see two feminine hockey teams, dressed up in Maroons' or Canadiens' colours, play here some night. Why not bring the Preston girls' team, Eastern champions, to Toronto some night…. It might be the starting point for real girls' hockey in Toronto…. Do you think we could approach Connie Smythe on the matter? Would he say yes?"

Smythe said no, but the Montreal Forum said yes just a few weeks later. In March 1936, the Rivs played a two-game Eastern championships series against the Montreal Maroons, not to be confused with the NHL entry of the same name, which shared Forum ice with the Montreal Canadiens. As usual, the only man on skates was the referee, but for the first time this was an NHL official, Leo Heffernan. The Maroons carried little white elephants with them for good luck, but buoyed by the excellent refereeing the Rivs won both games convincingly, 4-0 and 5-2, before crowds of 2,000. Afterward, one local reporter called Hilda Ranscombe the Aurel Joliat of women's hockey, for both her speed and celebrity, and the Maroons offered contracts to her and Marm Schmuck. Since women didn't play at the Olympics and there were no women's pro leagues, the idea of offering financial inducement was neither illegal nor unethical, but the Rivs' stars rejected the money just the same and returned home to Preston.

This victory in Montreal set up a Dominion finals against the Winnipeg Olympics, this time in Manitoba, but for once the Rivs had to default a series because they couldn't afford the necessary expenses for the games. At the start of the 1937-38 season, the Rivs secured a commercial sponsorship that almost proved disastrous. The Preston Springs Hotel agreed to pay the team's bills for the season, but in return the Rivs were required to wear sweaters that featured "Preston Springs" on their crest to promote the hotel. They did, but the rest of the league protested, arguing that the promotion gave them an unfair advantage. The Rivs then petitioned Preston's city council to change the name of the city from Preston to Preston Springs, but this was rejected. The "Springs" was removed from their sweaters and the money flow staunched.

(ABOVE) The Rivs pose for an unconventional team photo. (OPPOSITE) The Rivs: (BACK ROW, LEFT TO RIGHT) Molly Hamilin, Pat Marriott, Bing Wershing, Marg Gabitas, Herb Fach, Toddy Webb, and Beat Collard; (MIDDLE ROW, LEFT TO RIGHT) Marm Schmuck, Helen Schmuck, and Hilda Ranscombe; (FRONT ROW, LEFT TO RIGHT) Winnie Makcrow, Nellie Ranscombe, and Sheila Lahey.

In 1939 a promotions group in the United States tried to organize a tour for a Canadian women's hockey team to play a series of exhibition games against women's teams in the U.S. But the only Canadian team proposed was the Rivulettes, and the Rivulettes were just too overpowering. The tour idea was abandoned, and with war imminent, women's hockey stood last in the line of social and sporting priorities.

The Rivulettes had reached their zenith as a team just as their moment of glory was about to end. Once war was declared, the Rivulettes and most other women's teams disbanded and the LOHA more or less ceased meaningful operations. During their decade of existence the Preston Rivulettes had remained essentially the same team that first took the ice in the fall of 1930 in the Lowther Arena. Throughout the 1930s, the Ranscombes, the Schmucks, and Helen Sault wore the red and white team sweater, rarely missing a game. Others played with the Rivs for a game or even a season, then bowed out because they got married or had children. And now with the war on Pat Marriott and Helen Sault had the Rivulette-like temerity to join the armyOthers joined the legions of Canadian women who worked for the war effort. After the war there was no concerted effort to revive the Rivs, and no younger generation sought to follow in their footsteps.

During their reign, the Preston Rivulettes won five of the six national championships they played, six Eastern Canadian championships, and 10 Ontario championships. Only one tie and two losses blemished their 350 games played, a nearly perfect record accomplished during an era when women's activities more commonly formed around family hearths, not goal creases. The Rivs proved that women could play the game skilfully, could organize and sustain a league, generate enough countrywide interest to support a national championship, and compete with tenacity and pride.

Carl Liscombe, who grew up in Rivs country in the 1930s and later played for the Detroit Red Wings for nine years, formed an indelible impression as a teenager of these women and their skill. "I played with and against Hilda and her sister, Nellie, on the Grand River in Preston and Galt," he remembered. "Hilda was just as good as any boy, and better than most, myself included. When we picked teams, she was always the first one chosen." Today, the Preston Rivulettes remain in the first rank of women's hockey. Their place in history has yet to be usurped by any greater team.

# THE TEAM SMYTHE BUILT

1947-48 TORONTO MAPLE LEAFS

Prior to the start of the 1947-48 season, Leaf captain and star centre Syl Apps announced that the upcoming year would be his last in the NHL. He had spent 10 years in the league, interrupted by two years in the army. No one could have been more supportive of Apps's decision than his employer and friend, Conn Smythe, the Leafs' owner and builder of both the team and Maple Leaf Gardens. Smythe encouraged Apps while nonetheless asking him to reconsider as the year's end approached and the Stanley Cup playoffs beckoned. Apps entered the final game of the regular season with 198 career goals. He promptly went out and scored a hat trick against the Detroit Red Wings to pass the 200-goal plateau and ensure his place in team history as only the second Leaf after Charlie Conacher to reach that mark. In the playoffs, Apps's timing was equally fortuitous. In his last-ever playoff game he scored a second-period goal. Then, with the Leafs leading 7-2 and time counting off the clock, coach Happy Day put captain Apps out for one last shift, a gesture that had the whole team in tears. Once the bell sounded and the game and Stanley Cup were won, one of the greatest team men ever to play said his farewells to a remarkable group of players he himself had helped mould into the league's first dynasty.

APPS WAS NOT JUST A GREAT PLAYER; HE WAS A FINE MAN who had earned the Leaf owner's trust from the minute Smythe saw him play football at McMaster University in Hamilton. He signed Apps to a Maple Leaf contract without ever having seen him skate, a gesture of confidence not only in the player but in his own sense of player evaluation. The "Hollerin' Major" knew how to ice a Stanley Cup winner and how to turn the blue and white maple leaf into a Canadian cultural icon. Smythe and his Toronto Maple Leafs reached their apex during the few years following World War II, but to understand their success one must first understand the owner and his philosophy.

From a young age, Smythe believed that loyalty was the finest attribute a man might possess. He lived his life accordingly and expected those with whom he worked to do likewise. One of his first moves after he bought the Leafs in 1927 was to hire a childhood friend, George "Squib" Walker, as a part-time "bird dog," or scout, for the team. Smythe was the first to fully understand the importance of scouting as a means of building a team, not just for today but for tomorrow. He had scouts all over the country, friends who would simply call him if they spotted a young player of exceptional talent. Their connections to the Leafs ensured that any talented boy they discovered signed a contract on his 16th birthday, committing himself to the Leafs for the remainder of his skating life. Smythe's network guaranteed that the best young prospects from coast to coast, no matter how obscure their hometown, wound up wearing Toronto's dream-come-true blue and white, for no other NHL team held the same mystique in the hearts and dreams of Canadian boys.

Perhaps Smythe's ultimate act of loyalty came in 1940 when he hired Happy Day as coach of the team to replace the departing Dick Irvin, who was on his way to the Forum to assume the coaching position with the floundering Montreal Canadiens. Smythe had discovered Day playing with the University of Toronto while studying pharmacy and convinced him to join the Leafs. Since then, Day had played 13 seasons for Toronto, 10 of them as the team's captain. Promoting Day to the coaching job was a natural move for Smythe: Day had been loyal to the team, and now Smythe returned the favour.

As the war in Europe worsened, Smythe kept one eye on his country and one eye on Maple Leaf Gardens, as yet undecided what his contribution to Canada's war efforts would be. At the arena, he was more certain. That summer Smythe made Walker the team's first head scout, a full-time job that required travel virtually every day of the hockey season and daily contact with local bird dogs from coast to coast. Without Walker's hockey acumen and utter devotion to Smythe, the Leafs likely wouldn't have been so successful in the 1940s and beyond.

By the time Walker assumed his position full-time, Smythe had a very effective system in place. Once a young player had been signed, he was sent to play for one of two junior teams in Toronto, the St. Mike's Majors (for Catholics) or the Toronto Marlboros (for Protestants). This way, Smythe could monitor each player's progress while provid-

## The "Hollerin' Major" knew how to ice a Stanley Cup winner and how to turn the blue and white maple leaf into a Canadian cultural icon.

ing him with the finest coaches available, usually former Leafs. From the juniors, a player stepped up to the minor pro leagues, again to be greeted by a former Leaf coach ready to prepare him for the demanding grind of the NHL. Smythe's formula for success was set: scout, develop, minor pro, NHL. Through all these stages, the players knew their mecca was Maple Leaf Gardens. They became devoted to the team, often working part-time at the Gardens and meeting the current Leaf stars. They were in every way the children of the Maple Leaf hockey family whose patriarch was Conn Smythe.

Smythe built his team not only on scouting but on his and the Leafs' reputation. He demanded loyalty from his players, but he gave it as well. When fourth-line forward Nick Metz heard of his father's death, Smythe let Metz leave the team and join his family out West for as long as necessary. Nick returned the day of a game and scored two goals in the third period of a critical comeback win over Chicago. On another occasion, captain Syl Apps broke his leg during a game and was out for the rest of the season. One day soon after, he came into Smythe's office on crutches, offering to return the balance of his salary. Smythe was dumbfounded. That kind of loyalty could not be bought; it was a kind of chemistry between owner and captain that inevitably filtered down to all the players.

Smythe's ability to fleece other owners and general managers in trades made a great team even greater. Goaler Turk Broda, for instance, had been discovered by Smythe himself during a scouting trip to Windsor, and Smythe stole him from Detroit's general manager Jack Adams for just $10,000 cash. Smythe got Harry Watson (no relation to the star of the 1924 Granites) in a brilliant trade from Detroit for Harry Taylor, who failed to do much in the Winged Wheel. Max Bentley was acquired in an astounding five-for-two swap with the Blackhawks that left many people wondering – not for very long – what Smythe was doing. In addition, the Metz brothers were scouted at Father Murray's Notre Dame Hounds in Saskatchewan, and Gus Mortson and Bill Barilko were found playing in Northern Ontario, key bird dog discoveries.

### A HIGHER CALLING

By 1941, with no quick end to the war in sight, Smythe felt an increasing sense of obligation to join in Canada's efforts overseas. On September 15, 1941, he named and organized the 30th Sportsmen's Battery, intending the unit to be made up of hockey players and other sportsmen. He encouraged his own players to join and promised that any who enlisted in the armed forces would be given a fair shot at making the team when discharged. In other words, fighting for his country would

(LEFT) One of Conn Smythe's innovations was this annual calendar, complete with a Leafs' schedule and photos of players and game highlights.

## CONN SMYTHE'S RÉSUMÉ

Conn Smythe, seen here in the Leafs' dressing room, played hockey as a kid, but realized early on that he'd never make the grade as a pro. Born in Toronto in 1899, he grew up on Mutual Street — just down the road from where Maple Leaf Gardens would be built under his aegis. During his 20s, Smythe turned to coaching at the University of Toronto. In 1926 he became general manager of the newest entry in the NHL, the New York Rangers. But within a year, after numerous run-ins with the team's owner, Colonel John Hammond, he was fired and returned to Toronto. There he joined forces with his good friend Bill MacBrien and three other business associates, who helped secure the financing to buy the local NHL franchise, the St. Pats. On February 17, 1927, Smythe and his partners became owners of the team, which they immediately renamed the Toronto Maple Leafs.

cost no man his hockey job. The first man to enlist was Ted Reeve, aka "The Moaner," one of the most popular sports journalists of the day. Soon most Leaf players followed suit: Syl Apps, Bob Goldham, Turk Broda, Don and Nick Metz, Wally Stanowski, Sweeney Schriner, Billy Taylor, Pete Langelle, Joe Klukay, Bill Ezinicki, Garth Boesch, and Gus Mortson, all of whom would go on to win a Stanley Cup with the Leafs. It was an incredible display of loyalty, as much to owner as to country.

Major Constantine Falkland Smythe shipped off to Europe for active duty in November 1942,

wearing, returning home in September 1944 partially paralyzed and unable to walk. It took him a full year to recover to the point where he could go to the Gardens every day.

In the spring of 1945 the Leafs unexpectedly won the Stanley Cup with many of their star players still in the armed forces, but in the spring of '46 failed even to make the playoffs. By the start of the 1946-47 season most of the Maple Leaf stars had returned to civilian life. Turk Broda, perhaps the greatest playoff netminder of all time, rejoined the team late in the '45-'46 season for a few games then resumed his spectacular career full-time the following sea-

and 1949. Four more played on two of the three championship teams. This was a lineup not just of the highest calibre but of remarkable consistency that flourished under coach Happy Day as a cohesive, hockey-playing family. The top three scorers all made unique contributions: Ted Kennedy was the exciting youngster, a superstar in the making; Syl Apps was the veteran captain and a dangerous playmaker; and Howie Meeker, who beat out Gordie Howe in the voting for the Calder Trophy as the league's best rookie, was a sign of long-term prosperity. In the 1947 playoffs the Leafs eliminated Detroit in five games, then Montreal in six.

(ABOVE LEFT) A Leaf practice in the 1930s during training camp, usually held north of Toronto and consisting most often of dry-land exercise. (ABOVE MIDDLE) Conn Smythe before the battlefield accident that almost killed him soon after he was promoted to major. A year later he was back at the Gardens and back in charge. (ABOVE RIGHT) Canadians during the house-by-house battle for Ortona in December 1943. Many Leafs joined up at Smythe's urging, happy to put their careers on hold for him.

leaving the daily operations of the club in the hands of his lifelong associate and friend, Frank Selke. In Caen, while Smythe was on a routine check of explosives, a bomb blew up nearby and the resulting shrapnel hit him and wounded him gravely. He survived thanks only to the heavy overcoat he happened to be

son. The Metz brothers – Don and Nick – Wally Stanowski, Syl Apps, Bill Ezinicki, Garth Boesch, Joe Klukay, and Gus Mortson all returned and, as Smythe had promised, all were put back on the team as soon as they were able. That first full season for the war-hardened Leafs proved them worthy both of Smythe's loyalty and his ability to build a great team. It marked the beginning of the NHL's first dynasty.

## A POSTWAR POWERHOUSE

On the 17-man roster of the 1946-47 Leafs were no fewer than 10 players who would stay with the team as it became the first NHL franchise to win three Stanley Cups in a row – 1947, 1948,

Winning the 1947 Stanley Cup was as much a tribute to Happy Day's coaching as to Smythe's managing of the team. Day was a fitness fanatic who skated as hard as his players in practice, walked faster than most people ran, and knew just when to push his charges hard and when to ease up on the reins. Broda in goal was a given. On defence, his first pairing was Mortson and Jim Thomson, called the Gold Dust Twins because they had played together at St. Mike's and were both rock solid. Day's second set of blue-liners was the impenetrable combination of Barilko and Boesch, two of the hardest hitters in the game. Stanowski was a fifth defenceman

**In 1947-48 the Toronto Maple Leafs were nothing short of overpowering, thanks in large measure to the extraordinary trade Smythe made just seven games into the season.**

whom Day inserted periodically. With his forward lines, Day knew how to keep his players fresh with quick, high-speed shifts. For the opponent, as Detroit GM Jack Adams discovered, there was no respite from the talent-laden lineup.

In 1947-48 the Toronto Maple Leafs were nothing short of overpowering, thanks in large measure to the extraordinary trade Smythe made just seven games into the season. In return for an unprecedented

Unquestionably the Leafs now possessed the best trio of centres in the game in Apps, Kennedy, and Max Bentley. The first line featured Apps, Harry Watson, and Ezinicki, a threesome with size, tremendous intensity, and great skill at moving the puck. The second had Ted Kennedy at centre between Vic Lynn and Howie Meeker. "Teeder" Kennedy was arguably the greatest faceoff man of all time, and puck control was this line's forte. The other four forwards – Bentley, Sid Smith, Joe Klukay, and Nick Metz – also saw plenty of ice time, all of them proud and reliable skaters in "Leafian livery."

In the 60-game season of 1947-48 the Leafs lost only 15 times, with Broda allowing the fewest goals of any "hemp guardian," as Ted Reeve wrote in his *Toronto Telegram* sports column. Turk played every minute of every game in both the regular season and playoffs. The team had eight players who scored 10 or more goals, and the Leafs finished first overall in the standings.

five players – Gaye Stewart, Bud Poile, Bob Goldham, Gus Bodnar, and Ernie Dickens – Smythe acquired Max Bentley and Cy Thomas from Chicago. Max "the Hat" was considered the best centre in the league not playing in Toronto, and Chicago's willingness to trade him was stunning. In return, the Hawks got four top-notch players (Dickens, like Thomas, was a prospect), but Bentley's arrival in Toronto gave an already strong team even greater depth. As Smythe explained: "I made it [the trade] because I could see possible centre ice weakness on our team in a year or two, with no likely prospects coming up. With Bentley, we'll be strong down centre. I know the deal will leave us short of reserve strength, and I shudder to think what may happen if we run into a string of injuries. But those are the chances we must take." Chances, schmances. An even greater risk was to lose Apps to retirement at season's end without having an adequate replacement for the following year.

*(ABOVE LEFT)* A Leaf defenceman delivers a hip check to an unlucky Boston Bruin during a game at Maple Leaf Gardens. The Leafs' blue-line corps, drilled relentlessly by coach Happy Day, were masters of defence. *(ABOVE RIGHT)* Young fans take in a game at the Gardens. Smythe skilfully built the Leafs and their hockey arena into a cultural powerhouse, and just about every Canadian boy dreamed of one day playing for the Maple Leafs.

**A CUP FOR THE AGES**

The 1948 playoffs may seem anti-climactic when recounted in summary form, but the game-by-game results paint a different picture and demonstrate more clearly the character and determination of this Maple Leaf team. In the very first game of the semifinals against the Bruins, Boston scored early to take a 1-0 lead. Ezinicki scored to tie, but Boston scored again. Then Max Bentley tied the game again. Early in the third, Boston scored twice to take a 4-2 lead, their third lead of the game, but Apps and Thomson scored to even things up again. In overtime Broda would not surrender another goal; Nick Metz scored the winner. Five different players had goals

## THE HOUSE THAT SMYTHE BUILT

As soon as Maple Leaf Gardens was completed in 1931 it became the most important hockey building in the country. The Gardens was a marvel of architectural accomplishment, both for the rapidity of its construction and for the fact that it was the first NHL rink with no obstructed sightlines. Smythe had just acquired King Clancy, the league's marquee player, from Ottawa — with money he won at the track, no less! He ensured that Foster Hewitt's broadcasts of Leaf games were transmitted from Victoria to Halifax at a time when perhaps only Prime Minister Bennett himself enjoyed such country-wide exposure. During the era when the only other Canadian team in the NHL was the French-Canadian-dominated Montreal Canadiens (1942-67), Hewitt's voice converted the hearts and souls of the rest of the country into Leaf fans.

Smythe built his Maple Leafs both on and off the ice, creating a commercial and cultural empire from coast to coast that survives to this day. Smythe had been publishing a Maple Leaf souvenir program ever since he bought the team. The program not only informed Gardens game-goers of the lineup and sweater numbers each night, it also provided a way for fans right across the country to keep in touch with the team, the players, and the hockey news from around the NHL. In the late 1940s, for instance, the cover featured Turk Broda one night, Bill Barilko the next, Syl Apps another. Subscriptions numbered well into the tens of thousands, reaching fans right across Canada and overseas. The program also generated huge profits, which Smythe poured back into the team and its building.

Smythe also happily loaned the Gardens' ice to "kid teams," all the many high school leagues and organizations in the city. As a result, thousands of youngsters realized their dream of skating on that most sacred sheet of NHL ice. It was an act of generosity, to be sure, and no boy left the building without feeling awed and overwhelmed by the experience.

Smythe ran the Gardens as he ran the team, with the highest of professional standards — an approach that helped create and maintain the Leafs' winning attitude. He initiated virtually every sig-nificant off-ice innovation in the game, among which was film. Long before Roger Neilson studied film footage in the late 1970s with the modern Leafs, Smythe used Shanty MacKenzie (a batterymate in Caen) to film every Leaf game and practice so as to assess who was doing what during games, on his team and every other. He secretly installed individual timers up in a private office to keep track of ice time for every player on both sides during a game, so that he knew exactly who was on ice the longest. He assessed player performance using one credo above all others: if a player looked bad in a loss, he was a bad player; if he looked good in a loss, he was a bad player; but if he looked good in a win, that was the kind of player Smythe wanted on his team.

Smythe broadcast games on television long before anyone else. He was first to install Plexiglas above the boards and a proper scoreboard above centre ice. He painted the ice white so fans could see the puck better. He was the first to install escalators, in 1948, to get people up to their seats all the faster and more easily. Whenever hockey changed, chances are it changed at Maple Leaf Gardens before anywhere else.

Under Smythe's ever-watchful eye, the building was always in pristine condition. Every seat was hand-washed once a week, the floors were mopped daily, and Smythe even had two cats living in the building to ensure mice would never scamper along the Gardens' hallways. The pretty usherettes who worked in the high-society Reds wore smart uniforms and white cotton gloves, and they knew every subscriber by name. Alcohol was strictly forbidden on the premises (though, of course, bottles were smuggled into the Greens and Greys) and patrons were requested, by letter, to dress in a manner befitting Maple Leaf Gardens (jacket and tie for the men, evening gowns for the ladies). Smythe did everything to ensure the game-going experience was a culturally refined one. He was director of both the audience and the production of every Saturday night in his hockey theatre. "The best fans in the world deserve the best team," was Smythe's belief. And the best arena.

## SATURDAY NIGHT ON THE RADIO

Saturday night excitement for hockey fans began at 6:30 p.m. with the broadcast of Wes McKnight's half-hour pre-game show on CFRB radio. The avuncular McKnight's program was as popular as the game itself – a compendium of information about the night's combat, news from around the league, and the popular Beehive interview ("Remember, fellas, you get lots of food energy from Beehive Golden Corn Syrup"). By the time Foster Hewitt came on the air at 9:00 p.m – always with the words "Hello, Canada, and hockey fans in the United States and Newfoundland" – the game was already half an hour old. Between periods, McKnight was back as co-host of the Hot Stove League with Elmer Ferguson and Bobby Hewitson, who talked hockey and continued to promote Beehive: "Ask Mom to get some Beehive Corn Syrup for you tomorrow and start collecting your free hockey pictures right away."

For many listeners, however, the highlight of Saturday night on the radio came with Foster Hewitt's signature finale: "And now, while Fergie's on his way to the microphone with the Three Star selection, here's Court Benson!" The announcement of the game's best three players was sponsored by Imperial Oil and intended to promote Esso's Three Stars gasoline. To this day, the three-star selection remains a fixture of every hockey game played in Canada.

for Toronto, and the Leafs served notice that they would never give up.

In game two, the first two periods replayed game one in reverse. Twice the Leafs went ahead, twice Boston scored to tie. Then the Leafs scored two to go up 4-2. Once ahead, however, Toronto scored again and refused Boston a comeback of its own. This time the Leafs had a single hero – Ted Kennedy – who scored four of the Leafs' five goals. In game three, the Blue and White hammered the fighting spirit of Boston, winning 5-1. The final game, won by the Leafs 3-2, was almost a formality. Having eliminated Boston in four straight they advanced to face the Detroit Red Wings for the Stanley Cup.

The Leafs were undaunted by the challenge. Although Detroit scored an early goal to go up 1-0 in game one, the Leafs scored five in a row and cruised to victory. Again five players accounted for the scoring – Watson, Klukay, Apps, Mortson, and Meeker. In the remainder of the series the Leafs never trailed for another minute. Game four, the Stanley Cup clincher, was a cakewalk. Toronto led 3-0 after the first period, thanks to Kennedy, Boesch, and Watson, the three goals symbolizing all this Leafs team stood for. Kennedy, who led the playoffs in scoring with eight goals, scored on an early power play that put the Wings on their heels. Boesch's goal was a short-handed backbreaker, scored with Nick Metz in the penalty box serving a rare infraction and Detroit seeming poised to even the score. Instead, Boesch blocked a shot by Jim Conacher, who was positioned just inside the blue line. As the puck bounced out to centre ice, the normally slow-footed Boesch chased it down before any Red Wing could get to him, moved in on goal, and beat Harry Lumley with a quick shot. With the Wings now thoroughly demoralized, Watson's goal more or less sealed their fate.

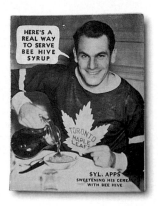

*(ABOVE)* This Syl Apps hockey card came with Beehive Corn Syrup. *(OPPOSITE ABOVE)* Fans crowd Toronto's Bay Street for the 1948 Stanley Cup victory parade. *(OPPOSITE BELOW LEFT)* Leaf players jump onto the ice after winning in 1947. *(OPPOSITE BELOW RIGHT)* Happy Day drinks from the Stanley Cup.

The Leafs led 6-1 after two (Syl Apps scoring Toronto's fourth goal) and they coasted in the third to a 7-2 victory made poignant by Apps's final shift as a Maple Leaf. Seven goals in all, seven different scorers. This was a team in every sense of the word, one that began with Squib Walker watching teenagers play house league hockey all over the country and ended with Conn Smythe's blue and white family crowding around the Stanley Cup hearth at centre ice in front of a disappointed crowd at the Detroit Olympia.

"If this team wins the Stanley Cup," Smythe had declared before game four, "it is the greatest club our organization has ever had." Amid the happy confusion after the game, he reconfirmed his assessment. "There's no doubt about it. This is far and away the greatest of the Toronto teams. They never failed to do what we asked. Not once did this bunch require a pep talk; they keyed themselves to rise to every occasion."

The entire season, like the team, seemed seamless, almost inevitable. The 1947-48 Leafs won the Cup not on any one night or in any one period or because of any one spectacular goal. Victory came as the culmination of years of careful planning, based on Smythe's experience and intelligence, great scouting, and brilliant trading. He had built a hockey system so giant and so perfect, one wonders how the Leafs didn't win every Cup for years to come. "The difference is in player depth," NHL president Clarence Campbell asserted during the Cup celebrations. "There's no question but that the Leafs had superior strength. Detroit simply couldn't match them."

That superior strength, though, was internal as much as external. Smythe judged his players not just in terms of goals and assists but in terms of character. He relied on the leadership of Apps because he knew Syl Apps was the kind of leader a team needs. He relied on Squib Walker's advice because he knew there was many a great player not living in a big city. And he relied on Happy Day's coaching because he knew Day's qualities as a player and a captain and a man. Thanks to Smythe's genius, his Leafs team was one of hockey's very greatest.

Stanley Cup victory came as the culmination of years of careful planning, based on Smythe's experience and intelligence, great scouting, and brilliant trading. He had built a hockey system so giant and so perfect, one wonders how the Leafs didn't win every Cup for years to come.

# THE PRODUCTION LINE

## 1949-50 DETROIT RED WINGS

One of the first on-ice decisions Red Wings coach Tommy Ivan made at the start of the 1947-48 season was to put veteran centre Sid Abel on a line with rising stars Ted Lindsay on the left side and second-year man Gordon Howe on the right. Ivan saw the three as a perfect blend of youth and experience, whose skills ideally complemented each other. Abel, the oldest by many years, was fast and smart, a passer first and shooter second. Lindsay had terrific speed and a quick shot, but didn't handle the puck as well. Howe was quickly developing into the league's first power forward, at 19 already possessing tremendous skill and strength and tenacity. A tireless and effortless skater, he could switch hands in a second to shoot either left or right. The three would struggle for most of their first year together, but in their second season they blossomed into the best line in hockey. Soon nicknamed the Production Line for their scoring prowess, they owed a large part of their success to a set play they invented, the so-called angled shoot-in. Ironically, however, Howe would be out of action for his team's most important victory. Yet even seriously injured, he helped inspire the Red Wings to win the 1950 Stanley Cup, the first of four they would win in the first half of the decade.

AT THE BEGINNING OF THE LINE'S FIRST SEASON TOGETHER, coach Ivan had trouble convincing the two youngsters to overcome their awe of Abel. The three worked well as a unit occasionally but inconsistently. Although they showed tremendous promise and superb natural instincts, they were unable to build any momentum in their play. While it may now seem hard to believe that the Leafs' Howie Meeker had beaten Howe for the Calder Trophy as top rookie the previous year, Detroit general manager Jack Adams had elevated Howe to the Red Wings roster at age 18 when he was still developing. As *The Hockey News* reported at the start of the 1947-48 season, Howe's second in the NHL, "Gordie Howe at 19 is bound to improve, for he has youthful stamina along with professional style." In December 1947, Abel was named the NHL's Player of the Week, the only significant sign that the trio was gaining a measure of respect around the league.

A player's ascension to the NHL seems easily accomplished in retrospect, but during his teenage years it is the rare aspiring player who takes turning pro for granted. In 1944, at 16, Gordie Howe had been invited to the New York Rangers' training camp. But the shy farm boy, who'd never been away from home, was extraordinarily unhappy. When he returned to Saskatchewan it seemed he might never play in the NHL. But the following year GM Jack Adams convinced the now 17-year-old forward to attend the Detroit camp, where he made such a superb impression that his place with the Red Wings was assured. Howe played that 1945-46 season in Omaha, for Detroit's farm team, becoming more comfortable with travel and sleeping away from home, and the next year made the big team.

Ted Lindsay originally seemed destined for the Maple Leafs, not Detroit. During his teens he played for St. Mike's in Toronto, right under the nose of Conn Smythe and his Maple Leaf Gardens empire. But for once Smythe failed to spot a star in the making, and Detroit bird dog Carson Cooper placed young Lindsay on the team's negotiation list, automatically making him Detroit property. Lindsay had joined the Wings in 1944, two years before Howe.

The senior member of Detroit's new line was seven years older than Lindsay and a decade older than Howe, but had joined the Detroit organization in like manner. Sid Abel was playing junior for the Flin Flon Bombers when Detroit scouts got to him before anyone else. He was assigned to the team's American League affiliate in Pittsburgh, and the next year to Indianapolis before joining the Wings near the end of the 1940-41 season. In his early days with Detroit, Abel played with Eddie Wares and Don Grosso; the youthful trio was jokingly known as the Liniment Line and became Detroit's best pre-war unit.

Abel's two postwar linemates soon earned nicknames to match his own. Abel was called "Bootnose" because his nose was so gnarled from countless fistic fractures. Lindsay was "Scarface" because of the dozens of sutures that had helped hold his face together during his young career, and Howe was "Blinky" because of a facial tick that sometimes caused an eye to flutter without warning.

**A player's ascension to the NHL seems easily accomplished in retrospect, but during his teenage years it is the rare player who takes turning pro for granted.**

## THE ANGLED SHOOT-IN

At the start of the 1948-49 season, coach Tommy Ivan tried putting youngster Max McNab at centre between Howe and Lindsay, thinking the three young players would develop into another Liniment Line. Abel moved to centre on a line with Marty Pavelich and Pete Horeck. The experiment ended five games later, in the third period of a game against the Rangers with the score tied 2-2. Hoping to inspire his team to victory, Ivan decided to reunite his threesome. Exactly 37 seconds later, after a beautiful three-way passing play, Abel scored on a 40-foot shot that beat goalie Charlie Rayner to the glove side. The line remained together for the next five years.

In 1947-48 the Red Wings had made the Stanley Cup finals against Toronto on the strength of great goaltending from a young Harry Lumley and a core of emerging stars. In addition to Lindsay and Howe, other young notables included Pete Horeck, Jim Conacher, Leo Reise, Jim McFadden, and Marty Pavelich. As the 1948-49 season evolved this young team continued to hone its skills, and the line of Howe-Lindsay-Abel quickly emerged as the star trio of the corps. The Wings finished the 60-game regular season first overall and led the league in scoring with 195 goals, 18 more than second-place Boston. They eliminated the Canadiens in a seven-game semi-finals, then ran headlong into the immovable force that was the Toronto Maple Leafs, losing the Stanley Cup in four straight games for the second year in succession. But all four games were close, three being decided by 3-1 scores and the fourth 3-2. True to form, Howe and Lindsay were one-two in playoff scoring. This was a Wings team clearly on the rise as its number one line improved by leaps and bounds.

Lindsay and Howe were opposites in many ways. Off ice, Howe was hyperconscious of how he was perceived by the public, striving to be a gentleman at all times. Lindsay could have cared less about what others thought of him. He was opinionated and confident, a man of principles whose principles didn't always sit well with the majority. On ice they both played with an innate ferocity, but Lindsay needed to fight to assert himself – he saw it as a way to victory – while Howe fought only to make a point. Once that point was made, he had no need to fight again unless challenged. Regardless of the differences, both could score as well as anyone in the league.

Howe and Lindsay may have been contradictory personalities, but their similar upbringing helped make them the best of friends. Lindsay was born with hockey in his blood, the youngest of five sons of Bert Lindsay, an NHL goalie

(OPPOSITE, LEFT TO RIGHT) Marty Pavelich, Sid Abel, Harry Lumley, Gerry Couture, and George Gee whoop it up in the dressing room with Canada Dry ginger ale.

Abel's two linemates soon earned nicknames to match his own. Abel was called "Bootnose" because his nose was so gnarled from countless fistic fractures. Lindsay was "Scarface" because of the dozens of sutures that had helped hold his face together during his young career, and Howe was "Blinky" because of a facial tick.

with the old Montreal Wanderers and Toronto Arenas. The first four boys had all gone off to war, leaving "Terrible Ted" to do his prideful fighting on the ice in Detroit colours. Howe came from an even larger family. He was one of eight children, four girls and four boys. Both men grew up in small towns, and with a strong sense of family loyalty. This was an important value they shared with the older Abel – born in small-town Melville, Saskatchewan, a stone's throw from Howe's hometown of Floral – a value that helped establish their relationship both on the ice and off.

In Detroit, Howe and Lindsay shared an apartment; on road trips they roomed together. When Lindsay eventually got married, Howe moved into the couple's basement. Their friendship was as true and solid as the Winged Wheel on their sweater was round. "You never saw Ted without Gordie," teammate Red Kelly once remarked.

The more Howe, Lindsay, and Abel played together, the more they understood each other's skills and strengths. The hockey rink was their living room and front porch, and their fraternal relationship had more meaning than just three men playing on a hockey team. By the start of the 1949-50 season, the line was head and shoulders the best trio in the league. And it was during this climactic year that the unit invented and perfected a set play that lay at the heart of their team's success. From fooling around with the puck in practice to identifying entrenched styles of play of other NHL teams to enjoying each other's company in their most comfortable setting, they developed a stratagem that enabled them to generate even greater offence. What emerged from all these hours together was a play that changed the game.

Teammate Murray Costello saw the play work time and again: "Gordie would lead the charge down the right wing, and just after he crossed centre ice he'd fire the puck between the defencemen. If he hit that spot just right, and he was uncanny about hitting it, the puck came right out to the top of the left circle, and Lindsay would scoot in behind the defencemen and get a point-blank shot on goal." The play worked because goalies seldom left their crease and would never have thought to come out and play the shoot-in the way they do today. Furthermore, if the

(OPPOSITE) Gordie Howe (LEFT) and Ted Lindsay (RIGHT) fight for possession in front of Hawks' goalie Al Rollins.

defencemen ignored the puck and interfered with the charging players – as is standard today – they would get a penalty.

The play may have looked simple, but it required endless practice. First, they marked a spot in the corner of the rink at which, if they shot the puck at just the right angle, it would carom off the boards and slide directly in front of the net. They worked on this play over and over again after every team practice until they could do it at top speed without thinking. In a way it was a play that was an extension of their friendship and love of the game. The extra time spent perfecting what came to be known as the angled shoot-in was time spent together; the extra practice was just more hockey.

When Detroit had the man advantage, the three were even more intimidating. In this situation, Abel would simply stand in front of the net and tip shots fired at him from all angles by either Lindsay or Howe on the wings, near the boards, in the corners. This simple strategy made the unit deadly on the power play. Together the two set plays added years to Abel's career. "The way we set Abel up for shots," Lindsay quipped, "he can play in a rocking chair – which is where he belongs anyway."

## THE PRODUCTION LINE

During the 1949-50 season other players on the team were also reaching their prime, above all goaltender Harry Lumley. Lumley had begun his NHL career in 1943-44 at the age of 17, playing three games as the youngest NHL keeper ever. By training camp in 1949, he was 23 years old with five full years' experience as a number one goalie, including two playoff series against the intimidating Toronto Maple Leafs. As for Lindsay, Abel, and Howe, they placed one-two-three in that order in league scoring for the 1949-50 season with point totals of 78, 69, and 68. (The fourth-place scorer on the Wings was defenceman Red Kelly with 40.) Detroit led the league in goals scored, and the team finished first overall in the standings.

It was during this season that it became clear to all that the threesome wasn't just another fine line. The first sign of immortality came when writers and fans started to coin nicknames for the unit. At first, they settled on the traditional though banal "Abel Line." (The centre of a star line always had the line named after him.) Alternative names included the Able Line, the Motor Line, the

## JACK ADAMS

Jack Adams was that rarest of hockey heroes, a man who won the Stanley Cup as a player, a coach, and then a general manager. As a player, he first won with the Toronto Arenas at the end of the NHL's inaugural 1917-18 season. After playing for a number of years with the Vancouver Millionaires of the Pacific Coast League, he returned to Toronto in 1922. In 1926 he signed with the Ottawa Senators and won his second Cup the following spring, before retiring. At the urging of NHL president Frank Calder, Adams took on the coaching job in Detroit, a franchise entering its second season in the league. He helped the Red Wings make their first Stanley Cup finals in 1934.

Early in his bench-bossing days Adams earned the facetious nickname "Jolly Jack." His temper was famous throughout the league, as were his screaming matches with referees. He constantly shuffled players between the big club and the farm team, giving rise to the players' grim joke that Adams always had two train tickets to the minors in his jacket pocket. In 1946 Adams hired Tommy Ivan as coach while he maintained his GM portfolio. Under this setup the Red Wings quickly entered their golden age, winning four Stanley Cups in the first six years of the 1950s.

(ABOVE) Enjoying some home cooking here are (LEFT TO RIGHT) Gordie Howe, Bob Goldham, Metro Prystai, Ted Lindsay. (OPPOSITE) Detroit's other production line featured row after row of cars to be sold throughout America.

Assembly Line, the Power Line, the Work-horse Line, and the Big Three. But toward the end of the season the "Production Line" was first coined, and that name stuck. It was an apt moniker for a line now famous for its scoring ability that played in a city famous for its car manufacturing. (Meanwhile, Howe's nickname changed from the immature "Blinky" of a rookie to the more intimidating "Power" of a superstar and team leader.) As the Production Line went, so went the Red Wings.

GM Jack Adams had nothing but praise for this Production Line that he himself had single-handedly scouted and signed and that was now developing into such a great playing combination. Ordinarily, Adams was as famous for his cantankerous personality as his hockey acumen. Behind his back, the blackly humorous joke was that he always carried two train tickets to Indianapolis in his breast pocket, Indianapolis being the Red Wings' farm team. Adams frequently demoted players from his NHL Wings to jolt them and the rest of the team. The Production Line needed no such motivation. "Abel is one of the finest athletes I've ever handled, a smart hockey man and a real team player. Lindsay is the best left wing Detroit has ever had, and as game a boy as they come. Only 165 pounds, and he meets them all. Howe [in his third

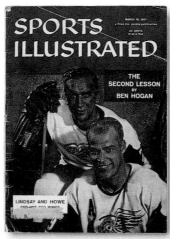

season] is becoming one of the greatest players in the history of hockey. And, all three of these men are two-way players. They are as great on defence as on offence."

## A TUMULTUOUS PLAYOFFS

As the 1950 playoffs began, the Wings were in top form for what would prove to be perhaps the most psychologically complex post-season in the history of the Original Six NHL. Each game was a battle fraught with emotional challenge. The chase for the Stanley Cup began with a series against the dreaded Maple Leafs, a team that had won 11 consecutive playoff games against Detroit since 1943.

The first game of the series, in Detroit, began as if Toronto's dominance would continue unchecked. By the third period the Leafs had built an insurmountable 4-0 lead. Then, on a routine play, Gordie Howe charged at Leaf captain Ted Kennedy along the boards near centre ice. Opinions vary, but one way or another Kennedy avoided what was going to be a terrific check. Howe piled into the boards face first, losing consciousness upon impact. Lindsay came over and slashed at Kennedy, but both players quickly separated when they saw the severity of Howe's injury. The young star was put on a stretcher and rushed to hospital, a pool of frank blood remaining on the ice as a grim reminder of what had just happened. Howe had fractured his skull, smashed his cheekbone, broken his nose, and scratched his eye.

**Howe's injury had been avenged, the curse of the Maple Leaf lifted, and this promising young Detroit team headed to the Stanley Cup finals for the third time in as many years. But whether it could carry through without Howe was another matter.**

Stunned by the accident, the Red Wings gave up another goal and lost the opening game 5-0. During the night, doctors performed a life-saving operation to release pressure on Howe's brain and stop the hemorrhaging. Once his teammates knew that he would live, their shock turned to anger. A number of them thought Kennedy had tripped "Power" or butt-ended him in the collision. Kennedy denied any wrongdoing, save getting out of the way in the nick of time. Regardless of who was right, Detroit approached game two with fury and purpose, turning it into a brawl-filled riot that saw Lindsay and Leo Reise go after Kennedy with their sticks. To his credit, Kennedy didn't back down, but Detroit emerged with its pound of flesh and a 3-1 win. Howe, now conscious and lying in his hospital bed, was not even allowed to listen to the radio broadcast, under doctor's orders to avoid all excitement. His fight to live was successful, but the war on ice was just beginning.

As the series shifted to Toronto, Howe was inundated by fan mail and letters of support from all over the continent. His condition was serious but stable, and soon he was allowed to follow his team by radio. At Maple Leaf Gardens, goalie Turk Broda shut out the Wings 2-0 as the Leafs won game three, but Detroit won the next game 2-1 to even the series once more. The teams exchanged shutout wins again, forcing game seven in Detroit on Easter Sunday, a game Howe was permitted to watch on television. The teams proceeded to play 60 minutes of scoreless hockey, ensuring the entire series would come down to overtime. Midway through the first overtime period, Detroit's Leo Reise scored on a lucky backhand that bounced twice before hopping over Broda's pads and into the net. But they all count. Detroit had eliminated the Leafs for the first time since 1943.

Howe's injury had been avenged, the curse of the Maple Leaf lifted, and this promising young Detroit team headed to the Stanley Cup finals for the third time in as many years. But whether it could carry through without Howe was another matter. Joe Carveth and Gerry Couture had taken turns at right wing on the Production Line, but neither man had been effective. Detroit had scored just 10 goals in the seven games against Toronto and been been shut out three times by Turk Broda. Without the heroic play of their own goaler, Lumley, the Wings never would have eliminated the Leafs.

## THE FINAL TEST

Detroit now faced a more unpredictable but nonetheless formidable opponent, the New York Rangers. The Rangers had lost more games than they'd won during the 1949-50 season, but their goalie, Charlie Rayner, was one of the best in the game. At season's end Rayner would win the Hart Trophy as most valuable player in the league, only the second goalie to do so. During the semi-finals against Montreal he had surrendered only seven goals as the Rangers eliminated the Canadiens in five games. Although the Broadway Blueshirts were underdogs, Rayner gave them a legitimate chance to win.

For the finals, Detroit gained a huge advantage due to a strange scheduling quirk. Madison Square Garden was booked each year at this time for the circus – a more rewarding and reliable booking than Rangers' playoff dates – so the Blueshirts had to play their home games somewhere else. Not surprisingly, they chose Toronto, the city that more than any other hated the Red Wings, hoping to elicit support from Leafs' fans. In another oddity, the standard format of two home games and then two away games was also altered. Instead, the first game was played in Detroit, a solid 4-1 win for the Wings, but then games two and three moved to Maple Leaf Gardens, where each team won once. The next two games were played back at the Olympia, both won by the Rangers in overtime on heroic goals by Don Raleigh. In the

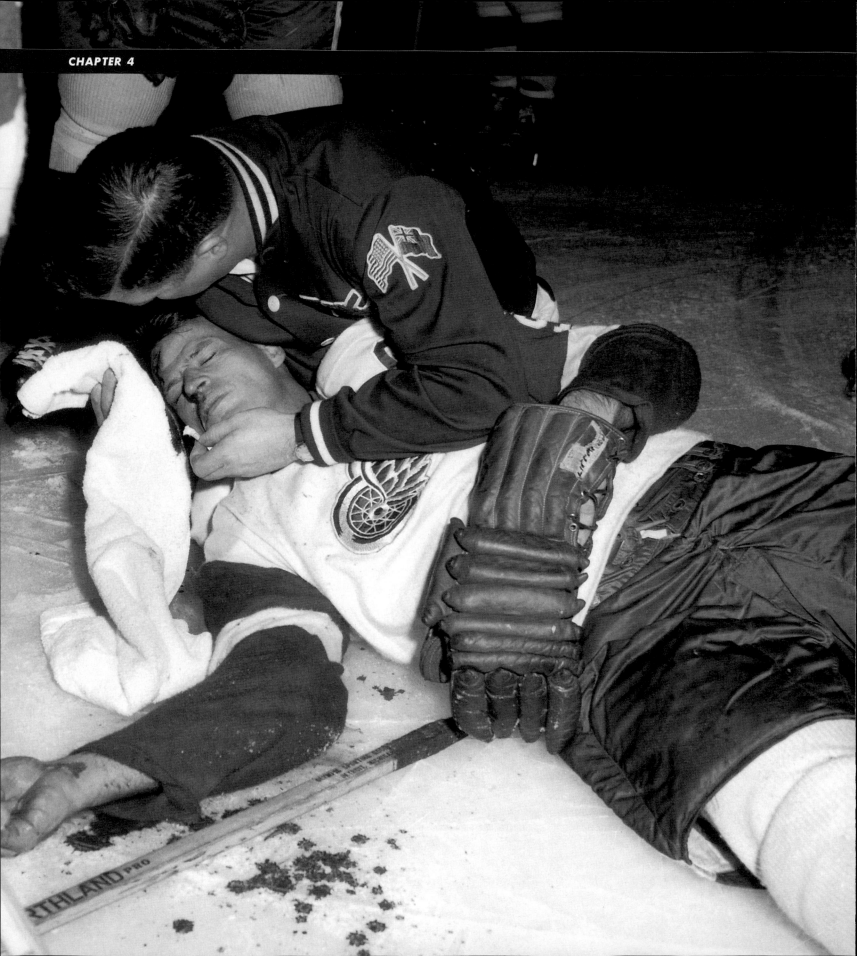

Detroit cage, Harry Lumley's playoff magic seemed to be wearing off, while the forwards in front of him generated little offence without Howe, who was still in hospital.

Leading 3-2 in games going into game six, the Rangers needed only one win to claim the Stanley Cup. As a result another strange NHL rule came to the Red Wings' aid. According to the league's constitution, a series-clinching game could not be played at a neutral arena. Since the Rangers were just one win from the Cup, they would have to play the remaining games of the series at the Olympia in Detroit, even though the crucial game six was technically a home game.

By the second period of game six, the Wings were down 3-1 and Stanley Cup victory was just a period and a half away for the New Yorkers. But Abel and Couture at last came to life, each scoring for the makeshift Production Line to tie the game. Tony Leswick put the Rangers up again early in the third, and the Blueshirts were leading with less than a period left. Now Terrible Ted Lindsay raised his play a playoff notch, tying the score just a couple of minutes later.

Midway through the final period, Abel scored an incredible goal that turned out to be the game-winner. Dashing down the left wing, he cut in on the net. Rayner held his ground and stopped the low shot, but the puck came loose. Just as Abel tripped over Rayner, he shovelled the puck into the goal while still in mid-air. The Wings held on for a 5-3 win to force a seventh game to decide the Stanley Cup. The Production Line, which had been ineffective for most of these playoffs without Gordie Howe, had come to the rescue in the nick of time, accounting for four of Detroit's five goals.

By game seven, Howe had been discharged from hospital and was well enough to go to the Olympia to watch the fifth of the series played in Detroit. It was a match that started out much like the previous one. In the first period New York went up 2-0, but in the second the Wings came out with unvanquishable determination, tying the score on quick goals by Pete Babando and Abel. But the Blueshirts weren't to be so easily overcome, scoring midway through the game to go ahead 3-2. Jim McFadden scored late in the second for the Wings to tie the game again, then the defence settled in for a long spell. A scoreless third period sent the game to overtime, and the fourth period yielded few good chances for either team. It wasn't until 8:31 of the second OT that Babando took a pass from George Gee and put a 20-foot backhander past the screened Rayner, Babando's second goal of the game. It was the first time a team had played two seven-game series in

the playoffs and won both. It was also the first time the Stanley Cup had been won in overtime of a seventh game.

The 13,095 fans in the sold-out Olympia went berserk with joy and many players tossed their sticks into the crowd. As the table bearing the Stanley Cup was wheeled out to centre ice the fans chanted, "We want Howe! We want Howe!" And so the convalescing Gordie, in suit and tie, came down from his seat to acknowledge the cheers and celebrate with his teammates, who were joined by Jack Adams and Tommy Ivan. Lindsay tossed Howe's fedora into the crowd to reveal a shaved head and remind everyone of the injury that had kept their great "Power" forward out of the lineup.

The dejected Rangers could only shake their heads in disbelief as they congratulated the victors. They had played just two of 12 playoff games at Madison Square Garden, earning the nickname the Orphan team. They had put up a brave fight, taking the lead each time after they had squandered it. But just as the Leafs had shown during their 1948 Stanley Cup victory, the Red Wings proved that their ability to come from behind and overcome adversity was the most important quality a great team could possess. As Marty Pavelich remarked during the post-game pandemonium "Fight and lots of spirit are what pulled us through out there tonight. Champions … just think of it … we're champions!"

As the organist played Detroit's theme song, "Pretty Red Wing," Ted Lindsay took the Cup from the presentation table, and, in a moment of inspired spontaneity, hoisted it high above his head. With arms upstretched, he skated around the rink to show off the sacred silverware to adoring fans in all corners of the building, establishing a tradition that has become emblematic of victory ever since.

(LEFT) Gordie Howe lies semi-comatose on the ice, seconds after missing Ted Kennedy with a vicious check and falling into the boards.
(ABOVE) Howe's close-cropped hair is the only hint of his injury as he embraces the Cup.

Ever the general manager, Jack Adams started looking ahead as soon as the Cup was won. "This is a team that shouldn't collapse," he said. "It's the youngest team in the league. Men like Ted Lindsay, Gordie Howe, Marty Pavelich, Lee Fogolin, Harry Lumley all appear to have 10 years of NHL play ahead of them." Indeed, the Wings would go on to win three more Stanley Cups in the next five years, but the first one, the one that established Detroit as a team capable of winning and not simply coming close, was the most important. That it was won without Gordie Howe, the team's 21-year-old superstar, was the truest sign of this team's greatness.

# CHAPTER 5

# THE FORGOTTEN AMATEURS

*1952 EDMONTON MERCURYS*

At first glance, the 1952 Edmonton Mercurys hardly seem like a team to rank alongside the 1924 Toronto Granites, the 1947-48 Toronto Maple Leafs, or the 1949-50 Detroit Red Wings. Yet these little-known players formed the only amateur team ever to win both a World Championship gold and an Olympic gold, accomplishments all the more startling given that they lacked even one star who could single-handedly win a game. The Mercs, as they were known to their fans, were amateur hockey players in the best sense of the word. Everyone on the team had a day job, many with a local car dealership, because as amateurs they couldn't be paid for playing. Like the Preston Rivulettes before them, they practised in the evenings after putting in a full day's work. Following road games, they often spent half the night coming home by bus so they could be back on the job the next day. They were a first-rate team in their league, but not one player aspired to play in the NHL. None has been inducted into the Hockey Hall of Fame, none is a household name, and none ever gained more than marginal renown outside his hometown. Today, almost a half a century after they conquered the world, they are all but forgotten. Yet as a team they rank among international hockey's greatest.

THE EDMONTON MERCURYS EXISTED BECAUSE OF ONE MAN'S love for his city. Jim Christianson, a local dealer in farm machinery for a company called Waterloo Equipment, had done well enough in the postwar boom to add a car dealership, Waterloo-Mercury on Jasper Avenue, to his portfolio. Although he didn't play or follow sports, he was a civic-minded Edmontonian who in 1947 decided to sponsor a basketball team and a Junior B hockey team, which he called the Mercurys, after one of his big sellers on the lot. Naming a team for its commercial affiliations was common enough. The Oshawa Generals got their nickname from General Motors, the Detroit Auto Club from the city's auto-building reputation, the Toronto Goodyears and Whitby Dunlops from tire manufacturers. There have been countless other teams in hockey history, from the obscure Los Angeles Global Ice Cream to the Mighty Ducks of Anaheim of the modern NHL, to be so named.

But at first blush, the Mercs seemed to belong more with the Ice Cream than with the Generals. They began play in 1947 as a Junior B hockey team competing in the Western Intermediate League against opponents from cities such as Lacombe, Camrose, Red Deer, Calgary, and Wetaskiwin. They never played in a top amateur league, and never played for the Allan Cup, which represented the pinnacle of amateur achievement in the country. The Allan Cup champions still regularly represented Canada at the Olympics, but the Mercs never aspired to play abroad for their country. Their first opportunity to do so came only by chance.

The Mercs won the Junior B Western Canadian finals in March 1949 under coach Jimmy Graham, the best result they could hope for at their level of play. But that autumn, Doug Grimston, president of the Canadian Amateur Hockey Association, lobbied on the team's behalf to send them to England for the 1950 World Championships. Grimston's was an unusual request, since representing Canada was an honour usually reserved for the Allan Cup winners. Clearly the Mercs had made a favourable impression on him.

As the CAHA president pointed out, there were several factors working in the Mercurys' favour. First, the 1949 Allan Cup-champion Ottawa Senators didn't qualify for the Worlds because their current roster included a number of former professional players. Second, it was a Western team's turn. Because there were many amateur teams in Canada that could be expected to beat any non-Canadian team, the CAHA representatives alternated from year to year between Eastern and Western cities. For the 1949 Worlds the Sudbury Wolves had got the nod, so it was expected that the West would earn the honour in 1950. Furthermore, the Wolves had lost to the Czechs 3-2 for the gold medal, the first Canadian hockey defeat to a team from the Continent. (Of Canada's two other international losses, one was to the United States at the 1933 World Championships and the

(RIGHT) The sweater the Mercs wore for the 1950 Worlds. (OPPOSITE ABOVE) Mercs founder Jim Christianson poses in front of a poster commemorating the team's 1949 Western championship. (OPPOSITE BELOW) The car dealership that inspired the Mercurys' name.

other to a Canadian-stocked British team at the 1936 Olympics.) But perhaps the Mercs' greatest advantage was monetary. As sponsor, Christianson promised to finance the trip. And so the Edmonton Mercurys became Canada's representatives at the 1950 World Championships in England.

## TAKING ON THE WORLD

Christianson didn't just pay for the team's transportation and accommodation; he covered the players' salaries for the three months they'd miss from work to ensure financial stability for their families. Since the trip included an extensive tour of the Continent before the championships began, the cost was considerable. But Christianson wanted the players to acclimatize to the larger European ice surface. He also hoped the tour would recoup some of his expenses.

By the time the Mercs arrived in London on March 13, 1950, they'd been in Europe almost three months and were ready to play at the world championships. Led by captain Billy Dawe and the high-scoring line of Leo Lucchini, Ab Newsome, and Hassie Young, the Edmontonians easily upheld Canada's honour, not only winning gold but demolishing the competition.

In the preliminary round the Mercs slaughtered Belgium 33-0, taking 114 shots on goalie Jacques Heylen, the team's reserve keeper, who played well despite the onslaught. In the five-game round robin the Mercs outscored their opponents 42-3, including a 5-0 whitewash of the United States, which took home the silver medal. In all, the Canadians allowed just 70 shots in the seven games played at the world championships. Their only disappointment was in not playing the Czechs, the only Communist country that participated in international hockey at this time, who boycotted that year's championships for political reasons.

Canada's deciding game of the round robin came against the hometown Brits – in Harringay, just outside London – where a capacity crowd watched their heroes fall behind 1-0 on the first rush of the game, then saw the Canadians cruise to a 12-0 victory. "Canada skated faster, passed better, and shot harder than they have done so far in the championships – and it had to happen to us. That's life," said British coach Lou Bates.

Had the Mercs won in 1950 and never been heard from again, their achievement in England would likely have been remembered as one in a series of impressive performances by obscure Canadian teams at a championships Canada has never taken too seriously. The Mercs had done their job, returned home to be feted briefly, then carried on quietly with their lives and playing the amateur game they loved.

The next year, the Lethbridge Maple Leafs won the Western Canadian Junior B finals then went a perfect 6-0 to win gold at the World Championships in France, but again the victory was compromised by the absence of the Czech team. In 1950-51, however, the Mercs were back on top of the league, still playing a notch below Senior A. That same year the Western Senior A league had gone from being an amateur organization to semi-pro, disqualifying most of the teams from Olympic eligibility. Thus the Mercurys' decision not to move up to

By the time the Mercs arrived in London on March 13, 1950, they'd been in Europe almost three months and were ready to play at the world championships. Led by captain Billy Dawe and the high-scoring line of Leo Lucchini, Ab Newsome, and Hassie Young, the Edmontonians easily upheld Canada's honour, not only winning gold but demolishing the competition.

a Senior or a semi-pro league made them eligible for the 1952 Olympic Winter Games. As the only top team not tainted by professionalism, and having previous international success, the Mercs once again became Canada's team, this time at the 1952 Olympics in Oslo, Norway.

The '52 Mercurys were substantially different from the team that had played in England just two years previous. A number of players could not afford to leave work this time, and under new coach Lou Holmes the roster had altered. Jim Christianson had also done some recruiting, convincing forward Frank Sullivan to join the Mercs. Sullivan, long considered one of the finest amateurs in the country, had

attended the training camp of the Montreal Maroons in the late 1930s but decided against turning pro in favour of a better-paying job as a technician for the Ciminco zinc mine in Kimberley, British Columbia. At 35, he was the oldest member of the Olympics-bound Mercs, a natural leader on a team whose players were mostly in their mid-twenties.

The best line of the 1950 World champions, Lucchini-Newsome-Young, had been replaced by the superior trio of Billy Gibson, David Miller, and George Abel. Fine players all, none was a star the equal of Harry Watson of the 1924 Toronto Granites. Of the 1950 veterans, Ralph Hansch was now the number one goalie, while Billy Dawe was still team captain

and head of the defence. The Mercurys still played as a group, won as a group, and relied on every man on the team to win. They possessed a balanced and consistent offence, a reliable and disciplined defence, and solid but not spectacular goaltending. The whole was unquestionably greater than the parts.

### THE EDMONTON OLYMPIANS

Christianson once again provided the financing, some $100,000 to underwrite the trip. The Mercurys flew from Montreal to Prestwick, Scotland, on January 5, 1952, the first time a Canadian team travelled by air. They deplaned in true western Canadian style, bedecked in white Stetsons. Less than an hour later they were on the ice playing their first exhibition game, a 6-3 win over the Ayr Raiders. After two more games in Scotland, then a series in London, they crossed to the Continent for more Olympic tune-ups.

The Mercurys' European tour was immensely successful. Much like the Toronto Granites in 1924, they amazed fans who had never seen such speed and strength coupled with such skating and puck-handling skill. And everywhere they went, they won – against the Raiders in Scotland, the Paisley Pirates in England, and national or all-star teams in Germany, France, Belgium, Sweden, Holland, Norway, Switzerland, and Italy. By the time the Mercs arrived in Oslo on February 15, 1952, just a few days before their first Olympic game, they felt ready to repeat their dominating performance of 1950.

As in previous World Championships and Olympics, the tournament consisted of a round-robin series of games between the competing nations, in this instance Canada, Sweden, Czechoslovakia (playing for the first time since 1949), Switzerland, Poland, Finland, Germany, Norway, and the United States. Before Canada's first game, however, forward David Miller was at the centre of a small dispute initiated by the Czechs, who claimed he had played semi-pro hockey several years earlier for Streatham in England. The International Olympic Committee listened to the argument but dismissed the protest, and Miller didn't miss a minute of action. Goalie Ralph Hansch also riled the IOC by adopting a zero as his sweater number, the first and only Canadian to have done so. Hansch had worn the number through peewee and the minors, and saw no reason to alter his good-luck digit now that he had arrived at the biggest tournament of his life. But the governing body frowned on the idea and asked him to switch to a "real" number. Hansch refused, and the IOC subsequently instituted a rule making the wearing of the goose egg illegal.

The Mercs began play with an easy 15-1 shellacking of the Germans, David Miller (five goals and an assist) and Billy Gibson (four goals and two assists) leading the assault. Because the Germans played most of the game behind their blue line, goalie Heinz Wackers earned accolades for staunching

what might have been an even heavier flow of vulcanized rubber. The only German score came when Walter Kremershof managed to surprise Hansch by getting off a quick shot just inside the Canadian blue line.

In their next game the Mercs recorded a victory over the Finns that was almost as easy, 13-3. That the Finns managed three goals on just seven total shots was more a sign of Canada's lack of concentration than of Finnish offensive ability. The soft effort was not lost on CP reporter Jack Sullivan: "The Canadians played it free and easy, roaming about the Finns' net and not bothering too much at times about opposition." Coach Holmes was not impressed with his team's defensive lapses and stressed greater focus for the tougher competition ahead.

After a complete dismantling of the hapless Poles 11-0, the Mercs faced their first tough opponent, the undefeated Czechs, whose predecessors had wrested the World Championships from Canada back in 1949. Two years out of the international loop, they were an unknown quantity but one not to be taken lightly.

More than an hour before the opening face-off on February 19, fans started streaming into Oslo's marvellous outdoor Jordal Amfi arena. The Canadians came out hitting, cleanly but heavily, for which they earned scornful whistles from the unsophisticated Norwegian fans, who knew little of bodychecking. With Sullivan in the penalty box the Czechs scored first on a Miloslav Charouzd shot from in close. "The Czechs," Jack Sullivan noted, "were artists at drop passes and fair at long-passing combination plays. They covered up well, and their only shortcoming appeared to be a good working knowledge of bodychecking." Undaunted by the early goal, the Mercs fought back, playing determined hockey for the first time at these Olympics. Billy Gibson tied the score eight minutes later when his shot caromed off a Czech defenceman and past the helpless goaltender, Jan Richter. After one period the score was tied 1-1. Early in the second, the Mercs had all the good scoring chances but converted none. They continued to press, and finally, midway through the period, after a terrific flurry around the Czech net, took the lead. Sullivan, Miller, and Dawe all had excellent shots, but it was Bruce Dickson who finished off the flurry by whacking the puck in off a rebound. Canada now had the lead, 2-1. In the third, Robertson and

Gibson put the game out of reach, 4-1. But this final score reflected the ever-narrowing gap in skill between Canadian amateurs and the Czech nationals.

The Canada-Czech game and the U.S.-Swiss game on the same day both garnered more ink for their supposed violence than for the calibre of play. Gordie Robertson of Canada and Joe Czarnota of the States both received major penalties for putative stick-swinging incidents, the more serious perpetrator being the American. The rough play disgusted many fans and critics, notably a writer from Zurich's leading paper, *Neue Zuricher Zeitung*: "We have neither the words nor the space to describe in detail what some of these rowdies drilled in circus business considered permissible. It is now time to ask whether this pollution of European ice hockey through overseas teams should not be halted. One can be certain that neither the Canadians nor the Americans would let themselves be criticized. However, what seems good enough for their players and their public need not be held up as a model for European circumstances." The editorial concluded by questioning "whether an ice hockey tournament under such unfavourable auspices might better be stricken from the Olympic program."

When asked to comment, Norway's Prime Minister Oscar Torp defended the brand of hockey provided by the North Americans: "Just ignorance of the mainly Norwegian crowd," he conceded. "People should understand that the penalties make ice hockey a human game. When the boys get so het up that they do something wrong or get too rowdy – okay, give them two minutes to cool down and think it over. Ice hockey is a terrific display, not only of teamwork but also of

## A CLASH OF STYLES

Although the IOC had adopted Canadian hockey rules in 1920, the one area of contention through the years has been European referees' interpretation of bodychecking. Europeans considered the bodycheck a goon tactic. Canadians saw things differently. Bunny Ahearne, president of the IIHF, summed up the European view: "We don't have any bodychecking in Europe and it's very difficult to form a comparison between our European teams here and your own teams in Canada. There's no question that the Czechoslovakian team is a first-class team, and if you eliminate the bodychecking, they would stand up to any team in Canada." The outgoing CAHA president put the Canadian position in equally diplomatic terms: "Hockey, as played in Europe, is a different game than what we play in Canada and I felt that our boys did exceptionally well under different rules and 'strange' refereeing. We play a more robust game, which is frowned on in Europe."

In Europe, checking in the offensive zone would be forbidden until 1968. In North America, hitting was always critical to forcing turnovers and generating chances in that offensive end. The difference in rules led to a difference in styles, with the European game emphasizing skill and puckhandling and the North American game putting more emphasis on the physical aspects.

technique and bodily strength. So, of course, the lads will hurt each other now and then." The next day, after an hour's meeting, the IIHF, under the directorship of Dr. Fritz Kraatz, decided that no suspensions would be levied.

After routing Switzerland 11-2, the Mercs faced their next tough opponent, the Swedes, who had stunned the U.S. 4-2 the previous day. The first period began as if a second, more stunning upset was in the works, with Tre Kronor ahead 2-0 before the game was 10 minutes old. The Mercs, shaking off an early bout of nerves, now started skating relentlessly, attacking with all their skill. Late in the first, Abel made a perfect pass to Lou Secco in front of the goal. Secco tipped the puck past goalie Tord Flodquist and the period ended with Canada trailing 2-1. The Mercs played inspired hockey for the rest of the game, prevented from a lopsided win only by the play of Flodquist. Abel scored the only goal of the second to tie the game, and for most of the third Flodquist held off wave after wave of Canadian attackers. The dominating Mercury offence seemed finally to have met its match, and with less than a minute to play a tie game seemed inevitable. But the team knew that a tie in the standings would jeopardize its gold medal chances. With just 20 seconds left, Billy Gibson took the puck into the Swedish end, curled behind the net, and stopped. This confounded the Swede defence long enough for Mercs captain Dawe to rush in on goal from the blue line. When Dawe reached the top of the crease, Gibson put the puck solidly on his stick. Dawe calmly deked Flodquist out of position and slid the go-ahead goal into the net. According to the *Toronto Telegram*, "In the remaining seconds, the Canadians hung grimly to the puck and at the final whistle Dawe's mates swarmed all over him." The Mercs had staged a dramatic 3-2 come-from-behind victory against a foe far stronger than any they had expected to face.

Another 11-2 cakewalk, this time over Norway, prepared the Canadians for the last game of the tournament, the gold medal match against the United States. Thanks to the Americans' loss to Sweden, however, the Canadians needed only a tie to finish first in the round robin. Dawe and Bruce Dickson

*(OPPOSITE)* The Mercs lift coach Lou Holmes high in the air while Jim Christianson looks on. Goalie Ralph Hansch, wearing his trademark "zero" sweater, has his back to the camera.

gave the Mercs a 2-0 lead in the first period, but the Americans tied the score in the second on goals by John Mulhern and Ruben Bjorkman. Don Gauf scored with just 1:57 in the middle period to give the Mercs a 3-2 lead, then the Canadians settled into a defensive game intended to keep the Americans off the scoreboard. But the red, white, and blue refused to quit, tying the game with just 2:09 remaining. They then threw everything at the Canadian net, knowing that only a win could give them the gold, but the Mercs held on and the game ended in a tie. At the final bell the Edmontons threw coach Holmes high in the air and sang "For He's a Jolly Good Fellow."

### LAST OF AN ERA

Despite the Edmonton Mercs' gold medal, Canada's international hockey dominance was coming to an end. As the Czechs and Swedes had shown, the days of slaughters and laughers against the emerging hockey countries in mainland Europe were all but over. "European teams have improved considerably the last few years and, with some proper coaching, could be mighty troublesome to Canada," Doug Grimston said after watching the progress of European teams during the Oslo Games. He went on to observe, "European teams lack stamina, especially on power plays, and they are timid when it comes to bodily contact." But if these problems could be eradicated, he warned, many could become superior hockey-playing nations. As the next Olympics would prove, his words were prescient. The Mercurys' 1952 gold medal was Canada's last of the century.

The story of the Edmonton Mercurys is unique among hockey's greatest teams. An anonymous group of players expected to win by simple virtue of their being selected to represent Canada at the Olympics, they went overseas as confident as the Granites some 30 years earlier. But unlike the Granites, their victory was hard-fought and fraught with unexpected challenge. Despite the absence of a star player and their surprise at the difficulty of the struggle, the Mercs prevailed. As Team Canada would do in 1972, the 1952 Edmonton Mercurys overcame obstacles they didn't know existed, fought battles they didn't expect to fight, and survived to retain a championship they had all along been expected to win.

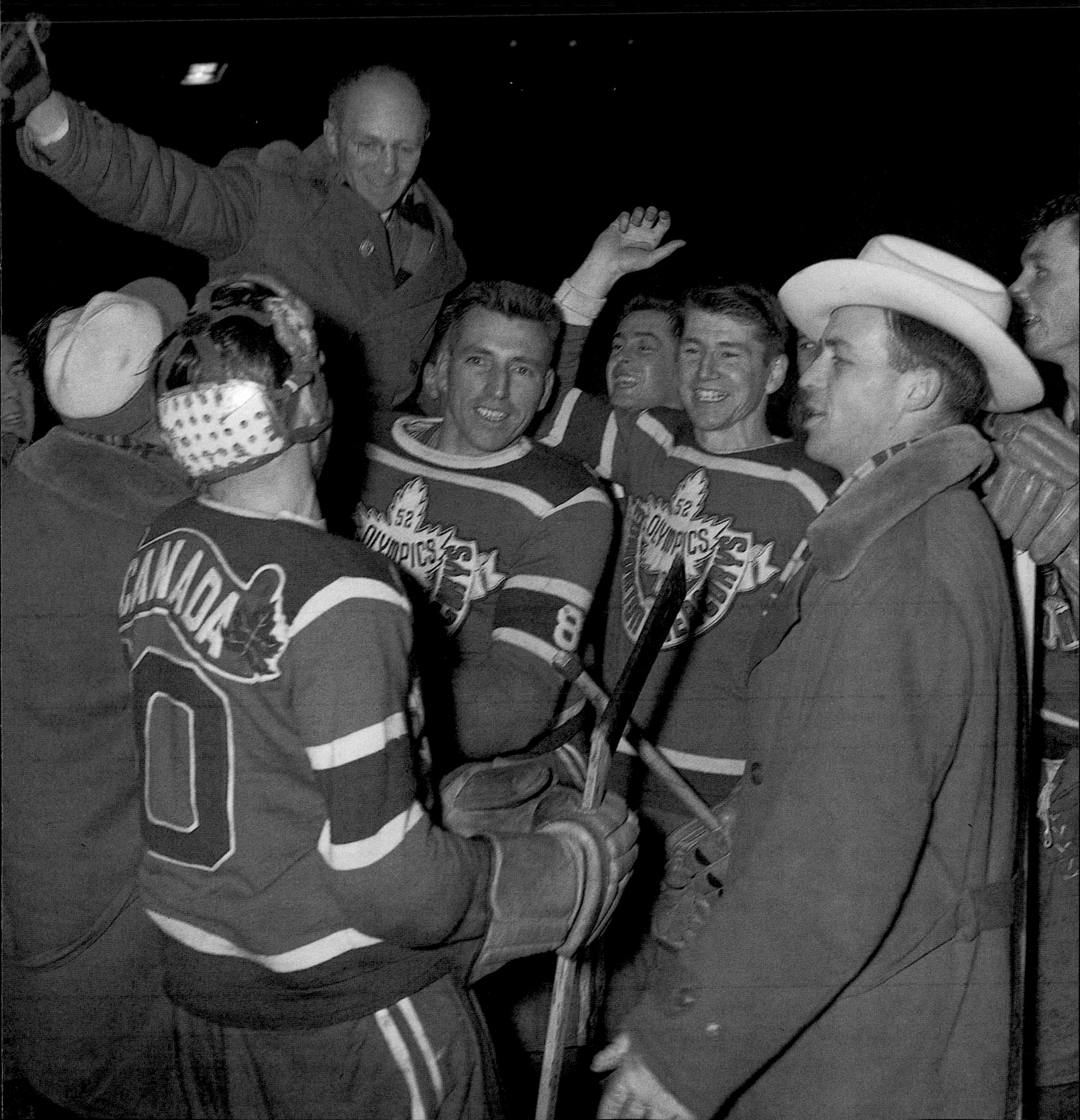
CANADA
52
OLYMPICS
8
52
OLYMPICS

# GREATEST OF THE GREATS

1959-60 MONTREAL CANADIENS

The Montreal Canadiens won five consecutive Stanley Cups from 1956 to 1960, a record unmatched before or since. The Toronto Maple Leafs had won three in a row from 1947 to '49, the first team to accomplish that feat, then added a fourth in five years in 1951. The Red Wings won four Cups in the six years from 1950 to '55. But five in a row was as inconceivable then as now. These were the greatest days of the "dynasty," the era when players would stay with one team throughout their prime hockey years, when scouting was intense and the competition to sign young talent ruthless. Of the 18 players on the 1960 Montreal team that won that fifth straight Cup, an extraordinary 11 were later inducted into the Hockey Hall of Fame, including the Richard brothers — Maurice and Henri — Jean Béliveau, Jacques Plante, Bernie Geoffrion, and Doug Harvey. Fourteen of the 18 were born in Quebec and eight came from Montreal itself. Equally remarkable, not one Montreal player was acquired by trade, and only one — Marcel Bonin — had not been developed in the Montreal organization under the Canadiens' astute general manager Frank Selke and their player-turned-coach, Toe Blake. Truly, this was a great team that reigned supreme because it was built to withstand change and challenge.

THE CANADIENS DYNASTY TOOK PLACE DURING THE ERA OF autocratic control, when the six NHL owners dictated every move of every player who wanted to make a career of skating, shooting, and stickhandling. A player's loyalty to the team was undeniable, yet it was a loyalty forced upon him contractually from the moment he started to play organized hockey as a teenager. Winning seasons came and went in other cities under these conditions, but they were the norm at the Montreal Forum.

Montreal took the first step toward building its dynasty of the late 1950s in the summer of 1955, when general manager Frank Selke named Toe Blake the new head coach, replacing the departing Dick Irvin. Along with Elmer Lach, Blake had been Maurice Richard's teammate on the great Punch Line – so named for its scoring punch – and Selke felt the key to continued success was to hire someone whom Richard respected, someone for whom he would play his best. The Rocket was not only the star of the team, he was revered by every aspiring player in the province, including his younger teammates who had idolized him from childhood – players such as Marcel Bonin, Claude Provost, and Jean-Guy Talbot. Selke's idea worked: the Rocket was one of the first to praise Blake's arrival behind the team's bench. And if Richard was happy, his team was happy.

Still very much in the prime of his career, Richard was one of the first public figures for whom the politically fiery epithet "French Canadian" was used regularly by members of the Montreal press. In the eyes of the city's French-speaking population, Richard embodied the hard-working, blue-collar man who put in his time and earned his pay. Born into poverty, the "Rocket" was one of the few to move out of his class. As a result, he became a hero off ice as much as on, both god and father to his teammates and to the people of Quebec.

Rocket Richard was an intense player among even the most intense, his competitive spirit impossible to hold in check. His emotions often propelled him to superhuman achievement, but sometimes they pushed him past rational action: he had been known more than once to push a referee or to hit a player on the head with his stick. Over the years he had many a run-in with NHL president Clarence Campbell, and the Rocket took each one very personally. In Campbell's early career as a lawyer following the end of World War II, he had helped convict war criminals. As league president, he played no favourites and acted in the interests of the owners. A brutally tough man, he was believed by many to be spiteful and vindictive. More than once Richard intimated an anti-French malice to the president's running of the league. These were smart tactics on Richard's part: his pride made the team and the city feel like hungry underdogs having to fight for respect of their culture and heritage against the rest of the league. It made Richard, and the Canadiens, even more competitive, and to players and fans alike it gave greater meaning to every game at the Forum in Montreal.

The cultural importance of the team gave the Habs a significant advantage. No proud French Canadian would play in Chicago or Detroit if he could play in Montreal. In 1959-60, for instance, there were just 12 players born in Quebec play-

## The cultural importance of the team gave the Habs a significant advantage. No proud French Canadian would play in Chicago or Detroit if he could play in Montreal.

ing on the five other teams. All of them had played junior in Quebec, and only a couple – Gump Worsley and Marcel Pronovost – were players Montreal might have signed. In other words, just about every NHL-calibre French Canadian played for the *bleu, blanc, et rouge*. Maurice Richard played right wing on a line with his younger brother, the "Pocket Rocket," Henri, and "Diggin' Dickie," Dickie Moore. (Richard himself was an anomaly in that he was one of the few left-handed shots ever to play right wing, a strategy that created a better shooting angle that often flummoxed goalies.) The second line featured "Le Gros Bil," Jean Béliveau, at centre, with wingers Bernie Geoffrion on the right side and Marcel Bonin on the left. These two lines alone produced more goals than most whole teams. The defence had Doug Harvey and Tom Johnson as well as Jean-Guy Talbot, Al Langlois, and the less heralded Bob Turner. Harvey doubled as an offensive threat, but as a group the Montreal defence followed the basics – taking the man and moving the puck out of their own end – as well as any in the league. In goal was the extraordinary Jacques Plante, a quiet man who knitted toques in his downtime and stopped pucks like few before. Without doubt, this Montreal team exuded dependability. Each player knew his role, and knew that if he fulfilled that role the team would win.

For all its star players, though, it was the team as a whole – its sheer dominance – that changed the game forever. In the very first year of coach Toe Blake's tenure Montreal won the Cup, and kept winning each successive season with increasing ease. In truth, les Canadiens were both the best and worst thing that could have happened to the NHL. They were supremely skilled and highly entertaining, but the ease with which they won sapped the league of playoff drama. As the dynasty continued unchecked, owners of the American teams begged NHL president Clarence Campbell to break up the Habs somehow, fearing their fans would lose interest if the Stanley Cup winner were more or less a *fait accompli* even before the start of each season.

### THE "MONTREAL RULES"
Montreal had such a tremendous roster that when the team went on the power play, the most feared fivesome in the game could be seen on the ice at one time – Maurice Richard, Jean Béliveau, Bernie Geoffrion, Dickie Moore, and Doug Harvey. The 1956-57 season was the first in which a penalized player was allowed to

*(LEFT)* In the pre-television era, hockey cards were one of the few ways fans could see what the players looked like, in this case the checking line of Hicke, Backstrom, and McDonald. Once television arrived, cards became cherished collectors' items. *(OPPOSITE ABOVE)* Crowds throng outside the Montreal Forum before a game. *(OPPOSITE BELOW LEFT)* Rocket Richard relaxes with Dickie Moore *(BESIDE HIM)* and brother Henri *(FAR RIGHT)*. *(OPPOSITE BELOW RIGHT)* Toe Blake, ever calm and in control, behind the bench.

A player's loyalty to the team was undeniable, yet it was a loyalty forced upon him contractually from the moment he started to play organized hockey as a teenager. Winning seasons came and went in other cities under these conditions, but they were the norm at the Montreal Forum.

Rocket Richard put up his dukes when he had to. Here he keeps the Rangers' Ivan Irvin at bay with a threatening gesture as Gump Worsley looks up ice from the safety of his crease. The Rocket became captain in 1956, replacing Butch Bouchard.

return to the ice after a power-play goal had been scored, a rule implemented in the hope of preventing Montreal from winning games with the man advantage. The Canadiens would frequently score two, sometimes three goals during one two-minute power play, after which the game, for all intents and purposes, was over. The new rule, intended to level the playing field, publicly acknowledged just how superior were the Canadiens during these dominant years. Even so, it had little effect on Montreal's ability to win.

Goalie Jacques Plante, whose superior skating and stickhandling abilities had earned him the nickname "Jake the Snake," played his position with intimidating confidence. A master tactician, he was a factor in every game he played, both in his crease and outside it. Plante became bolder and bolder as he learned the game, coming out of his net to make passes and clear the puck, thereby scuttling offensive thrusts that before had yielded many a great scoring chance or goal. He won the Vezina Trophy for fewest goals allowed in each of these five Stanley Cup-winning seasons, a tribute both to his ability to make big saves and his skill at preventing opponents from establishing possession in the Montreal end.

During the summer of 1959 Plante's prowess led to two other "Montreal rules" being proposed by the NHL Board of Governors, one of which was adopted. By now, the angled shoot-in, invented by Detroit's Production Line a decade earlier, was standard practice throughout the league. But Plante had neutralized the play by skating out to cut the puck off in the corners or to stop it behind his own goal. However, the other NHL teams argued that a goalie should be outlawed from playing the puck altogether. The Governors rejected this suggestion, but did introduce a rule penalizing a goalie for freezing the puck behind the end red line.

## THE ERA OF THE C-FORM

Without question, the C-form was the most misleading contract a teenaged hockey player ever signed. A boy who had no big-city agent or legal knowledge signed this agreement on his 16th birthday, usually in exchange for about $100 and the priceless promise of a National Hockey League career. The C-form committed him to one of the six NHL teams for the remainder of his pro playing days, at the discretion of the team.

Jacques Plante had become Montreal property in this way, as had almost every other player who made it to the NHL, with the notable exception of Jean Béliveau (second from left, strolling along New York's Broadway with Rocket Richard on right and teammates). When Béliveau's junior days were over, "Le Gros Bil" signed with the Quebec Aces, a semi-pro outfit in the Quebec senior league. (He had signed a B-form, which promised the Habs that

if he ever played professionally, he would play for them.) Montreal general manager Frank Selke was furious and red-faced, but Béliveau said he adored playing in Quebec City. Besides, his $10,000 contract was triple the Quebec league average and certainly more than many in the NHL were paid. Le Colisée in Quebec routinely attracted crowds of 14,000 to see Béliveau play, and he was treated as an icon in that city. Why should he leave?

After three years, the Habs did the unthinkable. They bought the entire Quebec Senior Hockey League, of which the Aces were just one team, and turned it into a professional operation. This meant that Béliveau was now a bona fide pro, and as per the B-form he would have to play for the Canadiens or not at all — at least, not with the now professional Quebec Aces.

**By now, the angled shoot-in, invented by Detroit's Production Line a decade earlier, was standard practice throughout the league. But Plante had neutralized the play by skating out to cut the puck off in the corners or to stop it behind his own goal.**

This rule change, implemented in time for the 1959-60 season, did little to diminish the Canadiens' drive to a fifth straight Stanley Cup. In fact, the Habs were responsible for introducing two more innovations that season, both quickly becoming important features of the game – the slapshot and the goalie mask – the one leading to the other. Montreal teammate Bernie Geoffrion was Plante's worst nightmare as well as his saving grace. During practice Geoffrion experimented with slapshots, the hardest shot a player could muster because it was taken with a full windup of the stick and a complete follow-through. Unfortunately, it was Plante who bore the brunt of each Geoffrion blast, and so Jake soon decided to carry out an experiment of his own: wearing a face mask in practice so as not to get injured and put himself out of meaningful games. Coach Blake didn't mind anything as practical and precautionary a piece of equipment as a mask – in practice. Meanwhile, Geoffrion's shot soon became all the rage as his goal-scoring increased dramatically. It earned him the nickname "Boom Boom" and helped make him just the second man, after Rocket Richard in 1944-45, to score 50 goals in a single season.

It wasn't a Geoffrion slapper, however, that turned a practice mask into a goalie's standard equipment. On the night of November 1, 1959, during a game in Madison Square Garden, Plante was hit in the face by a backhand off the stick of Andy Bathgate. He was screened, so never saw the shot. He fell to the ice in a quickly accumulating pool of blood, and the game was delayed while he was helped to the dressing room, where team doctor Kazuo Yanigasawa closed the wounds with a number of sutures. Plante then told coach Blake that he wasn't going back into the game without his practice mask. Blake,

Jean Béliveau was treated like a god when he played for the Quebec Aces. Here he entertains three female admirers before a game.

with no other goalie on hand, acquiesced, but only so that Plante could finish the contest.

Blake knew that his star goalie knew he expected the mask to come off for the team's next game. But Plante kept it on, refusing to play otherwise. The coach was furious, and a goalie of lesser skill and reputation would have been sent to the minors for good. But the Habs won the second game in which Plante wore the mask, and the next and the next after that. Blake didn't make a fuss because in his mind Plante, a renowned neurotic, was wearing the mask out of superstition. But Muzz Patrick, general manager of the Rangers, spoke for many in the league when he attacked Plante's protection: "Our game has a greater percentage of women fans than any team sport I know…. Those women fans want to see men, not masks. That's why I'm against helmets and masks. They rob the players of their individuality. We start out with goalies wearing masks. Every club has a defenceman or two who goes down to smother shots. Soon they'll want masks. All the forwards will wear helmets. The teams will become faceless, headless robots, all of whom look alike to the spectators. We can't afford to take that fan appeal away from hockey."

It wasn't until more than a month later, on December 2, 1959, that Plante finally lost a game wearing the mask – a slim 1-0 decision to Toronto. Perhaps it was that initial winning streak, combined with Plante's fame and skill as much as his pioneering genius, that helped make facial protection acceptable. In fact, the only barefaced performance he gave during the remainder of the season was March 8, 1960, when Blake convinced him to take off his mask. The Habs lost 3-0, and Plante never played barefaced again. "The decision over whether he wears the mask or not belongs to Jacques," Blake said after that game. "I won't force him to discard it any more."

Plante's ability to change Blake's stance on the mask was all the more notable because it occurred during an era when team management reigned supreme. The one attempt by the players to form a union had been crushed. The players were merely paid employees, bladed labourers who were offered take-it-or-leave-it contracts and who could be replaced with one long-distance phone call to the farm team. Plante's success at keeping the mask was both a personal and professional victory. It was as much about player versus management as it was about preventing injury, and was thus a morale booster for every player in the NHL. Even though a union was years away, Plante proved that if a player stood his ground, he just might win his fight.

Jacques Plante's first mask frightened many Montreal fans, though Chicago's Bill Hay doesn't seem appalled. Plante's battle to wear protective face gear was a rare example of a player prevailing over a coach in these Original Six days.

**As Rocket Richard's last year in the league and Plante's last with Montreal, the 1959-60 season represents not only the NHL's greatest team at the pinnacle of its existence, but the transition to continued success.**

## AN EASY ROAD TO THE CUP

With Plante at the height of his goaltending powers, Montreal finished the 1959-60 regular season in first place with 92 points, 13 more than second-place Toronto. The Habs scored more goals than any other team, 255, and allowed fewer as well – just 178. Three of the top seven scorers in the league were Canadiens – Béliveau, Henri Richard, and Geoffrion. (In this, his last NHL season, the Rocket missed 19 games with injury and had just 19 goals.) Plante played in 69 of the team's 70 games, and led the league in both wins (40), and goals-against average (2.54) to win his record fifth successive Vezina Trophy. Although Montreal had already won four Cups in a row, its lineup was almost the same in 1960 as it had been in 1956, the first of those victories, and there was no reason to feel that the team that had won the past four tries was all of a sudden going to lose this year.

In the semi-finals the Habs played Chicago, a team very close to becoming a championship outfit of its own. Under owner Jim Norris the Blackhawks had developed an excellent scouting system, and their lineup now featured high-scoring forwards Bobby Hull, Stan Mikita, and Tod Sloan, and the most reliable goalie of all time, Glenn Hall. Yet Chicago was not yet a match for Montreal, which swept the series in four games, the last two by shutouts. Blackhawks coach Rudy Pilous's frustration spoke volumes of Montreal's team strength: "I had Glen Skov tie up Béliveau and he did a pretty good job. I had Ted Lindsay on Boom Boom [Geoffrion] and he did okay. So what happens? Somebody named [Bill] Hicke came off the bench and scored."

In the days leading up to the much-anticipated Toronto-Montreal finals, Leaf coach Punch Imlach had been trying to soften the Montreal players' minds by declaring time and again that the Canadiens were hands-down the best team in the league and that they'd win the Cup with ease. Any other result would rank as an extraordinary upset, he intoned. Imlach's reverse psychology, however, had little effect on a team with such depth and experience. The Leafs, too, were gone in four straight, scoring only five goals in the entire series. In the last game, a 4-0 whitewash before more than 13,000 downcast fans at Maple Leaf Gardens, Béliveau and Harvey scored 29 seconds apart midway through the first period, and Plante would not be beaten after that. It was a bittersweet victory, however. Most of Rocket Richard's teammates felt certain this was his last hurrah. Slowed by age, injury, and now overweight, he was no longer the fiery Rocket of old, but was every bit the team captain as he held the Cup aloft one last time. This was how he would always be remembered – the very image of Stanley Cup glory.

## THE GREATEST OF THE GREATS

In winning their fifth Cup in a row, Montreal set a precedent for greatness no pro team in any sport has yet matched. Between 1956 and 1960, the Habs won 40 of the 49 playoff games they played, were never forced to a game seven, and only once lost a playoff game by three goals. As Rocket Richard's last year in the league and Plante's last with Montreal, the 1959-60 season represents not only the NHL's greatest team at the pinnacle of its existence, but the transition to continued success as the '60s progressed. As well as winning a remarkable five Cups in a row, the Canadiens had conditioned their young players for future Stanley Cup glory. In the 1960s, long after the departure of Plante and the Rocket and Harvey and Moore, the next generation was inspired by a winning spirit that had never left the dressing room.

Boom Boom Geoffrion hoists the Cup as Sam Pollock watches with delight. Across the table are goalie Jacques Plante and team captain Maurice Richard, while the rest of the team fights with fans for a good view in behind the proceedings.

# THE OVER-THE-HILL GANG

1966-67 TORONTO MAPLE LEAFS

Game six of the 1967 Stanley Cup finals came down to a faceoff in the Toronto end with 55 seconds to play. The Leafs were leading Montreal 2-1, and the Habs had their goalie, Gump Worsley, on the bench for an extra attacker. If Toronto could hang on to win the game, the Cup would be theirs. Toronto coach Punch Imlach sent out 41-year-old defenceman Allan Stanley to take what was the most important faceoff of the year. Also on the ice were 42-year-old goalie Johnny Bower, 40-year-old forward Red Kelly, 37-year-old captain George Armstrong, and the baby of the bunch, 31-year-old forward Bob Pulford. It was a preposterous sight, this cluster of "old" men on the verge of winning a trophy everyone thought they were a decade past competing for. Stanley won the draw cleanly from Jean Béliveau. He got it to Red Kelly, who moved it up to Pulford, who gave it to George Armstrong — and the Chief scored into the empty net. The Leafs had won the Cup with the oldest lineup in league history. This Over-the-Hill Gang, as they were nicknamed with both affection and a certain cynicism, owed their success to Imlach, for no other coach was prepared to give so many men so old a place in the lineup. They proved, however, that individual age was of secondary importance in a sport that emphasized teamwork and pride.

THAT FINAL YEAR OF THE SIX-TEAM NHL WAS UNDOUBTEDLY the last when Imlach's methods, combined with his veterans' pride, could have yielded a winning result. "The old players I have are the best," Imlach said. "Each one of them has tremendous desire. That's what keeps them in there … the ones who last a long time are the guys who work the hardest – the ones who really give out in practice. Bower is the greatest example in the world. Most people couldn't run around the block at his age."

Imlach's preference for older players looked both fresh and confounding to the hockey world of the Original Six, at a time when hosts of talented young players laboured in the minors dying for a chance to prove themselves in the NHL. Incredibly, no NHL coach had used such a strategy before. Other teams in the league that year were, on paper, more talented, but when the puck was faced off to begin play, talent ran up against desire and it was the Leafs' abundance of the latter quality that ultimately prevailed. Imlach's veterans weren't just an anonymous group of older players; they were future Hall of Famers all.

In February 1960, for instance, Imlach had acquired Red Kelly from Detroit for Marc Rheaume, a deal that quickly turned out to be arguably the most one-sided trade in team history. Kelly had won four Stanley Cups in Detroit, where he had played defence for more than a decade. At 33 he wasn't getting any faster, yet Imlach moved him from defence to forward, a position that was supposed to require more speed and younger legs. The move proved to be sheer genius, as Kelly played the best hockey of his life, thriving on a more offensive role and on the confidence Punch showed in him. (Rheame, meanwhile, never scored another goal in the NHL.) More improbably, Imlach had kept Johnny Bower in goal since 1958, the year Punch became coach, even though the "China Wall" was considered by everyone else in the NHL to be a career minor-leaguer and too old to hold the fort even when he first joined the Leafs. Likewise Imlach kept the aging, slow-footed Allan Stanley (hence the nickname "Snowshoes") on defence, and also claimed goalie Terry Sawchuk and forward Marcel Pronovost, both closing in on 40, from the Wings in the Intra-League Draft.

## TROUBLE IN TORONTO

Bower, Kelly, and Stanley showed up for training camp to begin the 1966-67 season at a time when most men their age were enjoying a quieter kind of life. And there was more going on in the dressing room that autumn than simply preparing for a new year of hockey. The Leaf players, with the help of Toronto lawyer Alan Eagleson, successfully formed a players' union, a development that made the autocratic Imlach apoplectic. "I didn't like the idea of anybody from outside having anything to do with my hockey club," was the most polite way he stated his opinion. At other times he was more blunt: "If I ever find a son-of-a-bitch in here [the dressing room] soliciting for that union – look out, you're gone."

In addition, the amateur draft was about to replace the notorious C-form. Under the system, the teams drafted young players in a predetermined order based on their league standing the previous season, with the last-place team always picking first in each round. The Leafs' current crop of St. Mike's and Marlies juniors were the last to sign C-forms, the last to develop under the old sponsored junior system in Canada. Although Imlach used his aging stars from bygone days and farewell teams, he also had on his roster many a graduate of the Leafs' minor-league system who was in the prime of his career: Dave Keon, Tim Horton, and Frank Mahovlich from St. Mike's; Bobby Baun, Jim Pappin, Bob Pulford, Ron Ellis, and Brian Conacher from the Marlies.

The 1966-67 season would be the last year a coach and GM could operate as an unchecked dictator, and make no mistake, Imlach was a dictator. The most extreme example of his omnipotence was his treatment of Frank Mahovlich, the high-scoring left-winger who was the crux of the team's offence and, without question, the most popular athlete in the city. Mahovlich was a player of elegance and grace who possessed an effortless stride and devastating shot. A veteran and leader, he was known by teammates and fans alike as the Big M. But Imlach always referred to him in public as "Maholovich" in deliberate disrespect for his superstar, and attacked him in the dressing room every chance he got. Mahovlich had been the only player to vote against the players' union, yet despite this seeming support for his coach, Punch still treated him badly. Imlach seemed to believe that by bullying the Big M he would make him even more productive. But Mahovlich was the kind of man who needed to be left alone. Twice during his years with the Leafs he left the team because of clinical depression brought about by Imlach's relentless prodding.

With the exception of the Big M, it was the younger players who tended to be Imlach's victims. If he could pick on his still relatively young superstar, he could be downright tyrannical with the younger, less proven players on the team. For instance, right-winger Jim Pappin had been called up from the minors to replace Ed Litzenberger on Mahovlich's line during the 1963-64 season, filling in superbly but never playing full-time with the team. Despite his NHL-calibre talent, during each of the next three seasons he was recalled from Rochester for only brief stints. The players felt sorry for the winger known as Imlach's "whipping boy," but he was more useful to the coach as a cautionary tale than as a Leaf regular.

Imlach's methods may have been shrewd and heartless, but his team had made the playoffs each year of his eight-year tenure and won three Stanley Cups. Paradoxically, the rocky relations between coach and players seemed only to draw the team together as the regular season approached. Part of the reason was that the 1966-67 season marked the end of an era. The following summer the league would double in size from six to 12 teams – all six new entries situated in the United States – and many of the older Toronto players knew they had exactly one year left in the hockey world they'd always known. All the veterans had won a number of Cups during their decades of play – many with Imlach's early 1960s dynasty when the Leafs won three in a row from 1962 to 1964 – and so the atmosphere in camp was already a mix-

Johnny Bower, aka "The China Wall," was one of several Leafs who had a brief recording career. Others included Eddie Shack *(Clear the Track, Here Comes Shack)* and Frank Mahovlich *(All My Hockey Secrets)*. *(OPPOSITE)* Veterans Terry Sawchuk *(LEFT)* and Johnny Bower played brilliantly long after their doubters had expected.

**All the veterans had won a number of Cups during their decades of play – many with Imlach's early 1960s dynasty when the Leafs won three in a row from 1962 to 1964 – and so the atmosphere in camp was already a mixture of nostalgia and inspiration. The team was also motivated by its over-the-hill reputation.**

ture of nostalgia and inspiration. The team was also motivated by its over-the-hill reputation. With a younger team Imlach's methods would have likely been a great obstacle to success, but these older players simply played largely for themselves.

## THE LAST SEASON

As the 1966-67 season began, critics wondered whether despite all the problems – the coach's mishandling of his superstar, the bad blood over the nascent players' association – Imlach would somehow find a way to win again. In the early going, the tension in the dressing room was palpable. When the team won only three of its first dozen games, sportswriters began to call into question both the abilities of the Over-the-Hillers and Imlach's coaching. By Christmas, the Leafs' record was just 11-9-7. They played inconsistently: one night they'd get hammered by Chicago 6-1, the next they'd trounce Montreal 5-1. The usually solid defence and goaltending were often betrayed by poor defence from the forwards, who seemed to have forgotten how to backcheck. All indications pointed to a lack of co-ordinated teamwork. On January 15, 1967, the

Leafs were shut out 4-0 in Chicago, then lost 10 games in a row, a record for incompetence.

Imlach was a winner who believed that results lay not just in shooting and passing but in motivation, in how he handled his players. During the losing streak, when it would have been easy to scream at Mahovlich or demote a lesser player, Imlach staunchly defended his team. "He could have blasted us in the news media, made a lot of lineup changes, and taken us apart verbally behind closed doors," Tim Horton later explained. "He did none of those things. Instead of criticizing, he went out of his way to try to build up our confidence and kept impressing us with the fact that we had too much ability to keep skidding."

Nevertheless, after finally puttting together a small three-game unbeaten streak, Imlach fell victim to his own pressure. On February 18 team physician Hugh Smythe – son of Conn – ordered Imlach to take time off. Like Mahovlich in 1964, the coach was exhausted and needed rest. King Clancy took over behind the bench, and the mood became suddenly sunnier.

Clancy's status with the Leafs and within the league was legendary. One of the league's first stars, in the 1920s, he also served as a

referee for a decade before becoming the Leafs' coach for two years beginning in 1953. He had been a member of the team's front office ever since. Clancy was a clown, a buffoon, a gregarious legend. He never drank a drop, but his spirits were always so high he seemed perpetually inebriated. His sense of humour and love of the game produced a more relaxed attitude in the Leaf dressing room. Where Imlach preached a defensive system as tight as the psychological vice he forced upon his players, Clancy released the tension altogether. For the players he was a weekend in Las Vegas after a lifetime in Calcutta. "He was just the opposite to Imlach," forward Eddie Shack said of the coaching change. "He just let the reins go. Everybody did what came naturally…. It was absolutely fantastic. And, he didn't work the crap out of you."

Between February 18 and March 11, with Imlach out of the picture, the Leafs went 7-1-2 in 10 games, a joyous three-week streak that seemed a clear indictment of him. By the time the coach returned for the last 11 games of the regular season the players were in a better frame of mind, and the team managed to finish with a middling six wins and five losses.

The Leafs ended the season in third place with a solid but unspectacular record of 32-27-11, but the emotional roller coaster had taken its toll, especially on Mahovlich, who had scored just 18 goals, his lowest total since 1959-60. The top point-getter on the team was centre Dave Keon with 52, while top goal scorer was winger Ron Ellis with just 22, the lowest team-leading total since the 1953-54 season. Jim Pappin, who finally got to play a whole season with the Leafs, came a close second at 21. Besides Bower and Sawchuk, the Leafs had employed three minor-league goalies for short-term duty – Bruce Gamble, Gary Smith, and Al Smith – candidates to inherit the crease once Ukey (Sawchuk) and the China Wall (Bower) retired. But none was particularly impressive, and in total the Leafs had given up more goals than they scored. The best that could be said as the playoffs got underway was that the team was back in one piece and still in the running.

## UNLIKELY HEROES

In the first round of the playoffs the Leafs faced first-place Chicago, a team loaded with talent but inconsistent of performance. Since winning the Cup in 1961 the Blackhawks had been the league's star underachievers. Statistically they were far superior to the Leafs, placing five of their players among the top nine in the league scoring race – Bobby Hull, Stan Mikita, Phil Esposito, Ken Wharram, and Doug Mohns – all of whom had scored more than 20 goals. Bobby Hull led the NHL that year with a record 52 goals, the first to surpass Maurice Richard and Bernie Geoffrion's 50-goal seasons. Hull had scored nine more goals

than the top two Leaf scorers combined. The Leafs' top point-getter, Keon, would have placed a lowly sixth on the Chicago roster. With 19 more points than Toronto in the regular season and four players on the First All-Star team, including the great Glenn Hall in goal (the Leafs had placed none), the Hawks looked like a cinch to move on to the finals.

And yet these Leafs believed they could win the series. Many of the Over-the-Hillers expected these playoffs to be their last games in the NHL. During their last meeting of the regular season less than a month before, the team had hammered the Chicagos 9-5. They knew the Hawks were far from invincible, even though their first-place finish gave them home ice advantage. Since 1961 Chicago had made the playoffs every year, losing to the Leafs in the finals in 1962 and losing in the semi-finals each year since. While they might have been the odds-on favourite based on their regular season performance, their playoff record revealed an inability to raise their game in the post-season.

The Hawks won the opening game of the semi-finals 5-2 in the raucous Chicago Stadium, but the Leafs played with confidence. They won game two in Chicago 3-1, thanks to timely scoring from the Armstrong-Keon-Mahovlich line and superb work in goal from Sawchuk. After splitting the next two games, both played in Toronto, they returned to Chicago tied two-all. In that pivotal fifth game the score was 2-2 going into the third period. Now the Leafs made their move by way of the Jim Pappin-Bob Pulford-Pete Stemkowski line. With Pulford on the left side and "Stemmer" at centre, the three had been the Leafs' most consistent trio all season. The line scored early and then late in the third period to give the Leafs a 4-2 win and a 3-2 lead in the series heading home. At Maple Leaf Gardens they battened the proverbial hatches under Imlach's claustrophobic defensive system and won 3-1, again on the strength of two third-period goals, from Brian Conacher and Stemkowski. Once again, Chicago had fallen short.

In the crease, the tandem of Bower and Sawchuk was nothing less than remarkable. Sawchuk had become Imlach's number one goalie for the playoffs, starting the first four games of the series. But Bower got the call for the crucial game five because Ukey's body had taken such a pounding that he'd asked for a night off. When Bower struggled in the first period, Imlach asked Sawchuk if he could go in for the second. Ukey nodded, and the Leafs went on to win the game and series. Both goalies played with pride – for themselves, for each other, for their position, and for their teammates. They competed against each other for the number one job, but in the knowledge that neither could go the whole way alone. Together they made the difference. Chicago's five 20-plus goal scorers accounted for just eight goals in six playoff games.

When the Leafs advanced to play Montreal the occasion represented far more than the last Stanley Cup contest played in the six-team league. Because both teams would play in the East Division the following year under the new expanded alignment, 1967 also represented the last year in the forseeable future when the teams could possibly meet in the finals.

As the only two Canadian teams in the league, their Stanley Cup matchup in Canada's Centennial year made for the perfect NHL finale. The rivalry between the Leafs and Habs was ancient and intense. The entire country was polarized culturally by a competition that pitted French against English, Quebec against the rest of the country. But above all, it was a contest between two cities. To every Torontonian, Montreal was the enemy, an arrogant metropolis that had won too often, too easily. To Montrealers, the Leafs were Anglos of the lowest order, a city that played a labourers' hockey lacking in aesthetics. They saw it as white collar versus blue collar, stylish skill versus brutish effort.

This was the 13th playoff meeting between the clubs since 1918. Each team had won six of the previous dozen. Since 1959 each team had won twice, the Habs taking the Cup in both 1959 and 1960, and the Leafs beating them in '63 and '64. The Leafs had won a total of three

Cups in the first half of the decade, but the Habs had won the last two with a team that seemed to be picking up where Rocket Richard's dynasty had left off in 1960.

While Montreal and Toronto finished with similar regular season records, Montreal's team speed – Jean Béliveau, Yvan Cournoyer, Henri Richard, Ralph Backstrom, Bobby Rousseau – looked a good bet to leave Toronto's fortyish defence corps wheezing. One comparison had Montreal's "jet fighters" playing Toronto's "Sopwith camels." In goal, the new Montreal superstar Rogatien Vachon looked sure to embarrass the Sawchuk-Bower duo. Although Vachon was a rookie who had played most of the year with a team called the Houston Apollos in the Central Hockey League before playing just 19 games with the Habs leading up to the post-season, he had performed so well that he had earned the starting playoff spot over veteran Gump Worsley.

The first game of the 1967 Stanley Cup finals seemed to bear out this hypothesis. A shaky Sawchuk was pulled after letting in four goals over the first two periods and Montreal coasted to a 6-2 win. In the next two games, however, Bower's experience got much the better of Vachon's youth; the old man shut out the Habs 3-0 on Forum ice and then made 52 saves in a 3-2 overtime win back at the Gardens. Sawchuk started game four after Bower pulled a muscle during the warmup, but struggled again in another 6-2 loss.

As the finals reached their climax, goaltending once again proved to be a deciding factor. Prior to game five at the Forum, with the series tied 2-2, Imlach intoned that no Junior B goalie – Vachon – would beat his team. The declaration was meant to be taken two ways: it told Imlach's players that they would be embarrassing themselves if they lost to this guy, and it served to intimidate Vachon, who was an NHL neophyte. Just as Imlach hoped, the Leafs played with added determination while Vachon let in two soft shots when the game was tied 1-1 in the second period. Coach Toe Blake as much as admitted defeat this night when he replaced Vachon with Gump Worsley to start the third period, and the Leafs won game five on the road by a 4-1 score.

With Toronto now leading the series 3-2, Imlach gave Sawchuk a crucial third chance, naming him the starter for game six at Maple Leaf Gardens. To start in goal for the do-or-die

## THE ALMOST-GREAT HAWKS

The Chicago Blackhawks were one of the most talented teams throughout the 1960s, yet during the decade they won only one Stanley Cup. Between 1959 and 1967, Bobby Hull (here pitching hay on his prairie farm) and Stan Mikita won the scoring race a combined seven of nine years. Goaler Glenn Hall won the Vezina Trophy twice and was runner-up four times in the '60s, and the team won more than 30 games every season. But after winning the Cup in 1961 they went into a tailspin during each succeeding playoffs. They reached the finals in 1962 and again in '65, but lost to Toronto and Montreal respectively. In every other spring they lost in the semi-finals, and in 1969 they didn't even qualify for the post-season. For all their talent, the Hawks lacked that killer instinct. Coach Billy Reay didn't seem to know how to push his players to the limit, and they acquired a reputation for relying too heavily on their top line of Hull, Mikita, and Ken Wharram. Check that line and the Hawks can be beaten, or so conventional wisdom had it. The result was a team that played through its prime without ever realizing its full potential. By the time it had developed a new generation of players in the late '60s, the Montreal Canadiens and Boston Bruins had built teams that were far superior.

Habs, Blake chose the more experienced, though in these playoffs seldom used, Worsley. The Leafs certainly wanted to win this game, for a loss would mean travelling back to the Forum in Montreal for a deciding seventh game. They seemed to relish their position: a team written off at the beginning of the season was now just 60 minutes away from winning the Stanley Cup.

Sawchuk atoned for his two weak performances earlier in the series and looked every bit the goalie who had stymied Chicago in the semi-finals. He was almost unbeatable, particularly in the first period when he stopped 17

tried a pass to Pete Stemkowski in front of the Montreal net. Stemmer was covered by Jacques Laperriere, but the puck hit the Montreal defenceman and dribbled past a surprised Worsley. The lucky goal demoralized the Habs, who now trailed 2-0 heading into the third period. Former Leaf Dick Duff scored on a nice solo rush at 5:18 of the third to make the score 2-1, but then the Leafs rolled out their stifling defence in an attempt to preserve the win.

The Over-the-Hill Gang was now less than 15 minutes away from a Stanley Cup no one imagined they could win. All year their aging defence had proved solid, but this was their

end. That Imlach would give 41-year-old defenceman Allan Stanley faceoff duties and surround him with veterans of similar vintage perfectly summed up his coaching philosophy. When Stanley won the draw from future Hall of Fame centre Jean Béliveau, no one was more relieved than Sawchuk, who watched Armstrong's empty-netter from the happy confines of his crease.

Great teams always rise to the challenge, whether they're expected to or not. They defeat the best competition that exists. These 1966-67 Leafs prevailed both because of and in spite of their coach, Punch Imlach. They

(ABOVE LEFT) Johnny Bower and defenceman Tim Horton, one of the hardest hitters in the game. (ABOVE MIDDLE) Centennial year not only featured an all-Canadian Stanley Cup but the country's historic Expo 67. (ABOVE RIGHT) Punch Imlach. (OPPOSITE) Captain George Armstrong hugs the Cup as (left to right) Allan Stanley, Frank Mahovlich, Bob Pulford, and Bobby Baun crowd around. Chief-Shoot-the-Puck was captain longer than any other man in team history.

shots to keep the game scoreless while the Leaf forwards struggled to find their form around the Montreal net. But as they did so often throughout these playoffs, the men in blue and white eventually managed to take control. Midway through the second period Ron Ellis gave the Leafs a crucial 1-0 lead. Then, with just 36 seconds left in the period, Jim Pappin

ultimate test. High-flying Montreal needed just one goal to send the game into overtime and keep its own Cup hopes alive. But judging from the regular season, the Leafs had the law of averages on their side. On the 28 occasions they had entered the third period with a lead, they had not lost once, recording 25 wins and three ties. There seemed little likelihood that the seasoned veterans would now relinquish even this slim lead. The defence corps of Horton, Stanley, Pronovost, Baun, and Larry Hillman possessed a combined 78 years of NHL experience, including 15 Stanley Cups.

And so it unfolded until there was only a minute to go and a faceoff deep in the Leaf

won the Stanley Cup despite a subpar year from their greatest scorer, Frank Mahovlich, and they won because players thought obsolete by every other NHL team played with a collective pride and inspiration. This team won not because of the incomparable skills of a single overpowering player like Harry "Moose" Watson or the prowess of an offensive trio like the Production Line. More than any other before and perhaps since, the 1966-67 Toronto Maple Leafs were a team whose combined efforts proved far superior to the sum of their individual talents. They may have seemed over the hill to others, but never to themselves.

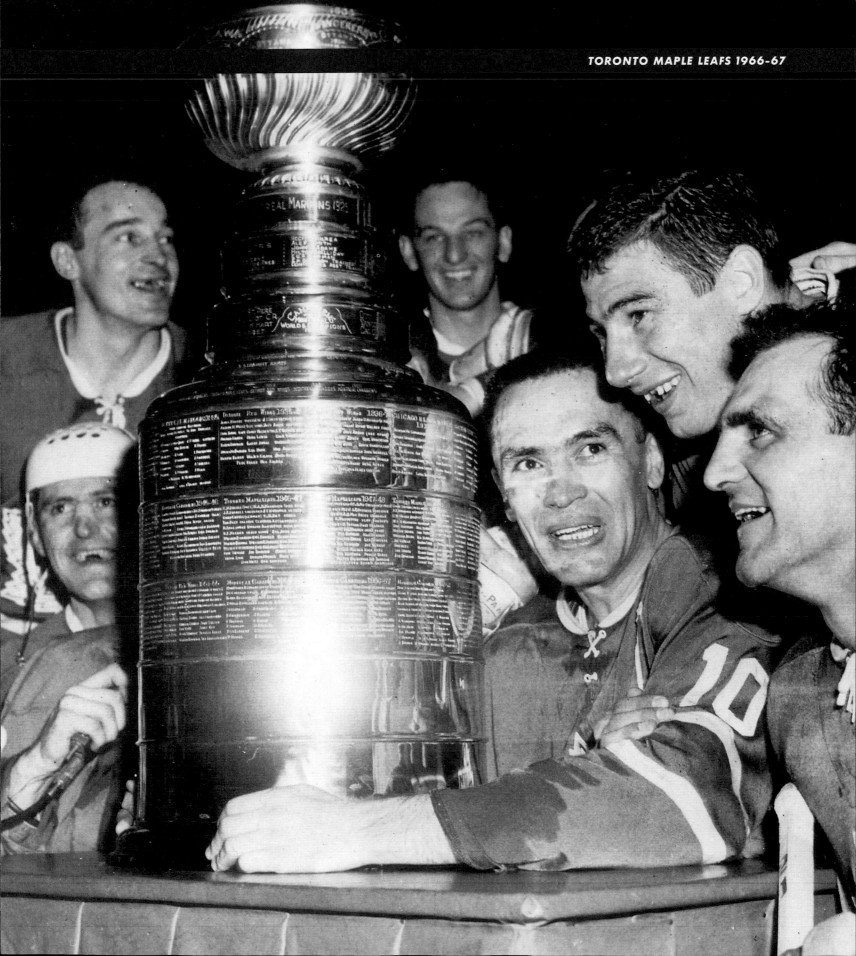

# CHAPTER 8

# BOBBY ORR TAKES FLIGHT

## 1969-70 BOSTON BRUINS

The image is as unforgettable as it is famous: Bobby Orr, flying through the air at the top of Glenn Hall's crease, having just scored 40 seconds into overtime to give the Boston Bruins the 1970 Stanley Cup. Orr's flight encapsulated a career full of dives and superhuman physical efforts. The moment defined his style, framed his skill, and expressed his character. On the winning play, Orr kept the puck in at the St. Louis blue line, but he didn't pass it right away or hammer it back into the corner or take a weak shot, as most defencemen would have done. Instead, he attacked. He moved down along the boards, abandoning his position and leaving the point open. He fed the puck to Derek Sanderson deep in the corner. Again, he didn't pass and retreat like any other defenceman would have done. Looking for the give-and-go, he headed straight for the net in anticipation of the return pass. When it came, he wasted no time in redirecting the puck past Glenn Hall. Noel Picard, the Blues defenceman in front, could only take a stick to Orr's skate after he scored. This served to lift Orr where he was going anyway: high into the welcoming air. Somehow he landed without hurting himself. The resulting mayhem was a tribute not just to Boston winning the Cup for the first time in almost 30 years but to how the Cup was won.

ALMOST FROM THE DAY ADULTS STARTED TO WATCH HIM skate in his hometown of Parry Sound, Ontario, Bobby Orr was hailed as the player of the future. When he was 14 years old he was already being scouted by the Leafs and the Boston Bruins. He was then playing major junior hockey, the league that was the prime feeder system for the Ontario Hockey Association, which was in turn where many NHLers came from. At 15 he signed with the Oshawa Generals, a junior team sponsored by the Bruins who were then the worst team in the NHL.

From the day Orr joined the Generals in the OHA in 1963, he was seen as the messiah who would come to save a franchise that hadn't been to the playoffs since 1959. As he matured, it became clear that he was unlike any other player scouts had seen. Orr had size, tremendous strength and toughness, and he could play defence. He was also the fastest, most skilled 18-year-old anywhere. And he could score. Instead of staying on the blue line and passing the puck to his forwards – like all other defencemen – he liked to carry the puck himself. He had extraordinary acceleration and changed his speed depending on game situations. He could lull an opponent into a slow pace and then zoom by with two quick strides; he could fly in a straight line faster than anyone, then feint and change direction without warning. He could circle again and again around his own goal to kill time on a power play or set up the perfect breakout. He could stickhandle like no other, and if someone tried to intimidate him Orr could intimidate right back. With the Generals he scored 29, 34, and 38 goals in his three seasons – astronomical, unheard-of numbers for a defenceman, who might normally score eight or 10, a dozen at most.

Orr arrived in Boston in the fall of 1966, but not without incident. He had an agent, a rarity even for a seasoned player let alone a rookie, and this agent was a young Toronto lawyer named Alan Eagleson. Eagleson wanted a $40,000-a-year contract for Orr, which would have made someone who had never played a single NHL game the highest-paid player in the league. Boston general manager Milt Schmidt, a superstar with the Bruins during the 1940s, had never encountered such outlandish demands and refused to acquiesce. Eagleson told the Bruins that they could either pay the asking price or Orr would play for Canada's National Team. Schmidt had little bargaining leverage and Eagleson knew it, the Bruins having now missed the playoffs the previous seven seasons. Orr got his contract.

Players throughout the league watched these negotiations with wonder and hope. Eagleson, fresh on the hockey scene, was breaking new ground as a player agent. Orr, a prized possession, not only deserved his contract but in getting it opened the way for other players to negotiate better deals. Imagine what superstar veterans like Gordie Howe, Jean Béliveau, Bobby Hull, or Dave Keon could have commanded with an agent.

Wearing what would be his trademark number four, Orr began his NHL season with games against first Detroit and then home-and-home against the Stanley Cup-champion Montreal Canadiens. Although the Bruins lost 6-2 to Detroit and both games to the Habs, 3-1 and 3-2, Orr had an assist in his first game and a goal in the third, a blistering slapshot from the point that beat Gump Worsley and earned the rookie a standing ovation from the Boston

## Orr had size, tremendous strength and toughness, and he could play defence. He was also the fastest, most skilled 18-year-old anywhere.

Garden crowd. Orr also established himself physically. Early in the season he pummelled Montreal defenceman Ted Harris, one of the league's toughest players. "I'd rather play hockey," Orr said afterwards, "but I'll never back away. If you do, they'll run you right out of the league." Over the course of the year he had 41 points and 102 penalty minutes, despite missing nine games with what would become his greatest adversary – a knee injury. Off ice, he comported himself quietly – a shy, good-natured, small-town 18-year-old kid. He won the Calder Trophy and was named to the Second All-Star team. Orr's 1966-67 season had fulfilled all expectations.

### BUILDING A TEAM AROUND THE STAR

Although Bobby Orr had proved himself, the Bruins finished in last place and out of the playoffs again. But GM Schmidt had a long-term plan and he wasn't about to lose focus. He would build a winning team around his young superstar through a combination of maturing juniors already in the Boston system and by making smart trades. During the course of the 1966-67 season Schmidt had used 33 players, a sign of discontent with his roster and of his desire to give a number of youngsters a brief audition.

One part of Schmidt's plan already firmly in place for Orr's rookie season was Harry Sinden, at 34 the youngest coach in the league. A defenceman on Canada's 1956 Olympic team, he was a minor-leaguer who, like many a great coach, never had the skill to play full-time in the NHL. Schmidt saw Sinden's youth and experience as the perfect mix for a team maturing in the modern NHL, where the increasingly powerful NHL Players' Association advocated sideburns and open collars over the jackets and ties and 10 p.m. curfews of the austere days of owner dictatorships. Sinden understood the modern player, had been a player-coach in the minors toward the end of his skating days, and knew how much social latitude to give the players while ensuring their on-ice performance remained at its highest.

The heart and soul of this Boston team was "The Chief," Johnny Bucyk. An NHLer since 1955 and a Bruin since 1957, Bucyk represented the experience needed to win. In goal Sinden could count on the young Gerry Cheevers, whom Schmidt had claimed from Toronto at the Intra-League Draft in 1965. "Cheesy" played junior with St. Mike's in Toronto, where he seemed destined for a pro career at Maple Leaf Gardens. But the Leafs thought themselves talent-rich in goal, with the likes of Bruce Gamble, Gary Smith, and Al Smith waiting to inherit the Bower throne. They left Cheevers unprotected and Schmidt grabbed him in the draft. Sinden could also

*(LEFT)* **A Boston Bruins pennant from the early 1970s.** *(OPPOSITE ABOVE)* **A teenaged Bobby Orr takes a diving slash at the puck.** *(OPPOSITE BELOW LEFT)* **Coach Harry Sinden.** *(OPPOSITE BELOW RIGHT)* **The Bruins' Kraut Line of the '40s** *(LEFT TO RIGHT)* **Woody Dumart, Bobby Bauer, and Milt Schmidt, represented the most recent superstars in Bruin sweaters before Orr.**

Schmidt saw Sinden's youth and experience as the perfect mix for a team maturing in the modern NHL, where the increasingly powerful NHL Players' Association advocated sideburns and open collars over the jackets and ties and 10 p.m. curfews of the austere days of owner dictatorships.

count on veteran defenceman Ted Green, one of the NHL's first enforcers. Green was a player with solid skills, but a true fighter who stood up for his teammates.

By the time Orr arrived in Boston, Schmidt also had a core of excellent prospects developing in the minors. Derek Sanderson, Don Awrey, Wayne Cashman, Ed Westfall, and Rick Smith all played for the Generals and Niagara Falls Flyers, both Bruins-sponsored teams. With the exception of Smith, all had played a handful of games with the Bruins over the previous two seasons. With this talented group ready in the wings, Schmidt sought to make trades that would fill the team's needs. During Orr's debut season, the Bruins had scored a league-low 182 goals, good enough to win only 17 of 70 games. So, first on his list of priorities was the need for goal scorers. After all, there was no point in having Orr join the rush if no one was waiting to put the puck in the net once he'd made his way deep into enemy territory. No matter how

Ed Westfall has the puck in front of the Leaf net, while Leaf forward Jim Dorey watches. In goal is Bruce Gamble. Hodge was part of the blockbuster deal with Chicago in May 1967 that brought Phil Esposito to the Bruins and more or less assured Stanley Cup success for a team that had missed the playoffs every year in the 1960s.

great he was, Number Four couldn't do it all by himself every rush.

On May 15, 1967, shortly after the season ended, Schmidt acquired Phil Esposito, Ken Hodge, and Fred Stanfield from Chicago for Pit Martin, Jack Norris, and Gilles Marotte. At the time, it was a blockbuster deal that saw the teams exchange terrific prospects of approximately equal value. While Espo and Hodge were solid, front-line forwards, so too were Martin and Marotte. In time, however, this proved to be one of the more lopsided deals in league history, more or less ensuring Boston's Stanley Cup victory. The three newcomers each took on prominent goal-scoring roles, while the players traded away by Schmidt did little to improve the fortunes of their new team, the Blackhawks. "This is a team that will learn how to win," Espo predicted when he arrived. "This first year, we'll make the playoffs for sure. Next year, we'll be second or third. The third year, we'll win the whole thing, Stanley Cup and all." Bold, though prescient, words.

Derek Sanderson (aka "Turk"), a confirmed playboy who adored wine, women, and scoring with equal relish, was just the kind of New Age player who would have lasted in the Original Six only as long as it took a Punch Imlach or a Toe Blake to demote him. "There are three things that make money in professional sports," Turk said when asked about his role in Boston. "The first is talent, the second is points, and the third is colour. With the Bruins, Orr and Esposito took care of the first two. That left me to look after the third." In exchange for his personal freedom, Sanderson became the best two-way player in the game, a genius on faceoffs and penalty-killing, and a true goal scorer with great passing ability.

## THE BRUINS MAKE THEIR MOVE

In Orr's second season, 1967-68, the Bruins made the playoffs. They finished a solid third in the East Division, having scored a whopping 259 goals, some 77 more than the previous year, while allowing 37 fewer. Esposito placed second in the league in scoring with 84 points, just three behind leader Stan Mikita. Hodge and Stanfield, the other ex-Blackhawks, had 25 and 20 goals respectively. Orr dropped to 31 points after missing almost half the season with his first serious knee injury, but still won the Norris Trophy and was named to the First All-Star team, tributes to his supremacy among the league's blue-liners. Without a healthy Number Four, however, the Bruins were eliminated in the quarter-finals of the playoffs by Montreal in an uneventful four-game sweep.

Schmidt made few changes during the off-season. He was fully aware that more than anything else his team needed time and patience. The talent was there; it was just a little raw. Orr was on crutches for much of that summer, and in his first exhibition games against Detroit and then the Rangers in the fall of 1968, players took runs at the 19-year-old with the tender knee until he made his point by holding his own against tough guy Reggie Fleming in a fight the young Bruin instigated. "He's learned that he has to stand up for his rights in this league," Fleming said

after taking a high-stick from Orr. "I can't blame him for that."

## ON TOP OF THEIR GAME

The 1968-69 season confirmed the wisdom of Schmidt's patience. The Bruins finished second behind Montreal in the strong East Division with 100 points. They increased their goal output to 303, tops in the league, thanks in large part to a healthy Orr who played 67 games and had 64 points. Now in his third season, Orr was developing his game in a way that even the most sagacious of scouts could not have envisioned. He was the league's finest rushing defenceman, generating offence from a position not traditionally noted for skating, puck skill, and speed.

Orr loved starting a rush from the defence because of all the open ice his position provided. He used defence as a starting point for lightning-fast forays that often resulted in either a scoring chance or a penalty to the other team. There had been rushing defencemen before – Detroit's Flash Hollett and Montreal's Doug Harvey – but Orr was special. His rushes were intimidating both for their sheer speed and their rate of success. Although Harvey rushed with the puck, he never scored more than nine goals in even his best season. Orr not only carried the puck, he routinely scored or assisted on a goal.

Beginning an attack from the blue line also meant that Orr could see the ice and players faster and more effectively, plot a strategy of movement that was both orchestrated (by his years of practice) and spontaneous (for his ability to read game situations as they arose). His speed and agility, however, did not make him invincible to vicious or illegal hits. He took a chance every time he had the puck on his stick, for he refused to stand still or get rid of the puck to avoid a check.

In the first round of the 1969 playoffs, the Bruins offered a glimpse into the near future when they routed the Maple Leafs in four humiliating games. The scores in the Boston Garden were the worst back-to-back losses in Toronto history – 10-0 and 7-0. At Maple Leaf Gardens the games were closer but still Boston victories, 4-3 and 3-2. In the semi-finals the Bruins again played Montreal, and lost the series in six games. However, three of the six went into overtime, the sixth going into a fifth period before Jean Béliveau scored to eliminate the ascending Bruins.

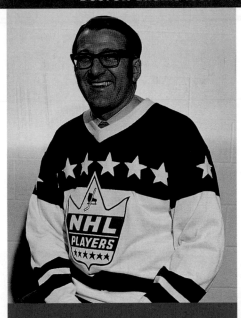

## THE EAGLE

Alan Eagleson quickly earned a nickname that evoked his negotiating skill. The Eagle clinched his position as a defender of NHL players when he ensured that the recently retired Carl Brewer was reinstated as an amateur following his sudden and tumultuous departure from the Toronto Maple Leafs. It was not an enormous achievement in practical terms — all that Clarence Campbell had to do was sign a piece of paper — but it represented a huge victory for the players over the dictatorial NHL president. Members of the Toronto Maple Leafs soon approached Eagleson about organizing a players' union, of which he became the first executive director. This position gave him enormous leverage with the NHL owners, ensured that most players would go to him first in the matter of representation at contract time, and put him in arguably the most powerful position in all of hockey because he not only looked after individual contracts but negotiated the NHL-NHLPA agreement as well. Above all, Eagleson represented the most promising player in the modern game, Bobby Orr, and had secured for him the richest contract in league history.

Once again Schmidt made barely a change over the summer, but the 1969-70 season began in a sickening way for Boston. During an exhibition game with St. Louis in Ottawa, Ted Green and the Blues' Wayne Maki were involved in a stick-swinging duel that put Green out for the year with a serious head injury and virtually ended Maki's career. It was a tragic and horrifying incident for all who witnessed it. Green was almost as important in his role as Orr was in his, and his friendships with the players meant that his loss helped bring the team together. A Ted Green Night had actually been planned by his

won was not accidental. Indeed, hockey has a long history of losing teams instigating fights against superior opponents, at least to show their unwillingness to go down to defeat meekly. Just as the Toronto Granites' Harry Watson was bludgeoned without warning because of his superior skills in the 1924 Olympics, and other women's teams played rough with the Rivs when being defeated for the umpteenth time, and the Red Wings brawled their way to victory after their star Gordie Howe had been seriously injured, so too were the Bruins so far superior to the rest of the league that they often wound up in

That killer instinct made the difference on the power play, during close games, and in pressure situations.

During the 1969-70 season Orr decimated the record books, scoring 33 goals and adding 87 assists for 120 total points, all records for a defenceman. It was the first time a defenceman had won the Hart Trophy as the league's leading scorer. (Orr won again five years later, and is still the only defenceman to have won even once.) True to his team's character, he also had 125 penalty minutes, the first player ever to reach the century mark in both points and penalty minutes. In addition to the Hart,

Referee Ken Bodendistel watches the stick-swinging duel between the Blues' Wayne Maki (LEFT) and the Bruins' Ted Green (RIGHT). In the days before helmets were standard equipment, such incidents were infrequent. This all but ended Maki's career and put Green out for the remainder of the season.

fan club to be held prior to a game early in the season. Obviously it had to be postponed, but it spoke volumes to his terrific popularity with the fans.

Although a rare example of serious on-ice violence, the Green-Maki incident was indicative of hockey at the time. While Boston was unquestionably the most skilled team in the league, it was also the most penalized, and the connection between games won and fights

bench-clearing brawls in defence of their hockey dominion.

They weren't called the Big Bad Bruins for nothing, and fans and critics alike described the team in a different but similar way. As general manager Bud Poile of Philadelphia observed, "When they drop the puck to start the game, the Bruins think it's a piece of raw meat." Boston's utility forward Glen Sather hung a sign in the dressing room with the motto "Think Kill." While seeming to advocate a strictly violent approach, the message was rooted more in the tenacity and competitive ferocity needed to complement the team's skating, shooting, and passing skills.

Orr was awarded the Art Ross, Norris, and Conn Smythe trophies, a feat not likely ever to be repeated. Above all, however, he had become the most exciting player in the game, a man of speed, skill, and strength, whose good looks and genuine humility only added to his star appeal. He had all his teeth, yet played tough; he maintained a small-town crewcut and innocent demeanour, yet played with the experience of a man years older. He skated like the wind, beautiful and untouchable. He was everywhere all at once but nowhere for long. He came to represent hockey's shift from black-and-white to colour, from radio to television, antique to modern.

His rushing style of play won hockey games as well as hearts. The threat of career-ending injury to his tender knees only added to the breathless anticipation that verged on terror each time he started another rush.

The supporting cast around Number Four was itself becoming more impressive. Esposito had finished second in scoring to Orr with 99 points, and the number-one line of Esposito-Hodge-Cashman led the league in points. The Bruins scored more goals than any other team, 277, and six players had 20 goals or more, testaments to an offence that was both potent and balanced.

years, only to lose in four straight each time to Montreal. In 1969-70 the top four teams in the East Division all had more points (92) than even the first-place St. Louis Blues in the expansion West Division (86).

In the quarter-finals that year the Bruins faced the Rangers, who had finished just seven points behind them in the regular season. Theirs was a formidable lineup in its own right, with goalie Eddie Giacomin recording one of the best goals-against averages in the league, and Walt Tkaczuk and Jean Ratelle finishing fifth and sixth in the NHL scoring race. Boston won the first two games of the

rest of the game." The Bruins won 4-1 to eliminate the Rangers and set up a semi-final meeting with Chicago.

As it turned out, the semi-finals against Chicago proved anticlimactic, yet another instance of an excellent Hawks team falling short of playoff expectation. The Bruins, playing with the poise and confidence of champions, swept Chicago in four games. In the first two, Boston gained 3-0 leads before Chicago could muster any sustained attack. In the third game the Bruins twice overcame one-goal deficits and rallied to win easily, 5-2. Orr averaged more than 30 minutes of play-

(ABOVE LEFT) **Ken Hodge** (LEFT), **Phil Esposito**, and **Wayne Cashman**, the highest-scoring line in the game in the late '60s and early '70s, worked their system to perfection. Espo's job was to station himself in the slot. When Hodge or Cash got the puck to Espo, he fired quickly and instinctively, scoring an astounding 76 goals in the 1970-71 season. (ABOVE RIGHT) **Gerry Cheevers** was often down but seldom out. (Rick Smith stands guard.)

When the NHL had expanded from six to 12 teams in 1967 it placed all the Original Six teams in the East Division, and all the new teams in the West. This ensured that each Stanley Cup finals would feature one new and one old team, but it also made for a great disparity in talent. For instance, the St. Louis Blues made it to the '68 and '69 finals both

series at home, then lost the next two at Madison Square Garden. In the pivotal fifth game Orr put the Bruins up 1-0 with an early goal, but by the third period Boston trailed 2-1. Phil Esposito, that magnificent slot-shooter, scored twice – one from a lovely Orr pass that sent Espo in alone on Giacomin – and the Bruins rallied to win the game 3-2. In the sixth and final game of the series Orr opened the scoring, and then, with the Bruins up 2-1, scored again on a low slapshot so hard it almost broke Giacomin's foot. "Bobby kept the puck low and it hit my right boot and went in," Giacomin said afterwards. "I could feel pain in my big toe for the

ing time a game, and goalie Gerry Cheevers, though not always busy, did his part with timely saves when called upon. The only close game was the last, with the series already virtually decided.

## BOBBY ORR TAKES FLIGHT
The finals against St. Louis, the best of the weaker West Division teams, proved to be not much tougher but certainly more dramatic. A team with much talent but little coordination of that talent, the Blues featured ancient warriors Glenn Hall and Jacques Plante in goal along with a host of memorable hockey-card heroes such as Frank St. Marseille and the

## THE NEW AMATEUR DRAFT

Officially, the drafting of minor league players began in 1963. But for all practical purposes it dates from 1969, the year the last player who had signed a C-form as a teenager passed through the junior system. In 1969 no team could sign a player unless it had drafted him. The rules of the amateur draft were simple. Once a player was 20 years old, he could be selected by any team if he were still available in the draft. The better a team's performance the previous season, the lower its draft placement. In the 12-team NHL of 1969, the first-place team at the end of the previous regular season chose 12th overall and the last-place team chose first, a system that gave the weakest teams a chance at the best young prospects. Rick Smith (above) was chosen seventh overall by Boston in 1966. Of course, prospects didn't always pan out. It was still up to a team's scouting staff to pick a future star. And since the poorer teams often had the weaker scouting departments, the more successful franchises drafted better than their draft placement would have suggested.

Plager brothers – Barclay, Bill, and Bob. But Plante and Hall, 38 and 41 respectively, could not be expected to win the series on their own, and the supporting cast comprised gifted but discarded veterans from Original Six teams – Jean-Guy Talbot, Phil Goyette, Ab McDonald – augmented by up-and-comers of middling ilk – Red Berenson, Jim Roberts, Gary Sabourin. Blues coach Scotty Bowman was a multi-Cup winner in the making, as was defenceman Al Arbour (also as a coach), but their great years were still well in the future. In 1970 there was some talent in St. Louis, but nothing comparable to Bobby Orr's Bruins.

As a result, the finals mainly showcased the superior talents of Harry Sinden's team. Boston won the first two games in St. Louis, 6-1 and 6-2, both cases in which Orr's contribution was subtle but essential. He had three assists in those 120 minutes of play, but was on the ice for seven of Boston's eight even-strength goals and for only one goal against. More important, he controlled the flow of the game and made scoring a goal a near impossibility for the Blues. As soon as the team returned to Boston, the players phoned Ted Green at his home in Winnipeg and told him to get down to Beantown – there was going to be a party. Green arrived for game three, won 4-1 by Boston with equal ease.

Game four was close. Boston scored first, then late in the opening period Berenson scored to tie. Early in the second, Sabourin gave the Blues the lead, then the Bruins' Phil Esposito scored his second of the series to tie the game 2-2. In the third, an early power-play goal by Larry Keenan put St. Louis up again, then a Johnny Bucyk goal at 13:28 helped send the game into overtime with the teams tied 3-3. From the opening faceoff of that overtime, Orr and the Bruins controlled play and quickly got the puck into the St. Louis end. The Blues tried to clear the puck around the right boards, but Orr was there to meet it at the point. He moved down the side, fed Sanderson in the corner, and made for the front of the net. Turk put the puck on his stick. Orr deflected it behind Hall without a moment's hesitation – and then took off

*(OPPOSITE, CLOCKWISE FROM TOP LEFT)* The Stanley Cup victory play: Orr (in front of net) has just deflected the pass from Derek Sanderson (standing, behind net) past Glenn Hall; a trip from Noel Picard launches him into the air; Orr takes flight.

while cameras around the rink captured his celebratory leap for the ages. How Orr landed without hurting himself is something only he knows, but the resulting mayhem was a tribute to Orr's fulfillment of all the hope and promise he brought to the club when he first arrived in 1966.

The Bruins had won the Stanley Cup for the first time in 29 years, and Number Four was the hero, just as everyone had expected from the day the 15-year-old prodigy began playing major junior hockey with the Oshawa Generals. Some critics have argued that Orr's spectacular goal was, in pure hockey terms, overrated. Although he scored in overtime, so the reasoning goes, he did so to wrap up a four-game sweep over a weak expansion franchise that was losing its 12th successive Stanley Cup finals game. That Boston would win this series and the Cup was inevitable. But the images of Orr flying through the air transcend the moment; they have come to represent the meaning of the glory of winning the Stanley Cup. No one, absolutely no one, could have finished a goal in like manner. For years Orr had been described as someone who was graceful, elegant, powerful, without fear – poetry in motion. All these epithets were captured and immortalized in the photos of the goal that won the 1970 Stanley Cup.

In playoff years before and since, the team that wins the Cup usually has a lead and as the clock ticks down the forward lines play solid defence and the defencemen chip the puck out to centre ice to kill time and protect that lead. When the game ends, everyone skates down to the goalie to congratulate him first. But in 1970 it was on Orr that the players focused their tributes. As he landed on the ice his linemates got down to hug their fallen hero. Goalie Cheevers skated the length of the ice to join them. Although the Bruins could not have won without the goaltending of Cheevers, the two-way play of Sanderson, the offensive power of Esposito, Hodge, and Cashman, and the effortless coaching of Sinden, it was Bobby Orr who made the decisive difference – with his ability to dictate the events of each game, then with his diving, flying, game-winning goal. Perhaps never before had a Cup victory been so much the product of one player's hockey genius.

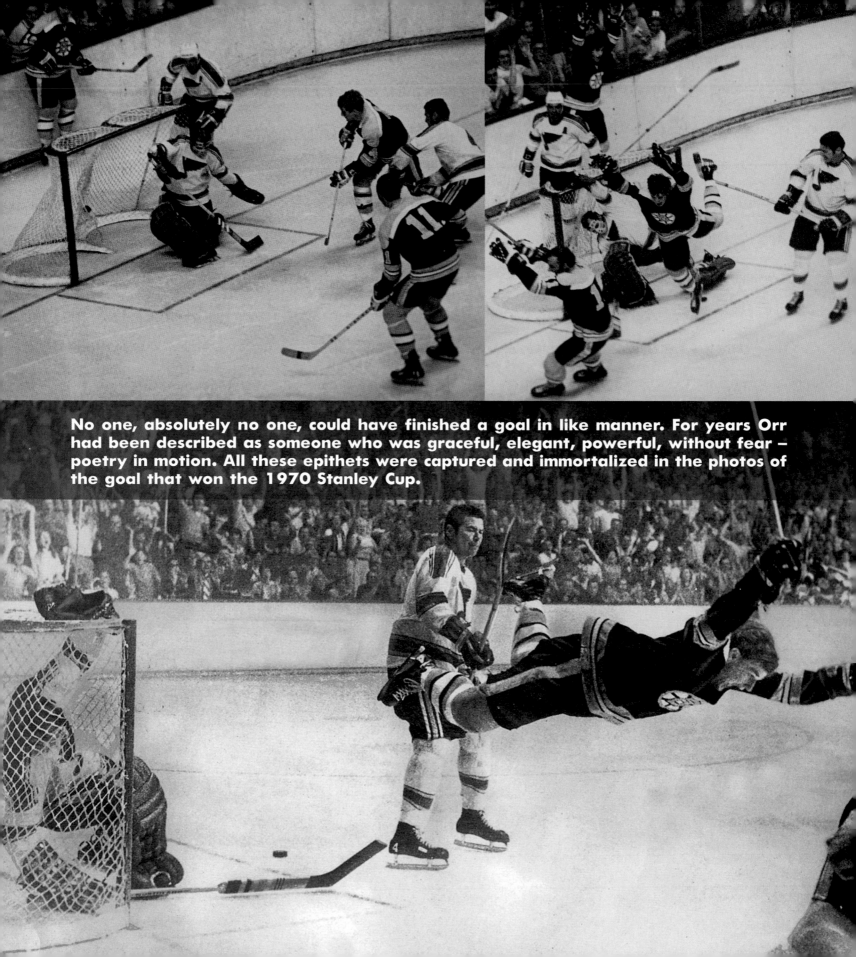

No one, absolutely no one, could have finished a goal in like manner. For years Orr had been described as someone who was graceful, elegant, powerful, without fear — poetry in motion. All these epithets were captured and immortalized in the photos of the goal that won the 1970 Stanley Cup.

# US AGAINST THEM

1972 TEAM CANADA

The five most important words in the history of hockey were uttered by Foster Hewitt on September 28, 1972: "Henderson has scored for Canada!" Hewitt's words not only meant that Team Canada had beaten the Soviet Union's national team and completed a miraculous come-back on foreign ice, they confirmed in the hearts of fans the superiority of democracy over communism, freedom over restriction, emotion over plan, Canadian-style hockey over Soviet style. But the words also announced the arrival of the Soviet Union as a true hockey power. A series that had begun in Canadian eyes as an eight-game exhibition of NHL superiority quickly turned into a national challenge. Not only did the Soviets stun Team Canada in game one, they went home with a seemingly insurmount-able lead. The rest is history, but of the most miraculous kind. Each game in Russia was as intense and demanding a game as these Canadian players had ever experienced. At the beginning of the series they'd been expected to win easily; by the time they arrived in the U.S.S.R., they looked like losers. When they lost the first of their four games on Soviet ice, all hope of ultimate victory seemed dashed — except in their own eyes. The manner in which they fought back and then prevailed in such spectacular fashion make them without question hockey's greatest team.

DURING THE DRAB, FROZEN WINTER OF THE EARLY PART OF 1972, a Canadian diplomat in Moscow named Gary Smith read an editorial in the newspaper *Isvestia* that suggested Soviet hockey needed a new challenge. The national team, it argued, which had won every World Championship and every Olympics since 1963, could not develop further without stiffer competition. Smith seized this opening. He approached the paper's editor, Boris Fedosov, and arranged to meet to discuss a possible Canada-Soviet Union hockey showdown. The diplomat and the newspaperman found themselves in agreement: the time was right for a tournament featuring the best players from both countries. The two communicated their accord to Soviet hockey leader Andrei Starovoitov, who set serious negotiations in motion. For CAHA president Joe Kryzcka and the rest of the Canadian delegation, simply having the Communists agree to sit at the same table with Canadians was akin to an international coup. In April, Canadians and Soviets met at the World Championships in Prague and finalized the terms of the Summit Series, most of which were settled to the disadvantage of the Canadians. The two sides agreed that international rules would prevail: fighting would carry a game misconduct, international referees would officiate, and the two-referee-no-linesmen system would be used. It was also agreed that the games would be played during the NHL pre-season, with the Canadian players in their worst condition of the year but the Soviets in mid-season shape. That the series would consist of eight games – four in Canada, four in Moscow – rather than the traditional Stanley Cup seven meant that a tie was possible.

It was at this point that Alan Eagleson, executive director of the NHL Players' Association, became involved. Eagleson was, after all, responsible for the well-being of all NHL players; if his members were to commit to playing, it would be on his terms. He got the NHL owners on side by having some of the income from the series put into the players' pension, money the owners would otherwise have had to ante up themselves. Eagleson, who had tremendous public relations savvy, also helped generate more than $2 million in television revenue for the series through ad sales, and ensured that all profits would flow into the pockets of the CAHA and NHL players. No question, Eagleson helped raise the public's interest in the tournament.

The Canadians had been so obliging during the negotiations because victory seemed so very certain. This series was what Canadian hockey fans had so long been waiting for – NHL pros versus the Soviets' "shamateurs." But Team Canada – a brilliant term coined by coach Harry Sinden in an effort to unite the entire country to his team's cause – received two serious blows before the opening of training camp. The great Bobby Orr's knee troubles meant he would likely miss the entire series (although he was with the team and practised lightly). And Bobby Hull, the highest scoring left-winger in NHL history, had signed a contract with the pirate World Hockey Association and so been barred from the series by NHL president Clarence Campbell.

Such was the furor over Hull's excommunication that Prime Minister Pierre Trudeau himself sent a telegram to all parties involved: "You are aware of the intense concern which I share with millions of Canadians in all parts of our country, that Canada should be represented by its best hockey players, including Bobby Hull.... On behalf of these Canadians, I urge Hockey Canada, the NHL, and the NHL Players' Association to take whatever steps may be necessary to make this possible." Trudeau's election campaign – whose defining slogan was "The Land Is Strong" – got underway the day before the series began. Although his petition was rebuffed, the prime minister's very involvement told the tale: For this international series there was no separation between politics, culture, and hockey. The barring of WHA players also cost the team the inclusion of goalie Gerry Cheevers, defenceman J.C. Tremblay, and forward Derek Sanderson, all of whom certainly would at the very least have been invited to camp. Nonetheless, when Team Canada's camp opened at Maple Leaf Gardens on August 13, 1972, 35 players vied for 19 spots on the roster.

Coach Harry Sinden had been out of hockey since winning the 1970 Stanley Cup with the Boston Bruins. But unlike active NHL coaches, he was available – no NHL coach could have committed to the series while his own league camp was underway. Sinden's Canadian camp was typical of those for NHL teams: it involved getting into shape and getting to know new teammates.

The big difference between the two countries leading up to game one was preparation. The Soviets weren't ready to play the NHL in 1954 when they first began to compete internationally. In 1972, they were. The Soviets were never *not* in top-notch condition. Two Soviet scouts attended every Team Canada practice, making detailed notes of every player and move. Meanwhile, Canadian scouting could be summed up by one headline that appeared in the *Toronto Sun* on August 24, 1972: "Russian goaltending weak, says scout John McLellan."

The most esteemed voices in Canadian hockey were anticipating this series with an ill-advised confidence. Red Burnett, a distinguished sportswriter for the *Toronto Star* for 45 years, was one of the few who predicted a series that would be more than a cakewalk: "Team Canada should win all eight games with the Soviet Union's national team. But, it won't be by the four- and five-goal margins that some National Hockey League executives are predicting." Burnett wrote the truth. The aforementioned McLellan, coach of the Maple Leafs, said simply, "If we play up to our capabilities, we can win every game." Scotty Bowman was equally sanguine: "Anything can happen in a hockey game or series, but we have the better players and should win all eight games." Al Arbour, coach of the St. Louis Blues and Bowman devotee, concurred: "Team Canada will win all eight games." In fact, every respected hockey mind in the country predicted Canada would win virtually

*(LEFT)* Treasured tickets to the final four games in Moscow.
*(OPPOSITE)* Prime Minister Pierre Trudeau *(MIDDLE)* greets Canadian and Soviet players on Montreal Forum ice prior to game one.

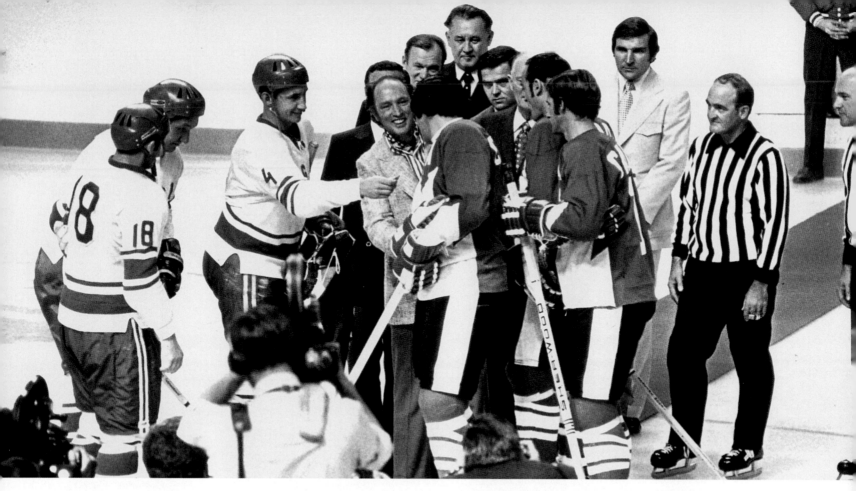

every game, with perhaps one Soviet win in Moscow on an off night for Canada. "I think even one victory for the Russians will be considered surprising success in the series worldwide," suggested former player and Los Angeles general manager Larry Regan. Only coach Sinden expressed real doubts. "I'm nervous as hell," he said prior to game one. "My main worry is the pace they play at."

## TEAM DISAPPOINTMENT

On September 2, 1972, the Montreal Forum was abuzz with tense anticipation as 8 p.m. approached. CTV was providing television coverage, and the revered Foster Hewitt, who had pretty much retired from broadcasting a few years earlier, was back at the mike to give the play-by-play to 12 million viewers across the country of 18 million. Prime Minister Trudeau took part in the pre-game ceremonies. Canada won the opening faceoff, then immediately got the puck deep into the Soviet end. After just 30 seconds of play, Phil Esposito scored on a quick shot. In 1972 Espo was a tower of dominance in the NHL and one of the men expected to lead the charge against the Soviets. The ease and speed with which he scored seemed to confirm the confident prognostication. Then six minutes later, Paul Henderson scored on a superb three-way passing play off a faceoff in the Soviet end with Bobby Clarke and Ron Ellis assisting. Henderson one-timed the puck into the lower right of the net past Soviet netminder Vladislav Tretiak. To everyone watching, it looked like the romp was on. Smiles adorned the bench and the seats in the Forum crowd.

But although the Soviets were down two goals, they couldn't be bumped off the puck. Instead they skated with a speed that showed they were in mid-season form, passing and circling with fanatical precision, generating one scoring chance after another. Line after line appeared, wave after indistinguishable wave playing a system as alien as the language they spoke. By the late stages of the opening period, the Soviets had tied the score.

Theirs was a game of puck possession: they waited for the perfect shot and recovered most of the rebounds. And then there was Valeri Kharlamov. Just 5'6", 155 pounds, he was a lithe streak of speed, and by the second period he had found his rhythm. He took a pass at his blue line from Alexander Maltsev, flew down the right wing as he crossed the Canadian blue line, and cut into the middle. The defence pair of Don Awrey and Rod Seiling were prepared for an inside move, but Kharlamov feinted left, cut right and blew past Awrey on the outside along the boards, then cut in on goal. As Canadian goalie Ken Dryden moved to cover the net, Kharlamov drove the puck between his pads. Soviets 3, Canada 2. By the end of the period Kharlamov had scored again to put CCCP up 4-2.

By the beginning of period three the NHLers' smiles had been replaced by huffs and puffs of exhaustion. Although Bobby Clarke scored another for Canada, the Soviets' superior conditioning allowed them to dominate, and by the final siren they had scored three unanswered goals to make the final 7-3. That night the Forum fans and all Canadians discovered that these Soviets were for real, especially the top two lines of Kharlamov-Maltsev-Vikulov and Yakushev-Zimin-Shadrin, sinewy reeds of harnessed steel who accounted for five of the goals. After the stunning opening night loss Canada's coach Harry Sinden was poetically succinct: "A little piece of all of us died today."

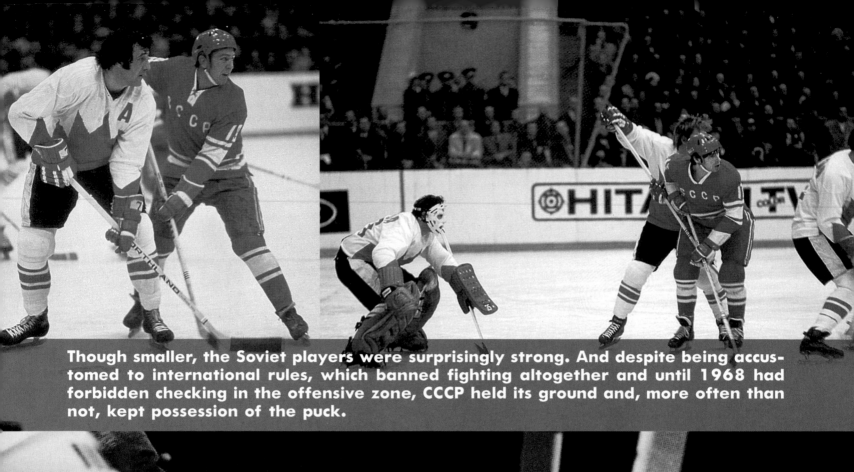

Though smaller, the Soviet players were surprisingly strong. And despite being accustomed to international rules, which banned fighting altogether and until 1968 had forbidden checking in the offensive zone, CCCP held its ground and, more often than not, kept possession of the puck.

The political differences between the two countries, which had been the major focus of the series, now gave way to the hockey differences, and these were huge. The NHLers were bigger than the Soviets, and they played a much more physical style that included fighting as necessary to earn their respect on ice. Only three Canadian players wore helmets, in contrast to the Soviets who all wore identical headgear. Though smaller, the Soviet players were surprisingly strong. And despite being accustomed to international rules, which banned fighting altogether and until 1968 had forbidden checking in the offensive zone, CCCP held its ground and, more often than not, kept possession of the puck.

It was easy for Canadian fans to turn the Soviets into symbols of communist culture: they wore steely expressions, and when the series began fans in Canada knew nothing about even one player. The Canadian players, on the other hand, were old friends who wore their hearts on their sleeves and whose red and white Team Canada sweaters seemed almost too small to contain the huge maple leaf that dwarfed the tiny "CCCP" the Soviets wore.

In retrospect, the Soviets had the advantage in game one: the element of surprise, not to mention the NHLers' overconfidence. But the longer the series went, the better the Canadians would become.

### THE FIGHT OF THEIR LIVES

Game two, in Toronto, was a resounding testimonial to the do-or-die playoff approach these experienced NHLers could bring to the rink. They knew the cardinal importance of rallying to win. If Canada went down 2-0, a series win would be next to impossible. So they came out roaring and registered a convincing 4-1 win in front of a sold-out house of delirious – and relieved – Maple Leaf Gardens fans. Game two set the emotional tone for the rest of the Summit. Again Phil Esposito scored the game's first goal. He assisted on the fourth, while his brother Tony was spectacular in the net. As much as anything the second game was a psychological

Phil Esposito jostles with a Soviet player for position *(OPPOSITE, ABOVE LEFT)* while Valeri Karlamov battles for his own space *(OPPOSITE, ABOVE RIGHT)*. *(OPPOSITE, BELOW)* A helmeted line of players on the Soviet bench. *(ABOVE)* A Summit Series hockey card featuring Espo.

**If Canada went down 2-0, a series win would be next to impossible. So they came out roaring and registered a convincing 4-1 win in front of a sold-out house of delirious – and relieved – Maple Leaf Gardens fans.**

watershed: Team Canada proved to itself and its opponent that it could win. And now it looked clear that, whichever team won, victory would be closer than previously imagined.

The first two games delineated two completely disparate styles of play. The Canadians liked to dump the puck in and chase after it, trying to tire and intimidate the Soviet defencemen as they gave chase. They crowded the front of the net and shot often, and took their man out whenever possible. In contrast, the Soviets circled forward and back with the puck, passing rather than sacrificing position in order to maintain possession. They waited for the perfect shot and absorbed, though rarely initiated, heavy hits. They played with discipline and took few penalties, but in the corners they were sneaky-dirty, kicking, spitting, spearing their opponents in ways that no NHLer had ever encountered. When the Canadian pros retaliated, in full view of the referee, he called the obvious fouls while ignoring the

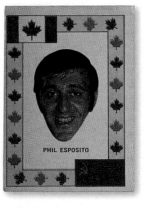

PHIL ESPOSITO

unsportsmanlike, secretive trangressions that so infuriated the Canadians.

By game three in Winnipeg, the refereeing was clearly becoming a factor. Before the game Soviets complained that in game two the officials had allowed Canada to get away with murder; the Canadians complained angrily of the despicable, cowardly play of the Soviets in the corners. But the complaining subsided by the time the puck was dropped. What followed was one of the finest games ever played.

For the third game in a row Canada scored the first goal, this time by J.P. Parisé less than two minutes from the opening faceoff. Not even a minute later, while on a power play, the Canadians surrendered a short-handed goal. Two more Canadian goals had the home side up 3-1 early in the second period, but again the Canucks let the Soviets score with the man

advantage. Although Henderson then scored to put Canada up 4-2, the Soviets scored two late goals to tie the game, further proof of their conditioning and relentless skating.

Team Canada came away from the tie with ambivalent feelings. The players knew they could have won – they blew a two-goal lead twice – but they had kept their heads and played superbly. As Sinden noted, "Aren't we all glad to be alive to watch that kind of hockey?"

In game four in Vancouver the Soviets defeated Canada 5-3 in front of a B.C. crowd that booed the home side lustily during the loss. At the end of that game, CTV commentator Johnny Esaw conducted a live interview with Phil Esposito at the players' bench. Sweat-soaked, exhausted, and at once frustrated, angered, and on the verge of tears, Esposito rallied not just his own emotions but those of a team and a nation:

"People across Canada … we tried. We gave it our best … all of us guys are really disheartened and we're disillusioned and we're disappointed in some of the people. We cannot *believe* the bad press we've got … the booing … I'm really, really disappointed … we're doing the best we can. But they've got a good team, and let's face facts … Every one of us guys, 35 guys who came out to play for Team Canada … we did it because we love our country and not for any other reason. They can throw the money for the pension fund out the window … We came because we love Canada. And even though we play in the United States, and we earn money in the United States, Canada is still our home, and that's the only reason we came. And I don't think it's fair that we should be booed."

Never had a hockey player uttered such a profound plea at the end of a hockey game, directly and passionately asking his team's fans and his fellow citizens for respect and support in a time of need. The team couldn't win without his country's support, Esposito was saying. The social and cultural context of shooting, passing, and skating did make a difference. The word "believe" was spat into the microphone with such a potent mixture of anger, love, and desire that it became a defining moment in Canadian culture.

## "FIFTY AGAINST THE WORLD"

Esposito's spirit helped renew Canadian confidence heading off to Europe, for by rights the series should have been lost. Team Canada had won but one game on home ice. Now they were heading off to play in a foreign country where the food was unfamiliar and the living conditions spartan and the ice surface larger than any they had ever encountered.

Team Canada had two weeks off before the first game in the Soviet Union, a hiatus that likely saved the series. Flying first to Stockholm, they played two exhibitions to familiarize themselves with the larger European ice surface and to adjust to the time difference. The games, against a Tre Kronor all-star aggregation, were violent and dirty, an opportunity to release the anger and frustration pent up during the first four games of the Summit Series.

After the loss in Vancouver, the Canadian press had been so hard on them that the players now formed a kind of autonomous country, a group that had to defend each other since no one else would. "When we were in Sweden," Ron Ellis remembered, "our party – players and coaches and others – numbered exactly 50. And we felt it was 50 against the world."

Vilified by the Swedish newspapers and called "gangsters" by the very Tre Kronor players who themselves speared and dove every chance they got, the Canadians stood up for each other and built a protective wall around themselves. Regardless of what happened outside the wall, inside they would endure. When the team arrived in Moscow, the capital of a country that not only depended on but encouraged insularity for its survival, the Canadians' emotional alienation found a physical counterpart. This sense of heroic isolation deepened when, unexpectedly, four of their own mutinied. Shortly after arriving in Moscow, Vic Hadfield, Rick Martin, Gil Perreault, and Jocelyn Guevremont abandoned the team in a huff owing to their lack of playing time. Sinden and Eagleson arranged to get them on the first flight back to Toronto, hopeful that the perceived betrayal by these four would solidify the resolve of those left behind. It did.

By the time game five of the series began at the Luzhniki Arena, on September 22, 1972, the team was in better physical condition and

mentally as tough as steel. And finally they felt supported by their home fans: thanks largely to Esposito's pleas, the Canadians received thousands of telegrams and letters of support in a form almost totally absent from the first half of the series in their own backyard. Meanwhile the mood of the Soviets had reversed. They were happy to be home, leading the series; they felt confident that they could continue to win.

The start to game five reflected the many changes of the past two weeks. After two periods Team Canada had built an impressive 3-0 lead and continued to press in the third. It was at this point that Paul Henderson's heroics began. After having already scored a goal and assisted on another in the second period, Henderson tripped and crashed heavily into the boards in the Soviet end, losing consciousness. In the dressing room the doctors diagnosed a concussion, advising him to head to the showers. But Henderson begged coach Sinden to let him play – which he did. Henderson then went out and scored Canada's fourth goal early in the third to give Canada a commanding 4-1 lead.

Ken Dryden and his wife Lynda take in the sights of Red Square.

But now Team Canada seemed mysteriously to fall apart, giving up three goals in six minutes. When the game was over the Soviets had won 5-4, and now led the series 3-1 with one tie. To win the series Team Canada would have to win all remaining games, a seemingly impossible task. Yet despite the late-game collapse, every player on the team felt certain they could win. "I never thought we'd lose another game," said Phil Esposito later.

The series took on a greater meaning two nights later, September 24, when the puck was dropped to begin game six. Everyone in the stands of Luzhniki Arena and watching in Canada knew that victory was the only option. While the Canadian fans in the Arena cheered wildly, the players retreated into an inner silence. They were focused and intent, able to turn the fear of losing to their advantage. There could be no more excuses, no more second chances. The team had played well in Toronto, their only win of the series so far; they had taken the lead in three other games, only to see the Soviets come from behind to win or tie. They knew they could beat the hammer and sicle. They believed they would win.

## THE COMEBACK CONTINUES

In contrast to the script so far, the Soviets scored the game's first goal – though not until early in the second period – then the Canadians stormed back in Soviet fashion, scoring three times in 84 seconds. The

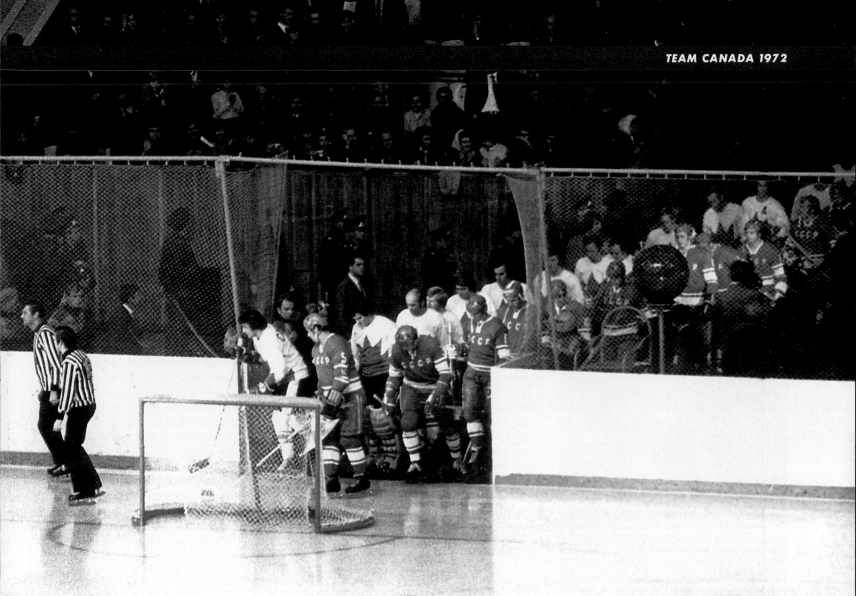

third goal was an incredible effort by Henderson, who played the whole series in Moscow like a player possessed. He danced between the two Soviet defencemen, and, while just inside the blue line, snapped the puck past a stunned Tretiak. The Canadians had announced their intention to defend their country to the limit. And now the war turned physical. West German referee Josef Kampalla assessed a total of 35 penalty minutes in the game, 31 of them to Team Canada. A whopping 27 of those minutes came after Canada went up 3-1. Playing two men short for two full minutes late in the second, Canada killed off the penalties masterfully and went on to

win the game 3-2. The second and third periods were the most violent of the series to date, with fierce but clean hitting and dirty stickwork on both sides, including Bobby Clarke's infamous slash that cracked the ankle of Soviet star Valeri Kharlamov. (Kharlamov missed game seven, then valiantly but ineffectually took the ice in game eight.)

As had become ritual, the Canadian players, management, and media pilloried referee Kampalla for what was clearly biased officiating, but Team Canada drew its strength from elsewhere. "I don't care how we win," assistant coach and GM John Ferguson said, "as long as we win."

Canadian and Soviet players take the ice in Moscow. In the stands Canada's few but boisterous fans sat side by side with Moscow's quieter hockey aficionados.

Game seven unfolded in ways both poetic and barbarous, at a level far beyond anything imagined by wide-eyed kids playing shinny on a frozen Canadian pond. It featured a fierceness of play that made the typical NHL playoff game look like a training camp scrimmage. Phil Esposito's two goals in the first period were acts of physical and emotional bravery – not merely good plays. On the first, he took a pass in the slot, then, shielding the puck with his body, spun and shot in one motion. Tretiak didn't see the puck until it

## CANADA CHEERS

Workplace absenteeism was at a record high across Canada the Thursday of game eight in Moscow, which started at 12:30 p.m. (EST). Virtually every school, among them Toronto's Gladstone Public School (above), had televisions set up so students could see the game. More Canadians watched Paul Henderson score his historic goal than had watched any other event on television in the country's history.

On ice, there would be no separation between sport and culture, game and politics. If the effect on the nation's psyche was profound, the meaning of Henderson's goal remains simple: In the face of defeat, when everything is going wrong and accomplishment seems impossible or untenable, when the world seems irrational and doing seems destined to failure, Canadians could now just think of Henderson's arms raised in triumph and the spirit from within would confirm the possibility of anything.

was past him. On the second, Esposito was knocked down in the slot but got up in a flash to handle a Serge Savard pass, then shot in one motion. Again Tretiak never saw the puck until too late.

As time ticked down in the third period, the score was tied 3-3 and chances of a Canadian victory seemed to be slipping away. Then Gary Bergman was grabbed by Boris Mikhailov after an offside whistle. Bergman went berserk, punching wildly at Mikhailov. The Soviet responded with kicks that left Bergman's socks torn and his legs bleeding. As the two players duelled, Canada's Yvan Cournoyer came to Bergman's defence, Yakushev tried to corral Cournoyer, and Esposito grabbed Yakushev. All players on the ice quickly paired off, though only the original two – Bergman and Mikhailov – received penalties, both majors for fighting.

Just a minute and a half later, Savard sped up along the boards in his end then hit Henderson with a pass at the blue line. Henderson split the defence and snapped a shot past Tretiak while falling to the ice, perhaps the finest goal of the seven games so far. Canada shut down the Soviet attack for the remaining two minutes of the game. Final score: Canada 4, Soviets 3. The series was now dead even – three wins for each side and one tie.

### HENDERSON SCORES

Game eight was a microcosm of the series. The Soviets scored first, but Canada tied. The Soviets went up 2-1, then Canada tied again; the Soviets went up for a third time, and Canada tied the game again. The score stood at 3-3 until, in the second half of the second period, the Soviets exploded for two goals and headed into the dressing room ahead a commanding 5-3. Team Canada knew that only a victory was good enough. To tie the game was to tie the series, a result unacceptable to team and country.

The political climax of the series came just past the halfway point of the third and last period of game eight. As so often in the series, Phil Esposito had scored a crucial goal to make the score 5-4. Cournoyer followed with a shot that apparently tied the game. But the red light signalling Cournoyer's goal never came on, and the referees made no move to

(OPPOSITE) Paul Henderson raises his arms after scoring the winning goal as Cournoyer embraces him.

acknowledge it. Perhaps a moment later referee Kampalla would have faced the puck off at centre ice ignoring the Canadian appeals. We'll never know. A livid Alan Eagleson left his seat to run at the timekeeper's table. Soviet soldiers grabbed him before he could reach his objective. All hell broke loose as Eagleson disappeared from sight and Pete Mahovlich jumped off the ice and into the stands. Mahovlich pulled Eagleson out of the soldiers' arms and hauled him onto the ice, then escorted him across the playing surface to the Team Canada players' bench. As he strode across the ice in his suit Eagleson raised his finger defiantly in victory. Once the confusion subsided, referee Kampalla had little choice but to count the goal. Now the endgame could begin: the score stood five-all, with seven minutes left to play.

Canada pressed and the Soviets counterattacked, and the clock kept ticking away. With less than a minute to go, and a tie (meaning a series loss) looming, Sinden wondered whether he should pull goalie Ken Dryden for an extra attacker. Then Paul Henderson screamed from the bench for Pete Mahovlich to come off the ice, a gesture a player would simply never, ever make in the National Hockey League. Equally amazing, Mahovlich complied. Henderson skated hard into the Soviet end, and the rest is history: "Here's a shot … Henderson made a wild stab for it and fell … Here's another shot! Right in front! They score! Henderson has scored for Canada!" The voice belonged to Foster Hewitt. Thirty-four seconds left in the game.

That September of 1972 the players on Team Canada aged a hundred years. They went to places they had never been, conquered demons previously unknown, summoned an inner strength they never knew they had. They represented themselves, their country, and their sport, but ultimately they stood for the human spirit. The expressions on their faces after the final bell conveyed a mix of anguish, exhaustion, and relief. They fought and won a battle that some had elevated to a contest between democracy and communism. It was a battle none could have imagined when they glided so overconfidently into training camp in early August. Now they were different men, and their country seemed different too, because "Henderson has scored for Canada."

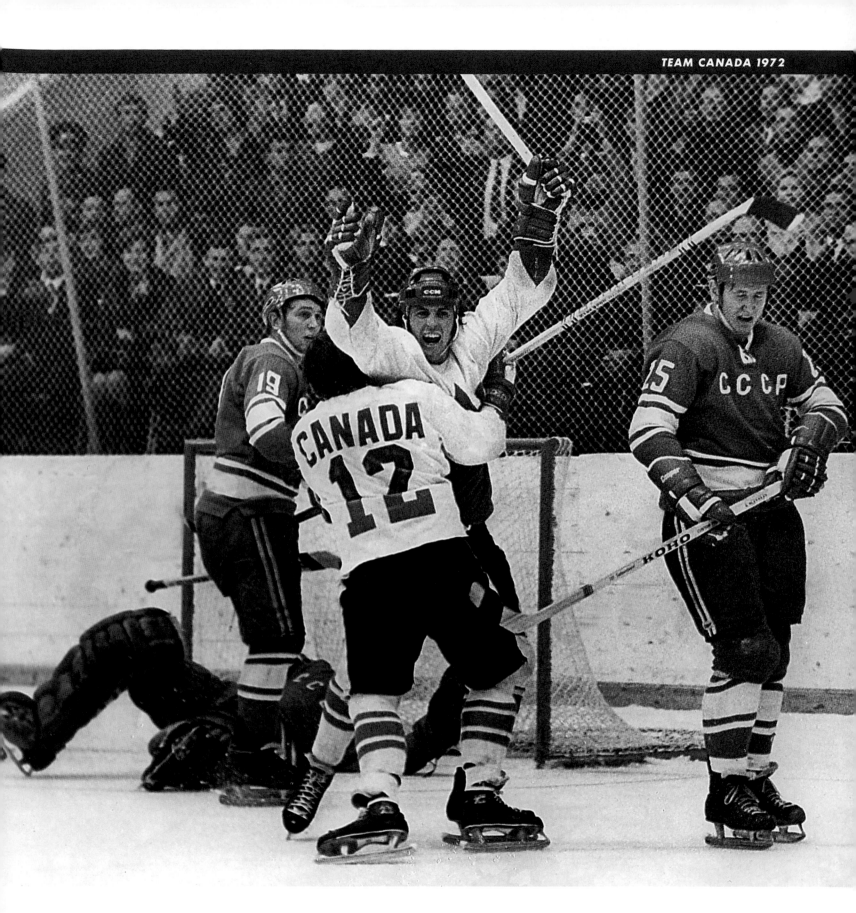

# CHAPTER 10

# THE EXECUTIVE CLASS

1976-77 MONTREAL CANADIENS

One day before a game in Vancouver early in the 1976-77 season, Montreal Canadiens roommates Serge Savard and Larry Robinson missed a game-day practice. That night, the two star defencemen were responsible for early give-aways that gave the Canucks a 2-0 lead after one period. During intermission, coach Scotty Bowman worked his magic: "It would seem," he began in thespian tones, "that some guys on this team think they're better than the rest.... It would seem that these guys got reputations in this league, they're all-stars and they love to read about how good they are in the papers. Obviously, guys like this don't have to bless us with their presence at practice ... like the rest of their teammates because they're too good for us and the rest of this league. Now can somebody tell me," he continued with a rising voice, "if these guys are so good, such *all-stars*, how come we're losing to the Vancouver Canucks? Could it be that the Canucks can't read, that not one guy on their team knows that we have such great stars in our room? Graves and Sedlbauer [the goal scorers] gotta be illiterate. If they knew how great Savard and Robinson are, no way they could have scored a goal like they did." It was a lesson the two learned as players that night, and one they and their teammates passed down years later as coaches, managers, and scouts themselves.

THE TWO ALL-STAR CULPRITS TOOK THE CRITICISM LIKE MEN and never missed another practice. Montreal came back to win the game, and went on to complete the most successful regular season in league history, losing just eight of 80 games before winning their second consecutive Stanley Cup a few weeks later. This remarkable Montreal team was coached by Scotty Bowman, by then the most successful coach in the business, but like most of his predecessors at the Montreal Forum he had plenty of talent to work with. "I've often wondered what makes this team so good," Ken Dryden would ask in his best-selling book *The Game*. "Management perhaps. Certainly the Canadiens are a textbook study: stability (three managers, five coaches in forty years), competence (professional managers whose qualifications aren't goals and assists; who are secure enough to hire the best people; who win), dedication (Pollock, Bowman, Ruel and others didn't marry until well into their thirties), attitude. They feel it's their 'God-given duty to be the best every year,' former coach Al MacNeil once said. It's a message we all sense. The team is a business, yet its bottom line seems only to win." That winning, prior to Dryden's arrival and since his departure, was made possible by the Canadiens' tradition of stability and intelligence. And this 1976-77 Montreal team was unique in that it produced an extraordinary number of front office men for the next generation of hockey.

Before the '70s team could establish itself as a new dynasty it had to defeat the Broad Street Bullies, Philadelphia's fight-obsessed, nearly talentless goon team that had brawled its way to intimidation and Stanley Cup victory in 1974 and '75. The turning point came during training camp of the 1975-76 season, on the night of September 21, 1975, in an exhibition game in the City of Brotherly Love. Late in the game, the Habs were winning 6-2 when Philly's captain Bobby Clarke collided with Doug Risebrough of the Habs near the players' benches. Risebrough had just one NHL season under his belt, but not only was he not intimidated, he started a fight with the Flyers' leader. This brought Dave "the Hammer" Schultz off the Philly bench, soon followed by the rest of the team. Montreal's bench joined the fray, and a full-scale brawl resulted. But the Habs got much the better of the Broad Street brawlers this night, and many a Flyer found himself on the receiving end of the many punches thrown. This turn of events came as no surprise to Habs' coach Scotty Bowman. He had dressed a number of the team's minor-league players, fighters primed for just such an on-ice battle. "We won the Stanley Cup that night," scoring star Steve Shutt said later. "It just wasn't official until next May. If you are going to beat the Stanley Cup champions, you have to beat them at their style because they dictate the game. Philadelphia was a tough team so we had to prove that we were tougher, to break them mentally.... Sitting in the dressing room after the game, a lot of guys were smiling. We knew we had them. Better still, they knew it, too. And once you beat them at their style, you could impose your style on them and we knew they could never skate with us."

And that's just how history played out the changing of the Stanley Cup guard. Montreal won the Cup that year with a feisty, fighting style, in the regular season, but by the time they got to the finals, fighting wasn't necessary. They swept the Flyers in a relatively tame

## Montreal won the Cup that year with a feisty, fighting style in the regular season, but by the time they got to the finals, fighting wasn't necessary.

series scarred only by a Moose Dupont-Mario Tremblay scrap midway through game two. Despite being Cup defenders, the Flyers tried to play Montreal's brand of hockey – with its fluid skating and passing – and lost badly. The Canadiens won each game on the strength of third-period goals, outscoring Philadelphia 6-2 in the four third periods of the finals and getting to play freewheeling hockey in the process. The Broad Street Bullies were clobbered, and the death knell for the bench-clearing brawl had been sounded. The Flyers never won another Stanley Cup under their anarchic coach, Fred Shero.

### POLLOCK BUILDS A POWERHOUSE

Now Montreal could focus on its strengths – speed, skating, finesse – and, as the Flyers had done with pure physical intimidation, use those strengths to set the tone of the game, a feat they managed for the rest of the decade. These strengths had been acquired through the singular drafting genius of general manager Sam Pollock, who was building his team under a completely different set of league rules from his predecessor, Frank Selke. Whereas Selke relied on bird dogs and French-Canadian patriotism to recruit his players, Pollock operated under the Entry Draft, a system of uniform dispersal of players within the league. His was the first dynasty created in this way. Almost every player on the 1976-77 team was drafted by the Canadiens – as opposed to free-agent signings or players acquired by trade – a fact that bespoke Pollock's shrewdness at the draft table at a time when every team had equal opportunity to scout and draft the same players.

The genius of Pollock and his scouting staff is best illustrated by the story of how the Habs came to draft Guy Lafleur. On May 22, 1970, Pollock traded Ernie Hicke and Montreal's first-round draft choice for 1971 to the Oakland Seals, the league's worst team, for François Lacombe and the Seals' first-round draft choice the same year. The exchange of players was of little importance to Pollock; he was after the number-one draft choice overall, certain Lafleur would be selected before any other in 1971. He traded with the Seals on the assumption they'd finish last in the league. Since draft selections were determined by reversing the order of the final standings (first place selected last; last place chose first), acquiring California's first choice would allow Pollock to pick first overall if his hunch was right. He planned to pick Lafleur.

*(LEFT)* In Montreal, once a hockey hero, always a hockey hero. As this cereal box promotion attests, Jean Béliveau remains one of the most popular figures in the city, even though he retired some 30 years ago. *(OPPOSITE ABOVE)* Flyers goalie Bernie Parent stops Bob Gainey on this close-in chance. Montreal defeated the Flyers to win the 1976 Stanley Cup. *(OPPOSITE BELOW LEFT)* The Habs' victory can be largely credited to the genius of Sam Pollock (here seen with Serge Savard). *(OPPOSITE BELOW RIGHT)* The Habs dynasty announced its intentions when it dropped its gloves in a pre-season game with the Broad Street Bullies in 1976.

Now Montreal could focus on its strengths — speed, skating, finesse — and, as the Flyers had done with pure physical intimidation, use those strengths to set the tone of the game, a feat they managed for the rest of the decade.

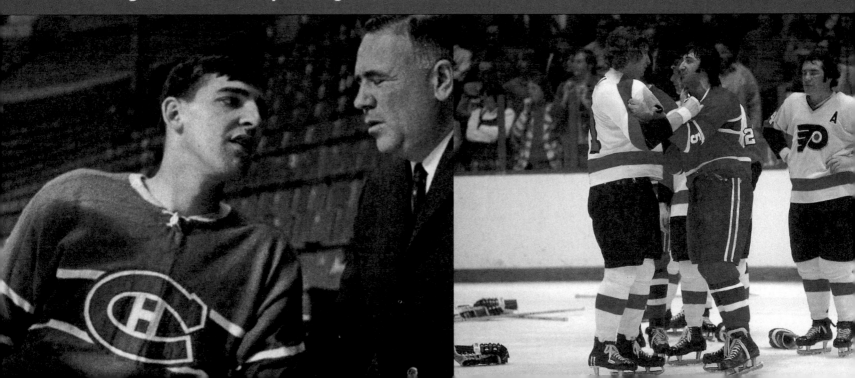

But as the 1970-71 season unfolded, Pollock's plan looked to be in jeopardy. The Los Angeles Kings were performing even more poorly than the Seals, and by mid-season looked certain to finish last themselves, something Pollock could not suffer. So the Montreal GM traded one of his star players, Ralph Backstrom, to Los Angeles for two journeymen forwards, Gord Labossière and Ray Fortin. Neither Fortin nor Labossière would play a minute in a Montreal sweater, but Pollock didn't care. He was interested only in improving the Kings enough so that they'd finish ahead of Oakland, thus preserving

**Pollock's play for Lafleur reflected his ability to plan. "I always tend to look at the overall or big picture ... very seldom was my philosophy to win a championship first," he explained.**

the time he drafted Lafleur, centre Jean Béliveau and left-winger John Ferguson had just retired. Dick Duff was in his 17th season, Backstrom and Henri Richard in their 16th, and J.C. Tremblay his 12th. Pollock needed two things, a young marquee French Canadian and an offensive superstar. Lafleur was unquestionably both. During his five

trading coups. In 1964, the year the Canadiens promoted Pollock to general manager after he spent some 18 years with the club's various minor-league teams, he acquired Dryden and a now-forgotten player from the Boston Bruins in exchange for two other also-rans. How did Pollock know that the then 16-year-old Dryden would become a star seven years later?

Guy Lafleur put together a string of six consecutive 50-goal seasons, thanks largely to a hard and accurate slapshot from his favoured right wing, and also not to having face his own Ken Dryden, one of the top goalies of the 1970s.

Montreal's claim to the first draft choice overall. Los Angeles, buoyed by the addition of Backstrom, rallied in the second half of the season, and just as Pollock had planned, the Seals finished dead last. Naturally, he used the first selection overall at the 1971 draft to choose Guy Lafleur. In a word, brilliant.

Pollock's play for Lafleur reflected his ability to plan. "I always tend to look at the overall or big picture ... very seldom was my philosophy to win a championship first," he explained. By

years of junior hockey in Quebec City – three with the Aces and two with the Remparts – he set every scoring record imaginable, including an extraordinary 130 goals and 209 points in his final year with the Remparts. Pollock knew he had to have Lafleur.

In goal, Pollock already had Ken Dryden, who had played just six regular season games with the Habs before backstopping the team to the 1971 Stanley Cup. Dryden became the first player to win the Conn Smythe Trophy for most valuable player in the playoffs before the Calder. With Dryden in net Pollock knew his goaltending was set for the rest of the decade. And Dryden was one of "Silent Sam's" first

During the 1971 Amateur Draft, after selecting Lafleur first, Pollock chose Larry Robinson 20th overall. At the next year's draft he took Steve Shutt and Bill Nyrop, then Bob Gainey in '73 and Doug Risebrough and Mario Tremblay in '74. The Stanley Cup was becoming more tenable.

### THE MOST HATED COACH

In hindsight, Pollock's hiring of Scotty Bowman in the summer of 1971 was his greatest stroke of genius. Pollock knew Bowman well – Scotty had apprenticed under him in junior hockey in Ottawa. He had watched Bowman develop as a coach with the expansion St. Louis Blues in 1967, taking the fledgling team to the Stanley Cup finals for three successive years. Pollock appointed him to the Canadiens when coach Al MacNeil decided to return to junior hockey, where the pressures were less and the living easier than in the fishbowl that was the Forum.

Bowman's task in Montreal was the complete opposite of his St. Louis challenge. There, he had taken a team lacking in skill and motivated the players to perform beyond their own expectations. In Montreal, Bowman had many of the most skilled players in the league at his disposal. His job was to ensure they played up to their ability and didn't self-destruct. As the decade advanced it became clear that the only team that could beat the Montreal Canadiens was the Montreal Canadiens. His was a psychological, not a physical challenge: "We had such a good team that petty little grievances could develop that might bring the team down," Larry Robinson later admitted. "So what Scotty did, he made himself the focal point. The one thing that we had in common was that everybody hated Scotty."

The players' communal hatred of Bowman created a team chemistry that produced a happy family. For this, Bowman was doubly grateful. He didn't need a team that loved him, only one that respected him behind the bench. Even though the players loathed him as a person, they held his coaching abilities in the highest regard. That was all he needed.

Bowman was at his best during close games when he could focus on the little things that separated victory from defeat. But when his Habs were leading by three or four goals and victory was assured – which was most of the time – he'd be pacing up and down the bench, barking at his players not to lose focus or let up because, really, he had nothing else to do.

Bowman also controlled the media better than any coach. He knew the power of the press, particularly in a hockey-mad city such as Montreal, and how to use it to motivate his troops. He would sometimes announce that a certain player would be scratched from a game. This inevitably upset the rest of the team, which would take the unusual step of approaching him en masse to ask him to reconsider his decision, which he would. The re-inserted player would then play a great game as the team rallied around him for a convincing win. In such ways did Bowman give his players the inspirational edge.

## TEAM INVINCIBLE

After winning the 1975-76 Stanley Cup and more or less eliminating fighting from the playoff agenda, the Habs worked on becoming not just great but invincible. For the 1976-77 season Bowman still had the incomparable Ken Dryden in goal, and his big three defencemen of Savard, Robinson, and Lapointe made the best blue-line trio in the league. Each of the four forward lines comprised a distinctive unit responsible for a different contribution to the team's success. The number-one line of Steve Shutt, Guy Lafleur, and Pete Mahovlich was the goal-scoring unit; the second line of Jacques Lemaire, Yvan Cournoyer, and Murray Wilson could score a bit and play solid, two-way hockey; the third trio, Doug Jarvis, Bob Gainey, and Jim Roberts, was the best checking line in the league; and the fourth line of Doug Risebrough, Mario Tremblay, and Yvon Lambert hit hard and chipped in with timely goals. (This last line was nicknamed "Piton's Raiders" for director of player development Claude Ruel, whose nickname was Piton and who often worked with the threesome.) In short, Bowman's Montreal Canadiens were a flawlessly organized team in which every player knew his role.

In 1976-77 the Habs' regular season record was 60 wins, 12 ties, and eight losses, the most successful regular season in NHL history. Four of those losses came before Christmas, four after: October 10 and March 6 at Buffalo, 3-1 and 4-1; October 17 and January 17 at Boston, 5-3 and 7-3; November 17 at Toronto, 1-0; December 12, 5-2 at New York; January 12, 7-2 at St. Louis. The only team to beat the Habs at home in 40 games at the Forum was Boston, on October 30, by a score of 4-3.

By 1976 Guy Lafleur had truly blossomed into "The Flower," as his adoring fans had inevitably nicknamed the man supposed to inherit the mantle of the great Jean Béliveau. A beautiful and fluid skater with a tremendous shot, Lafleur made slow progress during his first few years, but by 1976 had become the premier right-winger in the league. Unlike many stars before and since, he absorbed plenty of rough treatment from opponents without retaliating and without a bodyguard to do his fighting for him. He simply played through the hitting and checking, demanding respect and giving it to his opponents in return.

The master tactician, Scotty Bowman was both reviled and respected by his players. Still active as coach of the Detroit Red Wings, he has for years been the winningest coach of all time.

But Lafleur was not the only Montreal player who had to live up to excruciating expectations from the Montreal media and public. Ken Dryden was supposed to play like Jacques Plante, Larry Robinson like Doug Harvey. Herein lay the paradox of playing for Montreal, whose tradition of success was at once inspiring and stifling. In hockey terms, it was not a city for the meek.

## FUTURE EXECS

The Montreal Canadiens of the 1970s not only won with ease, they moved effortlessly and in unprecedented numbers into coaching, scouting, and managerial roles. Ordinarily, it is the less-talented player, the journeyman, the fighter, who excels as an executive. But this Montreal team of superstars was a training ground for more front office men than any other. These former players proved that coping with success could be as valuable a lesson as surviving as a fourth-line winger. Dealing with the remorseless expectations of the Montreal media and the incessant hero-worship from the city's faithful produced a psychologically tough businessman, scout, or coach.

Ken Dryden is now the president of the Toronto Maple Leafs. Bob Gainey (above) is the general manager of the Cup-winning Dallas Stars. Doug Risebrough was the GM in Calgary for many years, and Larry Robinson and Jacques Lemaire have been successful coaches in the NHL during the 1990s, among the very few to win Cups as both a player and coach. Mario Tremblay and Jim Roberts have also been head coaches in the NHL. Steve Shutt, Pete Mahovlich, Serge Savard, Guy Lapointe, Yvon Lambert, Doug Jarvis, and the late Bill Nyrop also became involved in the NHL or the minor pro leagues after retiring.

The 1977 playoffs, like the regular season, were a foregone conclusion. The Habs swept St. Louis in four games in the quarter-finals, trailing the Blues for not even one minute. In the next round, however, they were tested briefly by the up-and-coming Islanders, starring Bryan Trottier, Mike Bossy, Denis Potvin, and Billy Smith. The Islanders had the lead 3-2 after two periods of game one, but early in the third Montreal rallied and roared back to win 4-3 thanks to goals by Lafleur and Shutt. Two nights later the Habs won 3-0, and a sweep looked to be in progress. But the New Yorkers refused to concede so easily, winning games three and five. Like many great teams before them, the Islanders were announcing that sometime soon, they, too, would be legitimate Cup contenders. In game six, on Long Island, with the series still a close 3-2 in Montreal's favour, Bob Gainey scored only seven seconds into the game. From then on the Habs played flawless defence, skating to a 2-1 win to move on to the Stanley Cup finals.

In the finals the Habs faced a Boston team that was both outmatched and utterly jinxed. Since joining the NHL in 1926, the Bruins had played Montreal in the playoffs 13 times and had never – never! – won a single series. Fate, history, and timing conspired to ensure that these Bruins believed they would lose even before the first drop of the puck. Just 1:45 into that first game, Doug Risebrough scored, confirming those fears. The Habs then coasted to a 7-3 win. In fact, they won the first three games with intimidating ease, 7-3, 3-0, and 4-2. It wasn't until game four, with the series far out of reach, that Boston even once held the lead, and this was quickly erased. That fourth game went into overtime, but Jacques Lemaire took a quick, perfect Lafleur pass and drilled a shot

(ABOVE) After retiring, Ken Dryden wrote The Game, a literal analysis of the game he loved. (OPPOSITE ABOVE) Gerry Cheevers stops Pierre Mondou here, but Boston never beat Montreal in the playoffs during the 1970s. (OPPOSITE BELOW LEFT) In the 1970s in Montreal, Stanley Cup revelry was almost as regular as the seasons. (OPPOSITE BELOW RIGHT) Larry Robinson, Yvon Cournoyer, and Serge Savard celebrate their 1978 victory.

The Game

A reflective and thought-provoking look at a life in hockey

Ken Dryden

past Gerry Cheevers. A second championship for the future Executive Class. More would follow.

That year, Guy Lafleur won the Art Ross, Hart, and Conn Smythe trophies; the Habs placed four of the six positions for the First All-Star team; Bowman won the Jack Adams Award; Robinson won the Norris; and Dryden the Vezina. So many teams that had come before had won the sacred silverware because of grit or determination, through the dominant presence of two or three star players, with the help of a lucky break or fortuitous schedule, or because of good coaching. The 1976-77 Montreal Canadiens won because they were a virtually flawless team: pure talent and perfect execution. And thanks to the wiles of Scotty Bowman, the players were too preoccupied with hating him to take notice of their greatness.

Conn Smythe used to say that he didn't like players who looked bad in a loss or players who looked good in a loss. The players he went after were those who looked good in a win. The Montreal Canadiens of 1976-77 looked great in winning, and won more than any team before or since, nurturing as many great players as have ever shared a dressing room. "When a team wins once," Dryden wrote, "it can be for one central reason. When it wins for three consecutive years, nine times in fourteen years, it's for a crush of reasons. Winning brings with it such an immense momentum. Everything fits, everything works. Every new thing is made to fit and work. Everything just is. Reasons blur and disappear. It becomes a state of mind, an obligation, an expectation; in the end, an attitude. Excellence. It is that rare chance to play with the best, to be the best. When you have it, you don't give it up."

Perhaps the understanding of what makes a great team is in itself an important reason for being able to achieve monumental glory. From Bowman to Dryden to Lafleur and on down the line, this Habs team understood how to play their best. The 1976-77 season represents the very peak of their abilities.

# CHAPTER 11

# CANADA-SOVIET DÉJÀ VU

1987 TEAM CANADA

In February 1987 the NHL held a five-day "Rendez-vous" in Quebec City in place of its annual All-Star Game. The two-game series featured a team of NHL all-stars versus a team made up of the best from the Soviet Union, a format similar to the Challenge Cup staged in February 1979 in New York. The NHL team boasted such familiar names as Wayne Gretzky and Mario Lemieux; the Soviets, while less familiar, were no longer faceless: Viacheslov Fetisov, Igor Larionov, and Sergei Makarov had all played with distinction in previous meetings, and before long they and many lesser known teammates would be playing in the NHL. For now, however, a team of Soviet stars still held a real mystique for North American fans. The thrilling and well-played series saw the NHLers win the first game 4-3 on a late goal by Patrick Poulin with just 1:15 to play. In the second game, the Soviets scored three second-period goals to wipe out a 1-0 deficit en route to an exciting 5-3 win. After the handshakes, tournament MVP Wayne Gretzky waxed breathlessly enthusiastic about the competition: "Let's face it," he said, "people want more than two games. And they want more than Christmas tours. And when it comes to the Canada Cup, who really wants to see Canada play West Germany? People don't want to see those other countries. People want to see Canada and Russia."

**G**RETZKY KNEW THAT FANS WANTED ANOTHER SUMMIT Series featuring just those two countries. But although his lobbying didn't help produce another Summit Series, it did hasten the scheduling of another Canada Cup to a year earlier than planned. But by the end of the exhausting 1986-87 NHL season and another Stanley Cup win for his remarkable Edmonton Oilers, the Great One sounded considerably less enthusiastic: "It was the toughest year I've ever had ... I'm probably more drained now than I've ever been."

Just a few weeks later, when NHL Players' Association executive director Alan Eagleson invited Gretzky to report to Team Canada's training camp in August, number 99 was reluctant to commit. "If I cannot play my best hockey, then maybe I should let someone else play ... I'm going to have to sit down with Slats [Edmonton coach Glen Sather] and my father and talk it over. Everybody has a responsibility to play in the Canada Cup, to help out the Players' Association, but I've played twice now ... For the first time, it's not automatic."

Gretzky not participating in a Canada Cup? The idea seemed preposterous. Since playing at the World Junior Championships as a 16-year-old in 1978, he hadn't missed an international tournament to which he'd been invited. He had played at the 1981 and '84 Canada Cups; and after the Oilers were eliminated in the first round of the 1982 playoffs, he hopped on a plane that night and arrived in Finland the next day to play for Canada at the World Championships. But more important, Gretzky was the game's premier player, having broken every single-season NHL record imaginable and being well on his way to setting every career record.

While Gretzky hesitated, almost all the other invitees accepted: Oilers teammates Mark Messier, Paul Coffey, Glenn Anderson, and Grant Fuhr; and most other Canadian stars of the NHL, notably Pittsburgh's number 66, Mario Lemieux, nicknamed the Next One. The only significant absentees were New York Islanders forward Mike Bossy and Montreal Canadiens defenceman Larry Robinson, who both declined to play. On July 15 Gretzky finally agreed to come to the Team Canada camp, but only on two conditions: that he and the rest of the participants have a few days off after the end of the tournament before returning to their NHL training camps and that the next Canada Cup wouldn't be played until 1992. "It was time for somebody to take a stand that maybe we were playing these international games too often," he explained. With the Great One on board and Lemieux already confirmed, Team Canada '87 now had its nucleus. The host of scoring stars that filled out the roster left little doubt of the firepower coach Mike Keenan of the Philadelphia Flyers would be working with for the series. With Fuhr in goal, the only worry now was the defence. Besides Robinson, three key men would not be playing because of injuries: Paul Reinhart, Kevin Lowe, and Doug Wilson.

## MARIO'S LESSON

Team Canada's training camp opened in the August heat at Copps Coliseum in Hamilton, Ontario, with 35 players competing for 23 roster spots. The prospect of 12 of the best players in the world getting cut from any team created an uncomfortable competitive tension in camp,

**But more important, Gretzky was the game's premier player, having broken every single-season NHL record imaginable and being well on his way to setting every career record.**

especially between skaters accustomed to playing on opposing NHL teams. This tension flared on only one significant occasion, however. During an intense practice Philadelphia goalie Ron Hextall slashed Hartford's Sylvain Turgeon, breaking his arm. Turgeon believed there was intent to injure, and perhaps not coincidentally Hextall never played a minute in the tournament.

Team Canada coach Mike Keenan knew that no matter whom he cut, he would be criticized. Rather than simply pick the biggest stars, he decided to mould his team around specific needs. This led him to cut Steve Yzerman, one of the most skilled centres in the league but one high-scoring centre too many (the others were Gretzky, Lemieux, Mark Messier, Dale Hawerchuk, and Doug Gilmour). His fourth line needed to be physically intimidating and defensive-minded, which explained his inclusion of Gilmour, Rick Tocchet, and Brent Sutter – none as famous as Yzerman, but each well suited to the role to which he would be assigned.

As Keenan put the final touches on his roster, the players could focus more on the tournament to come – which could lead to a different kind of tension if a player didn't seem to be trying hard enough. To Wayne Gretzky this looked to be the case with Mario Lemieux. Now entering his fourth year in the league, Lemieux had possibly more talent than the Great One but a fraction of the competitive drive. Often brilliant during a game, Lemieux could be notoriously lazy at other times, merely going through the motions or even skipping a morning or off-day practice entirely. One day captain Gretzky loudly berated Lemieux in front of their Team Canada teammates for his lax approach to the series. This wasn't just another training camp, Gretzky admonished him; professional, cultural, and national pride were at stake. The 20-year-old Lemieux was embarrassed by the public tirade from the usually genial Gretzky, and he got the message. The world's greatest player was actually paying him a compliment, since Gretzky likely wouldn't have bothered trying to motivate a lesser player with less potential. Following the incident Keenan put the captain and the heir apparent on the same line, a move that would have a profound effect on the series.

On the eve of the tournament, Team Canada's confidence was high, a confidence bred of a long history of victory. They knew the Soviets were driven by superb conditioning, training, and discipline, but that they could crumble in the crunch. "The longer you stay with them," forward Dino Ciccarelli said, "the more they lose their composure." Defenceman Zarley Zalapski, another

A Canada Cup program, one of a variety of souvenirs that, along with television revenue, generated millions of dollars for the NHL players' pension fund and added to the lustre of Alan Eagleson, the players' association executive director who'd come up with the idea for the Cup.

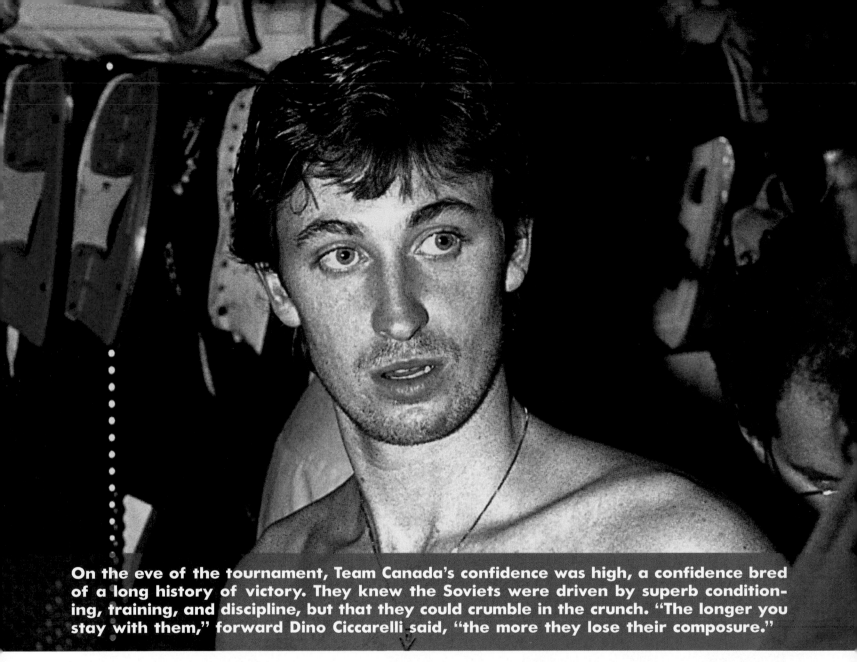

On the eve of the tournament, Team Canada's confidence was high, a confidence bred of a long history of victory. They knew the Soviets were driven by superb conditioning, training, and discipline, but that they could crumble in the crunch. "The longer you stay with them," forward Dino Ciccarelli said, "the more they lose their composure."

Canadian with international experience, agreed: "They get upset with each other when things aren't going well. They just seem to badger each other." Even the Soviets acknowledged the difference. "We do not have the spirit to draw on that these Canadians do," coach Anatoli Tarasov had said in 1972. "[They have] a light that cannot be put out. You defeat them sometimes, but you discourage them never."

## THE TOURNAMENT OF SIX

The 18-day Canada Cup tournament got underway on August 28, 1987. Featuring six nations – Canada, Sweden, Finland, Czechoslovakia, the United States, and Soviet Union – it began with a round-robin series of five games, from which the top four teams would advance to an elimination playoff round. Like any short tournament, the 1987 Canada Cup offered little margin for error and demanded that a team improve with each game. Canada's opening 4-4 tie with the Czechs certainly showed room for

Wayne Gretzky wasn't physically intimidating, as this dressing-room shot indicates, but he brought an unmatched intensity to the rink. In 1987, at the height of his hockey powers, he motivated those around him to raise the level of their play.

improvement. Defenceman Paul Coffey described the game as one in which Canada couldn't have played worse, yet one from which they earned a point in the standings. Canada held one-goal leads three different times during the game, and goalie Grant Fuhr demonstrated why he was the number one goaler in the world. His Czech counterpart was a 22-year-old named Dominik Hasek, not yet the Dominator of his future NHL years, but a formidable youngster all the same.

In their second game, against Finland, the Canadians showed some hopeful signs. The coaches had wanted the team to concentrate on playing as five-men units to counteract the Finns' style – all up or all back – and the Red and White used the counter-attack to perfection. They built up a 3-0 lead early in the second and cruised to a 4-1 win.

Sergei Svetlov of the Soviet Union skates away from Mario Lemieux during the finals. Super Mario led the Canada Cup in scoring with 11 goals and came into his own as a superstar.

The turning point for Team Canada came in the third game of the series, against their geographic neighbours. Until now, the United States had received little if any respect in the world of hockey, and for the most part rightly so. But in 1987 the American team was different, far superior to any it had sent to an international tournament, though not yet on par with Canada.

This Canada-U.S. matchup yielded a unique hybrid style of play: vintage North American hockey adjudicated according to international rules. There were hip checks and heavy hits, but there were also high sticks and cross-checks, though fighting was forbidden. The Americans took it to Canada in the first period, but led only 1-0 thanks to terrific goaltending from Fuhr. In the second the pace intensified, and the pushing and shoving began to continue after the whistle. Mario Lemieux tied the score early in the second, but the game's deciding moment came late in the period when forward Chris Nilan elbowed Lemieux. Mario responded with a high stick, Claude Lemieux stepped in and was punched by Curt Fraser, and all players became involved in a lengthy scrum. "We started playing for each other," Rick Tocchet said of the physical effort that had a greater emotional consequence than the score. Mario then broke the Americans' spirit with his second goal off a Gretzky pass just three seconds from the end of the period to give Canada a 2-1 lead.

In the third Lemieux scored again (another Gretzky pass putting him in scoring position), and although Corey Millen replied for the U.S. less than a minute later, Canada won 3-2 on the strength of Mario's hat trick,

Gretzky's passing, and the team's intensity in the face of adversity. The Americans had played gamely, but had fallen to a Team Canada that was, as hoped, getting better with every game. "It took a while for the team to develop," coach Mike Keenan remarked. "It didn't just happen, it evolved." And key to that evolution was the special tandem of numbers 99 and 66. "It's fun to play with Gretzky," Mario said afterward.

Prior to game four against Sweden, Gretzky told teammate and friend Mark Messier that it was time for him – Gretzky – to step up his game. The remarkable feature about the Great One's career was not only that people expected him to be great but that he almost always met those expectations. In this instance, he went out and scored the opening goal and assisted on three of Canada's next four goals in a 5-3 win over the Swiss. Gretzky's scoring aside, the Canadians were performing more like a team with every game, learning each other's moves and playing up to the level of skill that ran the length of the players' bench. Dale Hawerchuk, a superstar with the Winnipeg Jets, willingly accepted the role of a third-line checker. Likewise for Tocchet, Glenn Anderson, Doug Gilmour, and many NHL stars who took on parts in the supporting cast. Mario Lemieux, by virtue of being one of the team's best scorers, also became more of a leader than he had ever expected to be when the tournament began. Check your egos at the door was Keenan's philosophy, one the players happily adopted for a chance play for team and country.

The much-anticipated final game of the round robin featured Canada and the Soviets vying for first place in the standings. Although meaningless because both teams had already qualified for the playoffs, the

**A new generation of hockey lovers wanted an updated version of Paul Henderson's heroics; they wanted to savour a victory as sweet as Canada's last-minute win in the '72 Summit Series.**

game was psychologically important. In a pretournament exhibition the Soviets had hammered Canada 9-4, a reflection both of the Soviets' firepower and Canada's still-developing team play. This game certainly didn't figure to be 9-4 for either team.

Canada opened the scoring with a beautiful Glenn Anderson backhand over the shoulder of goalie Evgeny Belosheikin, a 1-0 lead that lasted until early in the second period. Then the Big Red Machine scored three goals in under seven minutes, with Sergei Svetlov, Vladimir Krutov, and Svetlov again doing the damage. Shortly after, Canada went on a power play and Gretzky made a perfect pass to defenceman Ray Bourque, who had snuck in to the side of the net. For the remainder of the game the Canadians attacked relentlessly. Finally, with just 2:27 remaining, Gretzky himself tied the game, which ended 3-3. The result and the manner in which it was achieved gave the Canadians confidence heading into the next round: They now knew they could match the Soviets' skating and scoring ability and play come-from-behind hockey.

One semi-final matchup saw Canada again face the Czechs, while the other game featured the Soviets versus the Swedes. The Canadians started their game as if preoccupied with a dream finals versus the Soviets, and by the end of the first period trailed 2-0. But now, with defeat and elimination only 40 minutes away, Team Canada went to work. "When they went ahead 2-0," Canada's assistant coach John Muckler commented, "the fear finally set in." This time, it was the rapidly maturing Lemieux and the veteran Mark Messier who led the comeback. Lemieux scored two goals in the second and Hawerchuk added one to give Canada the lead 3-2 after two periods. The go-ahead goal, scored on the power play, was vintage stuff. Gretzky feathered a pass to Bourque, who spotted Mario off to the side of the net. Bourque took a shot, but instead of directing it on net he put it to Lemieux, who merely redirected the puck behind Hasek. Canada

now had the lead and the momentum. The onslaught continued in the third, with Michel Goulet, David Volek, and Brian Propp scoring against the stunned Czechs. By the end of the game Czechoslovakia had been eliminated 5-3. In the other semi-final the Soviets had beaten the Swedes 4-2. The Canada Cup had come down to the Canada-CCCP series everyone had been waiting for.

As Wayne Gretzky had opined the previous February in Quebec City, fans wanted to see Canada play the Soviet Union. A new generation of hockey lovers wanted an updated version of Paul Henderson's heroics; they wanted to savour a victory as sweet as Canada's last-minute win in the '72 Summit Series. During the intervening 15 years of international play, the Soviet and Canadian styles had converged: the Canadians now played a more free-wheeling, high-speed game, while the Soviets played a more direct and physical game. But the two countries still produced the best hockey players in the world.

## THE DREAM FINALS

Game one of the best-of-three finals was played at the Montreal Forum on September 11 before the expected capacity crowd waving flags and banners and sporting painted faces with a red maple leaf on each cheek. The Canadians fed off their emotion early when Mike Gartner scored just 1:49 into the game – a patented bullet of a shot fired while rolling down the right wing – but the Soviets answered with four in a row by early in the second period. Once again, the fear of losing gave the Canadians some much-needed inspiration. Bourque scored late in the second to bring the score to 4-2. In the third Gilmour and Anderson tied the game before Gretzky put Team Canada ahead with just 2:59 left. It seemed that Canada had pulled off another remarkable, come-from-behind 5-4 win. But the Soviets, having learned a thing or two from Canada since 1972, staged a comeback of their own, tying the game just 22 seconds later to send it into overtime.

In that fourth period, centre Alexander Semak scored for the Soviets to give them the

win and a 1-0 lead in the finals. The familiar 6-5 score must have seemed sweet retribution for that game eight loss in Moscow some 15 years before. But the Canadians were not about to fold. "Coming back from a three-goal deficit," Ray Bourque explained, "that was really something." "One thing Canadians have always had is pride," Gretzky finished. "It's not over yet. There are too many winners in this room for us not to bounce back."

Injuries to Kevin Dineen, Claude Lemieux, and Rick Tocchet meant that Team Canada was down to 19 skaters for game two held at Copps Coliseum in Hamilton two nights later, but the losses seemed to rally the healthy troops. They took to the ice knowing that they'd either win the game or lose the series. Four times the Canadians took the lead, and four times the relentless Soviets came back. The teams contested each shift with fierce intensity, but there was little dirty play, just fervent skating and breathtaking scoring chances at both ends of the ice.

As in the first game of the finals, Canada led late in the third period, this time thanks to a Mario Lemieux power-play goal off a magical pass from Gretzky skating on his off wing. But with just 64 seconds left Valery Kamensky scored to tie the game. "We were really down in the dressing room," Gretzky said of the intermission between the third and fourth periods. "Two games in a row we had blown the lead in the final minutes and had to play overtime in two games we should have won. But Brent Sutter, Mike Gartner, and [backup goalie] Kelly Hrudey got us going. They wouldn't let us be down, and we went out for the overtime with smiles on our faces."

Despite the result of game one, overtime had long been Canada's domain – all too familiar for NHLers with playoff experience, but nonexistent in European hockey. With victory or defeat hinging on every rush, the first overtime produced end-to-end action, long stretches without whistles, and a palpable sense of excitement. Every shot or save produced anxious cheers and cries from the fans, but after 20 minutes of overtime, the game was still tied 5-5.

If possible, the second overtime featured even more pressure on both goalies. Canada's Fuhr stopped a hard slapshot from Vladimir Krutov and then a wraparound attempt by Viachelsav Bykov. Belosheikin gloved a hard

Lemieux shot and moments later the Soviets again came close. Alexei Kasatonov swirled around defenceman Doug Crossman and Fuhr came out to challenge him. The ensuing shot trickled through his pads and wobbled toward the goal line, but Fuhr reached back and put his glove on the puck as the fans screamed in helpless desperation. Finally, about halfway through the period, Gretzky smelled blood during a flurry in the Soviet end. Stationed to the side of the net, he took a blue-line pass from Larry Murphy and shot right away. The rebound came back to him and he moved closer and shot again. Belosheikin made that save, too, but the puck skidded to the other side of the crease and Lemieux was there to sweep it into the net in a single motion. Canada had won the game 6-5. Gretzky played 50 minutes that night, assisting on five of the six Canadian goals. Later in life, he called it the finest international game of his career.

To start the deciding game three back in Copps Coliseum, the Soviets came out flying and built up an impressive 3-0 lead after only eight minutes of play, the makings of an embarrassing romp. "Honest to God," defenceman Craig Hartsburg said after the game, "everyone will think we're all crazy, but we were never down. Even when it was 3-0, we knew we were coming back." These were words and feelings inherited from Phil Esposito after the first game in Moscow in 1972, spoken when the grandfather of all Team Canadas had won only one of the first five games of the Summit Series but somehow still believed in victory.

As the period evolved, Canadian determination gained the upper hand. The fourth-line superstars, Rick Tocchet and Brian Propp, each scored to bring Canada to within a goal. But the Soviets scored a disheartening goal just 28 seconds before the end of the first period and headed to the dressing room up 4-2. The second period was likely the best period the Canadians played. Grant Fuhr set the tone with inspiring stops on Fetisov and Bykov, and then his teammates found their legs. Gretzky got the puck behind the Soviet net, and with his usual patience controlled play until Larry Murphy snuck in off the point, received a perfect pass from the Great One, and snapped it behind Belosheikin. Two minutes later the goal was replayed, only this time it was Hawerchuk behind the net and Doug Crossman sneaking in from the point to take a perfect pass. A few minutes after that, Hawerchuk knocked in his own rebound and Canada took the lead for the first time in the game.

In the third period, in a scenario all too reminiscent of the first two games, Canada blew the lead on a goal by Semak at 12:21. But now the teams settled into a cautious checking game that had the feeling of over-

time to it. Finally, with less than two minutes left, Canada got the break it needed with a faceoff in its own end. "I saw Fetisov wasn't out there, and I was happy," Gretzky said later of his survey of the ice as he lined up on the wing. (It was Fetisov who had been matched against him all series.) Dale Hawerchuk won the draw and snapped it to Lemieux, who pushed it quickly to Gretzky, who led the charge out of Team Canada's end with defenceman Larry Murphy trailing and only Igor Kravchuk – not Fetisov – back on the play. Gretzky drew Kravchuk to him at the top of the Soviet faceoff circle and then gently teed the puck up for Lemieux, who skated in, looked, aimed, and fired into the top corner of the net. There was 1:26 left in the game.

Arms instantly upraised in celebration, Lemieux hopped over goalie Belosheikin's stick on the follow-through and leaped into the waiting arms of the much smaller Gretzky, while the rest of the team hugged the two superheroes who had given Canada the lead. There would be no comeback from the Soviets this time. Team Canada held on for a 6-5 win, as so often in the past the deciding score between these two great rivals.

The 1987 Canada Cup was Wayne Gretzky's finest hour as a mature player and marked Mario Lemieux's coming to maturity. Lemieux scored 11 goals in the tournament, nine of them assisted by the Great One, who led all players with 21 points in eight games. But it was also a supreme team effort. In goal, Grant Fuhr kept the Canadians close when they faltered. Behind the bench Mike Keenan deployed his lines with skill. On the ice the superstars relegated to unaccustomed roles did their jobs. But mostly it was a series won in the dressing room by men who knew the taste of defeat and did not want to taste it on the world stage. The series was won because Gretzky berated Lemieux in practice one day, because the players stuck together and fought the Americans in a fierce round-robin game, because they played with confidence each time they fell behind. And finally it was won because of an intangible sense of hockey lineage: that winning on the world stage is what Canadians are supposed to do. Every member of Team Canada in 1987 remembered exactly where he was the day Paul Henderson scored his historic goal in 1972. Then, they were dreamy-eyed kids; now, they were continuing the line of hockey greatness. Said Dale Hawerchuk after the game: "I'll be talking about this when I'm in a rocking chair."

(ABOVE) Homemade banners urge on the home team. (OPPOSITE, CLOCKWISE FROM TOP) Scenes from a victory: Lemieux and Gretzky celebrate a goal; teammates play defence earlier in the tournament; Mark Messier (aka "Moose") bears down on Soviet goalie Evgeny Belosheikin.

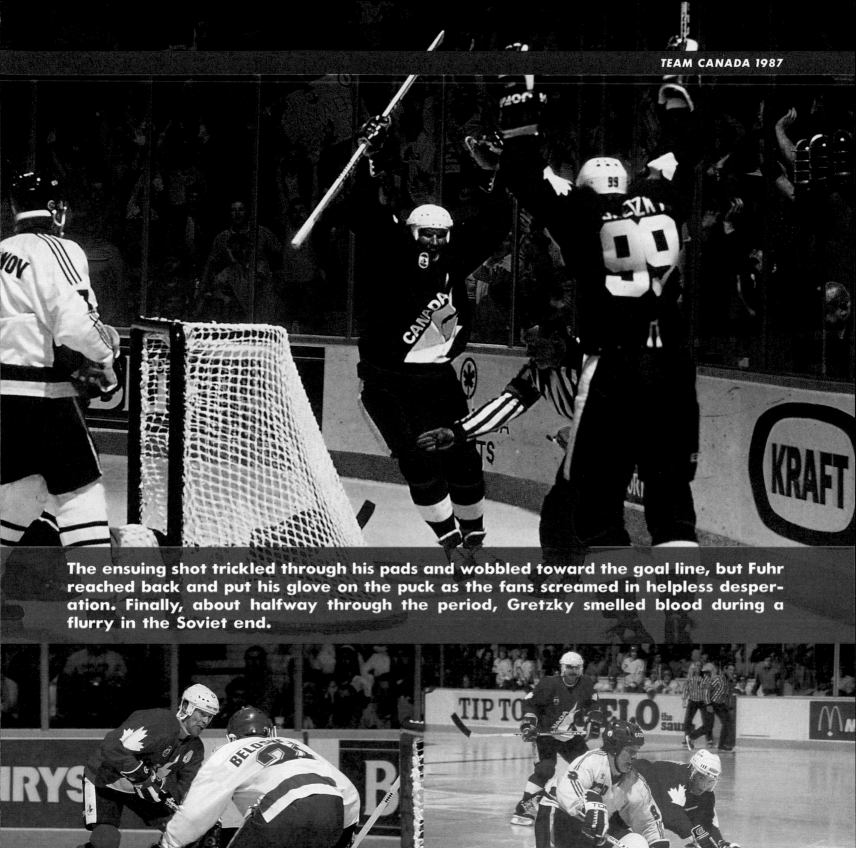

The ensuing shot trickled through his pads and wobbled toward the goal line, but Fuhr reached back and put his glove on the puck as the fans screamed in helpless desperation. Finally, about halfway through the period, Gretzky smelled blood during a flurry in the Soviet end.

# HOCKEY'S GREATEST FAMILY

## 1987–88 EDMONTON OILERS

It is the night of May 26, 1988, and the Edmonton Oilers have just won their fourth Stanley Cup, beating the Boston Bruins in four games straight to the delight of the hometown fans in the Northlands Coliseum. Captain Wayne Gretzky gathers his team near centre ice. The Cup is placed on the frozen waters and the players huddle around it while photographers snap thousands of team portraits. And these are family portraits, too, for perhaps more than any other team the Edmonton Oilers of the 1980s have grown up together on ice and off. The family had formed in the back-alley ice lanes of the World Hockey Association of the late '70s under coach and father Glen Sather, then reached maturity under the bright lights of the NHL in 1984 with its first Stanley Cup. At the centre of the picture is, of course, the Great One, but standing and sitting alongside him are many talented players without whom victory could not have been accomplished: future Edmonton captain Mark Messier; Paul Coffey, the best rushing defenceman since Bobby Orr; Grant Fuhr, the goalie under-appreciated by all save his teammates; Jari Kurri, the highest-scoring European in the game. Although the Oilers will win the Cup for a fifth time in 1990 sans Gretzky, it is this 1987-88 team, captured in hockey's first on-ice team portrait, that remains indelibly etched in our memories.

WHEN 17-YEAR-OLD GRETZKY JOINED THE WHA'S Indianapolis Racers in 1978, he was widely regarded as the best young player in the world. But just eight games into his first season, he was traded to the Oilers. Upon arriving in Edmonton he moved in with the team's young coach, Glen Sather. Late in the 1976-77 season Sather had moved from player to player/coach. At the start of the 1977-78 season he hung up his sweater and pulled his coach's whistle around his neck for keeps, a transition from skater to mentor that was swift and seamless.

At the Oilers' first NHL draft in 1979, Sather chose Mark Messier, future captain and the closest thing the NHL had seen to a power forward since Gordie Howe was in his prime; Kevin Lowe, a big, tough, reliable defenceman; and Glenn Anderson, whose blazing speed and left-hand shot from the right wing evoked memories of Rocket Richard. The next year Sather added Paul Coffey, the greatest blue-line prospect since Bobby Orr; Jari Kurri, a Finn with terrific speed and a superb shot; and goalie Andy Moog of the Billings Bighorns in the Western league. But all were supremely gifted teenagers whose greatest days were a few years away and who flourished under Sather's demanding and protective leadership.

Key to the team's development were the off-ice friendships fostered by the team's strict but good-natured patriarch. One player, veteran Colin Campbell, liked to prick a hole in the bottom of Sather's styrofoam coffee cup. Though furious, Sather would drink the coffee without acknowledging the spillage down his jacket and shirt. Later, he'd get Campbell back by putting talcum powder in his hair dryer or shaving cream in his comb.

Another NHL veteran, Doug Hicks, instituted the "Original Team Beer" night, a rite that brought the team together to hang out and talk about life. At the beginning of each season the second-year players had to take the newest draft choices out for dinner. The team also hired Joey Moss, the brother of Gretzky's girlfriend, Vicki, as an equipment assistant in the dressing room. Joey had Down syndrome, and his presence was a daily reminder to one and all how privileged they were to be playing in the NHL. "He worked his butt off for us doing simple tasks that weren't simple to him and he never complained," Gretzky once said. "How could we do anything but give our best, too?"

These young and rapidly maturing players learned their lessons on ice and off. During his first year, Mark Messier, clearly a team leader and emerging superstar, missed a team flight and was sent to the minors for two weeks. He never missed another trip. When the Oilers played the New York Islanders in the 1983 finals, it was clear the New Yorkers were the better team, but on the bench the Edmonton players tirelessly sang choruses of "Here we go Oilers, here we go!" to celebrate their camaraderie and their very appearance in the finals.

Sather saw his role as twofold. On the one hand, he had to develop his finest player, Gretzky, and push him to be better than the best, better than even he envisioned, better than anyone who had ever come before. On the other, the coach had to craft the entire team around his number one son while

## All were supremely gifted teenagers whose greatest days were a few years away and who flourished under Sather's demanding and protective leadership.

taking into account his strengths and weaknesses. Gretzky's strength was offence; his weakness, defence. That was what Sather kept in mind when he drafted or traded. He needed fast skaters who could keep up with Gretzky (whose sheer speed has never been given enough due), and he needed players who could find open ice in which to convert Gretzky's miraculous passes. The team that Sather reared had all the talent in the world to score at will, but such a team also needed reliable defence. And Sather always made sure to have a great goalie – Andy Moog, then Grant Fuhr – who could bail the team out defensively. His blue line was rock-solid with Kevin Lowe, Steve Smith, Charlie Huddy, Marty McSorley, Jeff Beukeboom, Paul Coffey, and Craig Muni, a group committed to defence with limited offensive skills, save Coffey, who was just the opposite.

### SCORE, SCORE, SCORE

Sather's system, though, was all about offence. Score first and score often. Use every puck possession to create scoring chances, even when killing penalties. Short a man, he would often send out his two premier centres, Gretzky and Messier, as much in the hope of scoring a goal as killing the penalty. The days of just clearing the puck down the ice to kill time off the clock were over. And he had Dave Semenko, a goon whose main job was to beat up and terrify anyone who tried to hit Gretzky. A barbaric strategy, perhaps, but one that worked.

Just as Gordie Howe was the league's first power forward and Bobby Orr the best rushing defenceman, Gretzky pioneered a particular style of offence. He was the first player to use the trailing man as the most dangerous in the other team's end. Previously, the idea was to head-man the puck, to always advance it on goal. But Gretzky would carry the puck across the blue line, then curl back, waiting for the fourth man, often Orr-like defenceman Paul Coffey, to join the rush. Gretzky's other

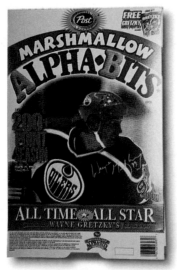

great innovation was the way he used the space behind the net, where it was toughest to check him. It was in "Gretzky's office" that he generated so much of the team's devastating offence. If one defenceman came after him, he could come out the other side and pass in front. If both came at him, at least one Oiler would be wide open in front of the net; and if no one came after him, an Oiler defenceman could sneak in on the play. Only Gretzky could work this play to perfection because only he could make the perfect, feathery passes required.

*(LEFT)* Wayne Gretzky's fame guaranteed him many lucrative commercial endorsements. *(OPPOSITE ABOVE)* Glen Sather stands behind the Oilers bench. Sather took over as coach from Bep Guidolin in February 1977 while still a player. *(OPPOSITE BELOW)* One of Sather's great drafts, Mark Messier *(RIGHT)* eventually became team captain. Craig MacTavish *(TO MESSIER'S RIGHT)* was perhaps Sather's finest reclamation project. MacTavish later became the team's coach.

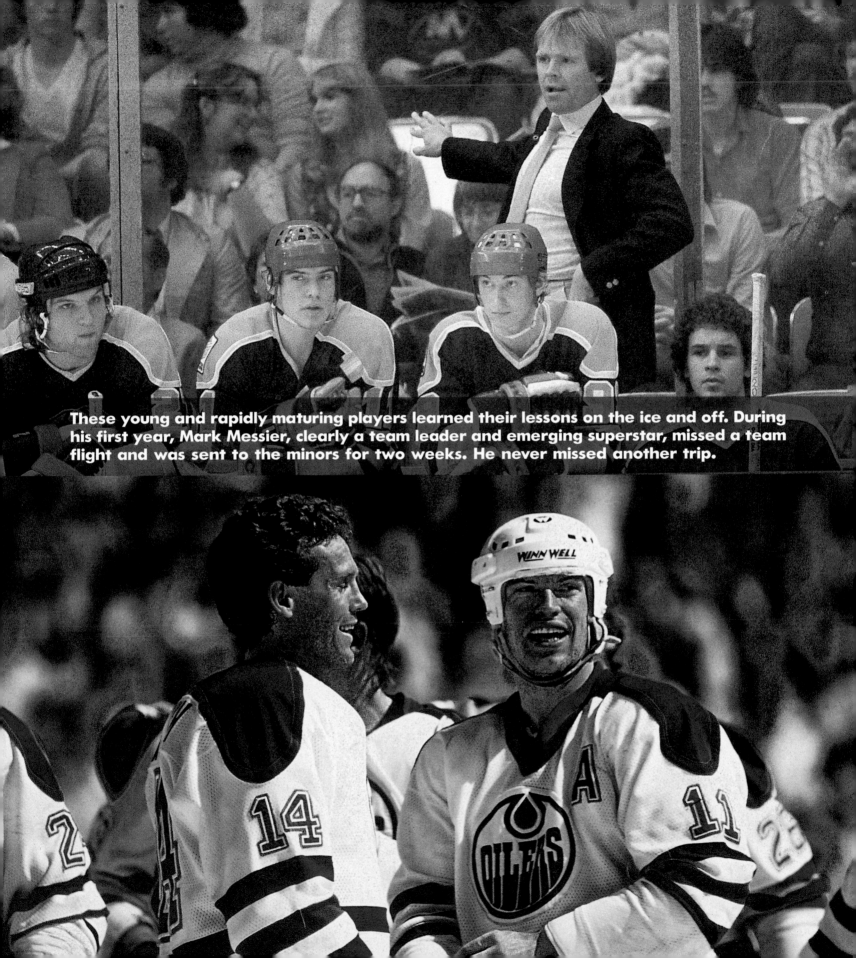

These young and rapidly maturing players learned their lessons on the ice and off. During his first year, Mark Messier, clearly a team leader and emerging superstar, missed a team flight and was sent to the minors for two weeks. He never missed another trip.

Wayne Gretzky tries to find some open ice, despite the presence of three Bruins, notably Steve Kasper (11) trying to crowd him along the boards. Gretzky's magic was never more evident than in the 1988 playoffs when he registered a record 13 points in the finals against Boston.

Sather's practices reflected the team's abilities and were in themselves completely unlike those of any other team. In a typical NHL practice the players stood around half the time and waited for instructions or performed at half speed because it wasn't a game. But on off days the Oiler practices were conducted at top speed, at game speed. Since Edmonton's style relied on player movement, precise passing, and skating as a form of intimidation, their practices were intense and all-out, so that game situations were nothing new. The Oiler style, a combination of possession-style Soviet play and the physically aggressive Canadian approach, was perhaps the perfect embodiment of how the game had changed since the Summit Series of 1972. Drop passes, circling players, and great shooters had meshed with heavy hitters, determined forecheckers, and offensive-minded wizards to form an Edmonton Oilers team that neither Team Canada nor the Soviet Nationals of '72 could likely have defeated.

Following the oft-travelled road to playoff perfection, the Oilers won the 1984 Stanley Cup after first experiencing bitter disappointment. They were eliminated in the 1981 quarter-finals by their nemesis, the New York Islanders, and the next year lost to the L.A. Kings in the first round. In 1983 they made it to the Cup finals only to be eviscerated by the Islanders in four straight. But in 1984 they were finally ready. When Edmonton again met the Islanders in the finals, the ascending Oilmen defeated the New Yorkers in five games to claim their first Stanley Cup. They won again the next year, then in 1986 were eliminated by the arch-enemy

Calgary Flames after an own goal by Steve Smith sent the team to defeat in game seven of their division finals. Unfazed, they came back to win for the third time in four years in 1987. After the Oilers-dominated Team Canada won the 1987 Canada Cup, Edmonton embarked on what would become their climactic run for the Stanley Cup in the fall of '87. It was a run that, for the first time, meant overcoming internal adversity within the long-lasting and supremely close Oilers family.

## THE LONGEST SEASON

Before the 1987 Canada Cup, defenceman Paul Coffey had got involved in acrimonious contract negotiations with the Oilers, becoming increasingly upset with remarks made by both Sather and team owner Peter Pocklington about his integrity. After the Canada Cup he refused to report to the Oilers' training camp. Mark Messier was another no-show, deciding not to report after contract talks stalled. Both were suspended by the team. Also missing as Edmonton's training camp got underway were Kent Nilsson and Reijo Ruotsalainen, who both returned to play in Europe for the season; Glenn Anderson, another contract holdout; free agents Mike Krushelnyski and Moe Lemay; and Randy Gregg, who joined the Canadian National team to realize a lifelong dream to play for his country at the Calgary Olympics in 1988. Goalie Andy Moog, an Oiler since 1980, also decided to join Canada's Olympic team rather than play another year as backup to Grant Fuhr. For a short time during training camp, the three-time Cup-champion Oilers were a team in utter disarray.

But Anderson and Messier soon returned to the team with new contracts. Sather ran his practices knowing Coffey wasn't likely to play

again for the Oilers, and by the start of the season the family had adapted to being without their 30-goal, 100-point defenceman. In November, "Coff" was traded to Pittsburgh in a deal that brought 20-year-old Craig Simpson to the Oilers. Although Coffey had long been considered the closest thing to Bobby Orr, his defence was always suspect and his loss not as keenly felt as the players might have feared. "It was easier to implement [team] discipline without Paul and his sometimes overly creative offensive talents," teammate Kevin Lowe admitted later.

The core of this great team had been together for years and these off-ice distractions didn't much affect the team's on-ice performance as the 1987-88 season got underway. By the end of December the Oilers were averaging nearly five goals a game and had a record of 23-12-3. But on December 30 Gretzky suffered the first serious injury of his career when he sprained his knee playing Philadelphia. He missed 13 games, but during his absence the team held its own with a record of 5-4-4. For Gretzky, the month-long absence proved a blessing in disguise. Gretzky's injury allowed Mark Messier to assume the captain's role, which he did admirably. Just a few games after returning, Gretzky got a stick to the eye and missed three more games from this scarier, though ultimately less serious, incident.

At the trading deadline, Sather sent holdout goalie Andy Moog to Boston for goaler Bill Ranford, a loss that might have meant something in the dressing room but showed no effect on ice. Fuhr was still the Oilers' number one man, at age 26 still in the prime of his career. And now, as the season reached its critical stages, the Oilers' team that would defend its championship in the playoffs was set. Edmonton had had to adapt to numerous changes in the roster during the last few months, but its core of great players remained intact. The team finished second to Calgary in the Smythe Division and third overall behind the Flames and Canadiens. For the first time since 1981, Gretzky did not win the Art Ross Trophy as leading scorer; this went to Mario Lemieux, who with 168 points finished 19 points ahead of the Great One (but played 13 more games). Heading to the playoffs, however, Gretzky was fresher than he'd ever been at this stage in the season. Ranford

was proving to be a spectacular backup to Fuhr, Craig Simpson was scoring more than the team might have expected, and the great players – Gretzky, Messier, Kurri, Anderson – were at the peak of their powers.

## A FOURTH CUP

In the first round of the playoffs the Oilers eliminated Winnipeg, the fifth successive series win by Edmonton over the Jets. They then faced a much tougher foe, their provincial neighbours the Calgary Flames, in another round of the "Battle of Alberta." The Flames had transferred to Calgary from Atlanta in 1980, a year after the Oilers joined the NHL. Since then, the two teams had met three times in the playoffs, the Oilers winning in 1983 and '84, the Flames in 1986. Head-to-head meetings during the regular season and playoffs had made this one of the most intense rivalries in the NHL. And now the Flames were a legitimate Cup contender, having won more games than the Oilers during the year, scored more goals, and finished higher in the standings.

It was during this series, however, that the 1987-88 Oilers defined themselves. Calgary, after all, had been the beneficiary of the horrid Steve Smith own goal two years before, and the Oilers wanted, if nothing else, to confirm that that series win had been a fluke. Because of their superior regular season, Calgary entered the series as the odds-on favourite, a situation that bred unhealthy overconfidence. The rivalry was, therefore, at its boiling point right from the start. "I'd rather have a sister in a brothel than a brother who's an Oiler fan," one sign read at the first game of the series.

Game one in Calgary featured phenomenal goaltending from Grant Fuhr and two goals from Gretzky. Edmonton won 3-1, and the humbled Calgarians were a little more cognizant of the Edmontons' abilities as they prepared for the next game, which was a classic. The Flames built a 3-1 lead, but the Oilers fought back to tie the score after two periods. Early in the third, the Flames again took the lead, but again the Oilers tied the score. In overtime, Glen Sather's advice was simple and consistent with the way he had coached his team since day one: "Play to win. Go after them. Don't hold back." In the fourth period, Mark Messier was given a rare OT penalty, giving the Flames a terrific opportunity to win. But it was the Oilers who dominated the attack

## NEARLY NEW YORK

Firmly buried between the Montreal dynasty of the 1970s and the Edmonton dynasty of the mid- to late-1980s sit the New York Islanders, winners of four Stanley Cups in a row from 1980 to 1983. The team had been expertly built by GM Bill Torrey, who drafted and traded with remarkable success. Bryan Trottier, Mike Bossy, and Denis Potvin, now in the Hall of Fame, were draft choices, as were Bob Nystrom, Duane Sutter, John Tonelli, Ken Morrow, and Dave Langevin. Goalie Billy Smith was selected from Los Angeles in the Expansion Draft. Clark Gillies, the angry giant other teams tried not to provoke, was picked up in the Waiver Draft, and Butch Goring and Bob Bourne were other superb acquisitions by trade. But there's a more remarkable fact about this team: Of the 19 players who appeared in the 1980 finals for their first Cup win, over incumbent Montreal, 15 were there for all four Cups. More than any other dynasty, this team remained virtually unchanged for four seasons. Yet, for all their success, the Islanders lacked the winning tradition of the Habs and never generated the extraordinary offensive excitement of the Oilers. Outside the New York area, they failed to capture a wider audience of fans. A great team, yes, but not one of the very greatest.

on the Flames' power play. Finally, Gretzky took a pass off the boards from Jari Kurri, and skating down the left wing drilled a slapshot over the collarbone of goalie Mike Vernon. The Oilers won the game 5-4, and Gretzky later called that shot "the biggest goal I ever scored." It gave Edmonton a 2-0 lead heading home. After allowing that short-handed goal in overtime, the Flames succumbed with greater ease, 4-2 and 6-4, at the Northlands Coliseum. The Oilers had swept their arch-rivals and now only the Detroit Red Wings stood in the way of another trip to the Stanley Cup.

Edmonton dispatched Detroit in five quick

The storyline of the Boston-Edmonton finals focused on the ever-important goal-tending matchup, featuring Andy Moog, now in a Bruins uniform, against his former teammate Fuhr. Could vengeance be a motivating-enough factor to give his otherwise out-talented Bruins team a chance? In the first two games Edmonton held Boston to just 14 and 12 shots, and in both games the Oilers scored first and went on to win 2-1 and 4-2. In game three, the Bruins scored first but Gretzky set up four of Edmonton's six ensuing goals, giving the team an easy 6-3 win to take full control of the series.

the sequel – left no doubt about the better team. The Oilers skated to a convincing 6-3 win.

After the final bell, the victorious Oilers team tossed sticks and gloves into the air and celebrated around Fuhr, the spectacular but under-appreciated puck-stopper whose value could not be measured only by his goals-against average. Then Gretzky gathered the players and coaches near centre ice for the now-defining on-ice family portrait.

This was the last photo taken of Gretzky in an Oilers sweater, for he was traded to Los Angeles just a few weeks later at the age of 26. The players he left behind – his teammates,

(ABOVE LEFT) Craig MacTavish (without helmet) takes on a Boston player. McTavish was invaluable as a checker during the 1988 finals. (ABOVE RIGHT) Only the scoreboard at the Boston Garden stayed dimly lit when the lights went out during game four, which had to be postponed. (OPPOSITE, ABOVE) Hockey's first on-ice team portrait, which started a Stanley Cup tradition. (OPPOSITE BELOW LEFT AND RIGHT) Gretzky and Mike Krushelnyski hold the sacred trophy high before the Great One takes a lap solo.

games. After the finale, an 8-4 slaughter, it was learned that a number of the Red Wings had been out drinking late the night before the last game. Detroit coach Jacques Demers blamed those players for the loss, but this act of irresponsibility highlighted the difference between the two teams.

Boston's last chance, game four on May 24 at home, was short-circuited by bad luck in the sweltering heat of the old, majestic Boston Garden. Through the second period the Bruins were playing their most impressive game of the series, with Moog superb in net. As the end of the period approached the score was tied 3-3. Then, at 16:37, a generator in the building collapsed, leaving both spectators and skaters squinting in the semi-dark. The game had to be postponed, and because NHL rules stipulated that a game that couldn't be completed had to be played at the end of a series, game four was rescheduled for Edmonton. Two nights later, in the well-lit Northlands Coliseum, game four –

roommates, friends, and hockey brothers – were still in their prime, but the team would never be the same. In a few years salary disclosure would make it virtually impossible for small-market teams to build a dynasty like these great Edmonton Oilers. Most of the players had been drafted within the space of just two or three years, and matured together under the watchful eye of coach and father Glen Sather. They'd made mistakes together, learned about losing and winning together. Gretzky's departure signalled a change, not just for one team but for the NHL. After nine years together, the family that was the Edmonton Oilers was irreconcilably torn apart.

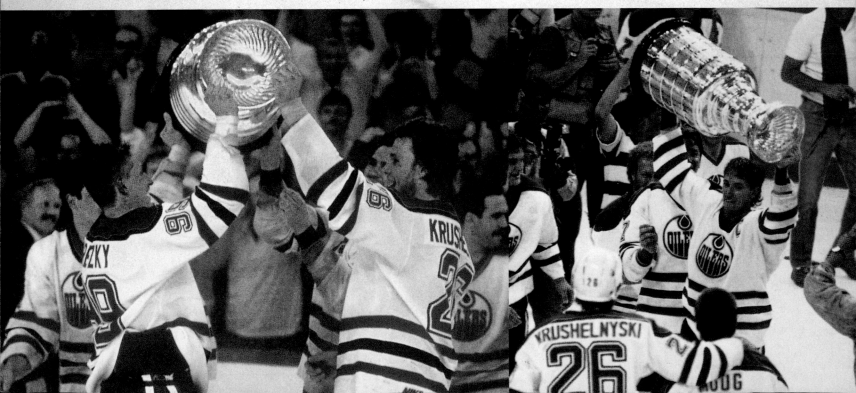

# CHAPTER 13

# PROGRAMMED TO PERFECTION

## 1995 CANADIAN NATIONAL JUNIOR TEAM

Shortly after the 1995 World Junior Championships began in Red Deer, Alberta, Team Canada's coach Don Hay held a dinner for his players. He brought along a hockey stick covered top to bottom with white tape. After dessert he took a black marker and printed R-E-S-P-E-C-T on the shaft, then handed it to one of his players. The player dedicated his performance at the Worlds to someone special in his life. After explaining the importance of that special person, he wrote the person's name on the stick, and handed the stick to a teammate. Each member did likewise until every one of them had promised a superior performance to someone near or dear. Alexandre Daigle dedicated the tournament to his parents, Jamie Rivers to his older brother, and so on. For the rest of the World Juniors the stick went where the team went, a constant reminder of their commitment. "It really is quite a thing to see," said Hay. "There are always a lot of dads' names on the stick, but there are a lot of different sources of inspiration. Moms, grandparents, some who have passed away, a brother who has been lost." By the end of that Christmas dinner the Team Canada players knew something private about every teammate, making them feel more like 22 brothers than a collection of individual hockey prospects.

THE BEGINNING OF CANADA'S 1995 JUNIOR TEAM CAME IN THE spring of 1994 when Hay was named the team's coach. He had been an assistant with the Kamloops Blazers of the Western Hockey League from 1985 to 1992, when he became head coach. During his years with the Blazers the team had won an extraordinary three Memorial Cups in four years, a feat accomplished neither before nor since. More than 50 junior teams across the country compete for the "Mem Cup," making it arguably the toughest hockey trophy to win. And because teams turn over an entire roster every three or four years, winning three times in four seasons is virtually unheard of. Thus, Hay had proved himself to be the finest coach in junior hockey and had very much earned the honour of coaching the national junior team.

Hay's first job was to hold a summer training camp for candidates across the country, who had been invited by a committee consisting of Hay, members of Canadian Hockey (formerly the Canadian Hockey Association), and one member from each of Canada's three junior leagues: the Western Hockey League (WHL), Ontario Hockey League (OHL), and Quebec Major Junior Hockey League (QMJHL). The players would return to their junior clubs in the fall, and if they played consistently well they'd be invited back to the final training camp in early December, leading up to the WJC that traditionally started on Christmas or Boxing Day. Hay's reaction to player performances at the summer camp was, typically, respectful but reserved. "I have a good feel we have the talent," he said. "But nobody stood out. It is going to be tough to make selections."

Assembling a team of juniors is completely different from putting together an NHL team. The World Junior tournament takes place over two weeks, during which a group of virtual strangers is expected to perform at its peak. So Hay had to figure out what kind of team he wanted: although the players were the cream of the junior crop, his job was not to pick the most likely NHL superstars but rather the 20 players who, together, would make the best team at that time. During the tournament NHL scouts and general managers would be watching their own drafts as well as the still-undrafted, assessing their play against the most demanding opposition the world could provide.

The players Hay invited to the Edmonton pre-tournament training camp included seven men from the previous year's team who could be expected to impart their experience and maturity to the younger players: Jason Allison, Jason Botterill, Alexandre Daigle, Jeff Friesen, Bryan McCabe, Marty Murray, Jamie Storr, and team captain Todd Harvey. In 1994 these seven had led Team Canada to a gold medal in the Czech Republic with an almost flawless record of 6-0-1. Daigle was the NHL's first overall draft choice in 1993, and, except for McCabe and Murray, every one of the other seven had been a first-round selection. These teenagers represented the next generation of NHL stars, and playing against their toughest opponents at their own level was essential to their development.

This year the juniors had one huge advantage in player personnel. As a result of an NHL dispute, the owners had locked out their players

## The World Junior tournament takes place over two weeks, during which a group of virtual strangers is expected to perform at its peak.

and the entire pro season was in serious jeopardy. Ordinarily, by the time they were 18 or 19 most of Canada's best juniors were already playing in the NHL, and usually unavailable to the national team. But the lockout meant that players such as Allison (Washington Capitals), Ryan Smyth (Edmonton Oilers), Harvey (Dallas Stars), Friesen (San Jose Sharks), and Daigle (Ottawa Senators) were only too happy to get some ice time and represent their country.

### THE LINDROS CUT

Before the team's first game Hay had to reduce the 34-player squad to 22, since according to IIHF rules the final roster had to be registered 24 hours prior to the opening faceoff. It was the most important task he faced as coach of the 1995 World Junior team. "I honestly believe the success of our team will depend on how close we are, how well we come together to become a team in the truest sense of the word," Hay said during the final camp. "The most important thing we do is to pick the right 22 players," he continued. "That's not necessarily the best 22 guys, but the best 22-man team. Chemistry is so important."

Those left off the team included goalies Eric Fichaud and Jocelyn Thibault, Christian Matte, Jamie Allison, Patrick Boileau, Brendan Witt, and Brad Church. But no matter who was cut and who was kept, one cut caused controversy above all others – NHLer Brett Lindros. Lindros, the equally large and equally skilled younger brother of the already famous Eric, had arrived at camp with enthusiasm and confidence: "Look around," he'd said upon entering the dressing room. "This is the next wave of players in the NHL." But Hay didn't let Lindros's reputation intimidate him. A star in the making, undoubtedly, Brett didn't fit into this particular team. When told of the news, Big Brett was stunned. "I felt I did well enough," he said bitterly. When asked if he was angry, he offered only two words: "Big time!"

But Hay defended his decision calmly. "Nobody is bigger than the team. I did what was best for the team. There were four guys – Jason Allison, Shean Donovan, Todd Harvey, and Eric Daze – who outplayed him. The bottom line is that he didn't show the speed for the international game." Of the 22 selected to play, 10 were from the WHL, nine from Ontario, two from Quebec, and one – Botterill – from the University of Michigan. All were either 18 or 19 years old, with the exception of 17-year-old phenom Wade Redden of the Brandon Wheat Kings (WHL).

The front page of *The Hockey News* celebrates Canada's gold medal in 1995, the third of five in a row that would set a World Junior record. The country's national program has been more successful at this tournament than that of any other nation, winning 16 medals — 10 of them gold — since 1977 when the WJC became an official IIHF event and provided seasoning for future stars, including Wayne Gretzky, Mario Lemieux, and Paul Kariya.

The Lindros cut, while admirable for its boldness, put more pressure on Hay. If the team lost the whole country would blame the coach for cutting Big Brett, clearly a superior player in the minds of many an armchair critic who hadn't watched a minute of training camp. Of course if the team won, Hay would look like a genius. "He did what he said he was going to do," Allison said of Hay's promise to choose the best 22-man team. "I respect him for that." As did the other players, and that respect would translate into a greater confidence in themselves.

## DEFENDING GOLD

At the 1982 World Junior Championships, Canada faced the Czechs in a game that would decide the gold medal. The Czechs had to win to claim gold, but if the Canadians tied or won the gold medal was theirs. After two periods the Canadians looked tired and were trailing 2-1. Team manager Sherry Bassin borrowed a gold medal from the awards

*Team Canada performs a pre-game warmup on the ice. Players stretch in the corridors and in the dressing room, but a show of team unity is important for morale. This scene is therefore as much about mutual support and mental edge as it is about physical preparation.*

table, took it into the dressing room to show his players and, like an hypnotist, let it swing gently in his fingers. Twenty minutes of hockey, he reminded them, and every player could have one. Seven minutes later the Canadians had scored two quick goals to lead 3-2, and then hung on for a tie. Gold was theirs. At the 1993 World Juniors the Canadians played Finland, and again a win over the Finns would more or less guarantee Canada gold. After the first two periods of the game they were leading 2-1, but the Finns had been the much better team. During the second intermission coach Perry Pearn came into the dressing room, cleared off the trainer's table, and placed on it his championship ring from the 1991 World Junior tournament. "That!" he said emphatically, pointing to the ring, "is what we're playing for." Tyler Wright scored four minutes into the third, and Canada went on to win the game and gold medal. For these young men the sight of the medal and the ring invoked the same magic as would the names inscribed on Hay's ever-present, white-taped hockey stick.

With the 1995 WJC roster in place and the team's emotions safely in the hands of coach Hay, Canada was prepared to defend the World Junior gold medal that it had won in Sweden in '93 and the Czech Republic in '94. The '95 tournament, centred in Red Deer, featured eight teams – Canada, Sweden,

**The advent of an international NHL in the early 1990s meant that the Canadian dream of playing in the NHL could now be realized by any young hockey skater in the world.**

Day and Germany the following night. Their easy victories – 7-1 and 9-1, respectively – couldn't yet be seen as clear indicators of the team's abilities, but they did confirm that Canada's greatest strength would be scoring. They outshot the Ukraine 59-15, scored five power-play goals, and scored four times in five minutes of the second period to take

rule," which demanded they be in bed two hours after a game; and the team motto was sacred: Keep the Eye on the Prize. Hay based his methods on experience. He knew that when Team Canada was playing on home ice the crowd support was without compare, but so too were the demands: a bronze or even silver medal was not acceptable. Gold, only

(ABOVE LEFT) Eric Daze moves to create some traffic in the crease. Daze led all scorers at the 1995 WJC with eight goals. His size and skill around the net were critical in beating the United States 8-3 in the round robin. (ABOVE RIGHT) Darcy Tucker eludes Sweden's Niklas Sundstrom during the final game of the championships. Tucker, a three-time winner of the Memorial Cup, provided solid checking and two-way play that helped his team preserve their undefeated tournament record, a first for Canada.

Finland, Germany, Russia, the Ukraine, U.S., and Czech Republic. They played a simple round-robin schedule, no overtime games and no playoffs. The final standings would determine the medal winners.

Canada began play with games against the two weakest teams, the Ukraine on Boxing

control. Against Germany they were even more overpowering, outshooting their opponents 59-20 and scoring six in the second to coast to victory. All the big guns were firing: Eric Daze, Marty Murray, Todd Harvey, and Jeff Friesen. The coach, however, took his encouragement from elsewhere. "The biggest thing we showed in our last two games," he explained, "has been our discipline. That's going to be a key in our next five games."

Ever since the start of the tournament Hay had instituted a series of rules that kept the players focused. Team activities were always group-oriented, with individual ones disallowed; players had to adhere to the "two-hour

gold, would do. Yet despite these expectations the players had all the distractions of the familiar. For a group of players coming together at the last minute, a trip abroad would have worked wonders: the players would have had to deal with jet lag, an unfamiliar language, being away from family. Developing friendships was an emotional necessity in this context, and a reliance on camaraderie would have carried over to the rink. At home, in Alberta, the best Hay could do was take his players out to a frozen pond in Grande Prairie to play a little shinny and so rekindle childhood memories of where their love of the game had begun.

Canada's third game, played December 29, presented the team's first significant challenge. Not only was the U.S. always an arch-rival, but many of the opposing players were teammates with Canadian players in the junior leagues. Team Canada's captain Todd Harvey, for instance, played on the Detroit Junior Red Wings with three of the Americans – Sean Haggerty, Jeff Mitchell, and Bryan Berard. But once the puck was dropped, they had to put their friendships on hold. "I told them it will be all business," Harvey said before the game. "I hope they feel the same way because I'm not going to let up." That was the mindset of a future NHLer.

Harvey wasn't fooling, either. He scored one of Canada's four first-period goals that sent the team to the dressing room with a huge 4-0 lead. The relentless maple leaf attack continued the rest of the game, resulting in an impressive 8-3 victory – an enormous confidence-builder leading to their fourth game against a strong Czech team.

While Canada was the over-whelming favourite to win the 1995 WJC, the Czechs were a team of like talent and equal confidence. The advent of an international NHL in the early 1990s meant that the Canadian dream of playing in the NHL could now be realized by any young hockey skater in the world. Increasingly, players from European countries saw the World Juniors as an important stepping-stone to the NHL, since scouts from each pro team attended the tournament. Each year it seemed that more players from around the world were being assessed based on their performance at the WJC. In 1995 every Canadian had already been drafted, with the exception of defenceman Wade Redden, who would go second overall at the '95 Entry Draft just a few months later. But other countries had produced many fine prospects as well. Some 13 of Sweden's 23 players had been drafted, most notably Mattias Ohlund, Niklas Sundstrom, and P.J. Axelsson. The Czechs had Petr Sykora, one of the top-ranked juniors in the world, as well as Milan Hejduk and Vaclav Varada. The U.S. featured Adam Deadmarsh, Jamie Langenbrunner, Bryan Berard, and Mike Grier. The Russians had Oleg Tverdovsky; the Finns had Kimmo Timonen; the Germans, Jochen Hecht. A few years before, scouts would have considered only Canadian and perhaps a few American teenagers. Now they looked everywhere.

The tough Czech team was particularly motivated to impress the scouts. It featured the number one line of Sykora, Zdenek Nedved, and Petr Cajanek, three of the fastest skaters in the tournament. For the first two periods the Czechs had the edge in both play and possession, but produced too few good scoring chances to break the game open. Still, after 40 minutes they led 5-4, and as the third period began it looked

Goalie Jamie Storr had a perfect 4-0 record at the WJC. In the championships played in the Czech Republic the previous year, he'd gone undefeated (3-0-1) and was named the tournament's best goalie.

as though Canada was going to let victory slip away. During three power-play chances the home team barely posed a threat, and with less than five minutes to go still trailed by a goal. But at 15:51 Wade Redden tied the game when he drifted a shot from the point that eluded a screened Michal Marik in the Czech net. Two minutes later, Jamie Rivers scored the go-ahead goal: after knocking down a clearing pass along the boards, then making a dazzling outside-in move on the sur-prised defenceman Jan Hlavac in the slot, he fired a low shot just inside the far post. It was a spectacular goal, eclipsed only by the late-game heroics of goalie Jamie Storr. Leading 6-5, the Canadians had to focus on defence after Shean Donovan was given a penalty at 18:04. With the Czechs on the power play and their goalie out for another attacker, Storr robbed Vlastimil Kroupa from in close. At 19:29 Jeff Friesen scored into the empty net to put the game out of reach.

Canada had rallied for an important 7-5 come-from-behind win before 19,465 fans at Calgary's Saddledome, the largest crowd in the history of the WJC. After the game coach Hay expressed tremendous satisfaction: "Being down to the Czechs going into the third period and coming back to get the win … that was our first bit of adversity and we came out with a win."

## THE FINAL HURDLES

The next game, a 6-3 win over the Finns on New Year's Day, left the Canadians with a perfect record after five games. But their final two games of the tournament would be against their toughest opponents, Russia and Sweden, each tied for second place with 4-1 records. Game six, against Russia in Red Deer on January 2, was the most anticipated game of the tournament. A Canadian win would guarantee first place head-ing into the final game; a loss would allow the Russians to move into a tie for the top spot.

For decades of international hockey it had been the Canadians who were given marginal penalties or who retaliated when restraint would have been the wiser course of action. But on this night the roles reversed. Late in the second period, with Canada holding a 5-3 lead in a tense game, the Soviets' Alexandre Koroliouk shot the puck on Storr in goal long after an offside whistle had been blown, an enormous faux pas in hockey. He then swung his stick at Canada's Lee Sorochan, who didn't retaliate. When referee Sold of Sweden assessed a five-minute major the enraged Koroliouk tried to get at Sold, earning himself a game misconduct. The period ended 5-3. But with their man advantage for the first

## THE BEST OF JUNIOR A

To win a Memorial Cup, a team must first be champion of its junior league (WHL, OHL, or QMJHL) and then win a tournament featuring the three champions plus a team representing the host city. In 1992 the Kamloops Blazers, a junior team owned by Peter Pocklington's Edmonton Oilers, beat Seattle, Verdun, and Sault Ste. Marie to win its first "Mem Cup." Coached by the experienced Tom Renney, that Blazers team included future NHL stars Darryl Sydor, Scott Niedermayer, and Darcy Tucker. Although the Blazers weren't in the running the next year, they went on to win again in 1994 and 1995 under new coach Don Hay, an unprecedented run of three championships in four years. Since the trophy's inception in 1919, only four players have played on three Memorial Cup teams. Three of these were Blazers: Tucker, Tyson Nash, and Ryan Huska. (The fourth, Robert Savard, won with Cornwall in '80 and '81 and Kitchener in '82.) But Junior A supremacy does not necessarily translate into WJC participation. Coach Hay selected only two of his Blazer players for the 1995 World Juniors, Darcy Tucker and Nolan Baumgartner.

four minutes of the third, the Canadians scored three goals in the first three minutes, upping the score to 8-3 and putting the game out of reach. Two late goals by the Russians made the game look closer than it was.

Eric Daze, one of the players who had been named to the team ahead of Brett Lindros, had led the way with three goals and an assist. But overall it was Canada's composure that earned them the easy 8-5 victory. Russian coach Igor Dmitriev put full blame for the loss on his penalized forward, Koroliouk: "This player is very emotional," he explained through a translator. "He is young and he cannot control his emotions." Hay's words about discipline had proved prophetic.

When the Canada-Russia game ended, the equally important Finland-Sweden game was still in the third period. A win for Sweden would give Tre Kronor the same number of points as Canada and thus a chance for gold in their meeting on the last day of the tournament, whereas a tie would leave the Swedes three points back of the Canadians and unable to catch them on the final day.

Hay's players went to the dressing room to watch the end of that game. As expected, Sweden was ahead 3-1 and it looked as though the final matchup of the tournament, between Canada (6-0) and Sweden (5-1), would decide the gold medal. But when the Finns scored to make it 3-2, coach Hay began summoning any stray players so that the whole team could watch the end of the game together. With just 2:19 left in the third, Jere Karalahti scored for Finland to tie the game. "It was the most nervous two minutes of my life," Daze said of the game's conclusion. Sure

enough, the final score was 3-3. Regardless of the result of their final game against the Swedes, the Canadians would be receiving their gold medals after the game. "Find out where Jere is staying," Daigle shouted jubilantly to his teamates. "We have to send him something!"

Although Canada's international hockey tradition is rich with victory, the country has had a habit of playing poorly in meaningless games. It would have been easy for Hay's team to go through the motions on January 4, the final day of the tournament, knowing that a loss wouldn't affect their gold-medal showing. But with captain Harvey's words still in the minds of his teammates, the Canadians didn't let up. They came out flying, and by the midway point of the first were up 2-0 thanks to goals by Harvey and Allison. The teams exchanged goals in the second, then Daze scored just eight seconds into the third. They skated to a 4-3 win, giving them the first perfect record for a Canadian team at the World Juniors and the first by any team since the Soviets went undefeated in 1986.

The Canadians had scored 50 goals in the tournament's seven games, and except for the second period against Sweden they had scored in every period of every game. The defence dominated physically and their puck movement was superlative. Goalie Storr was outstanding when he had to be. They even won the Fair Play Cup for being the least penalized team in the tournament. Nolan Baumgartner summed up the World Junior experience and how Canada had achieved perfection: "The guys in that room there, all 22 guys, they're all the guys who were picked for this team because they're willing to make the sacrifice. You know if you sacrifice for three weeks, you're going to have a gold medal around your neck and a gold ring on your finger. It's sacrificing for your country also. There's no better feeling than putting on a red and white sweater, the colours of your country, and playing for it."

(OPPOSITE ABOVE) **Todd Harvey** (LEFT) with Jeff Friesen and Marty Murray pose proudly with their gold medals. (OPPOSITE BELOW LEFT) Two future NHL adversaries — Canada's Ryan Smyth (20) and Russia's Vadim Sharifianov (19) — partake in the ritual post-game handshake before heading to their dressing rooms. The Canadians thoroughly dominated their Russian arch-rivals, virtually guaranteeing the home team a gold medal. (OPPOSITE BELOW RIGHT) Canada celebrates its WJC gold and its undefeated tournament record after holding on for a tie against Sweden in the final game of the tournament, played before a partisan crowd in Red Deer, Alberta.

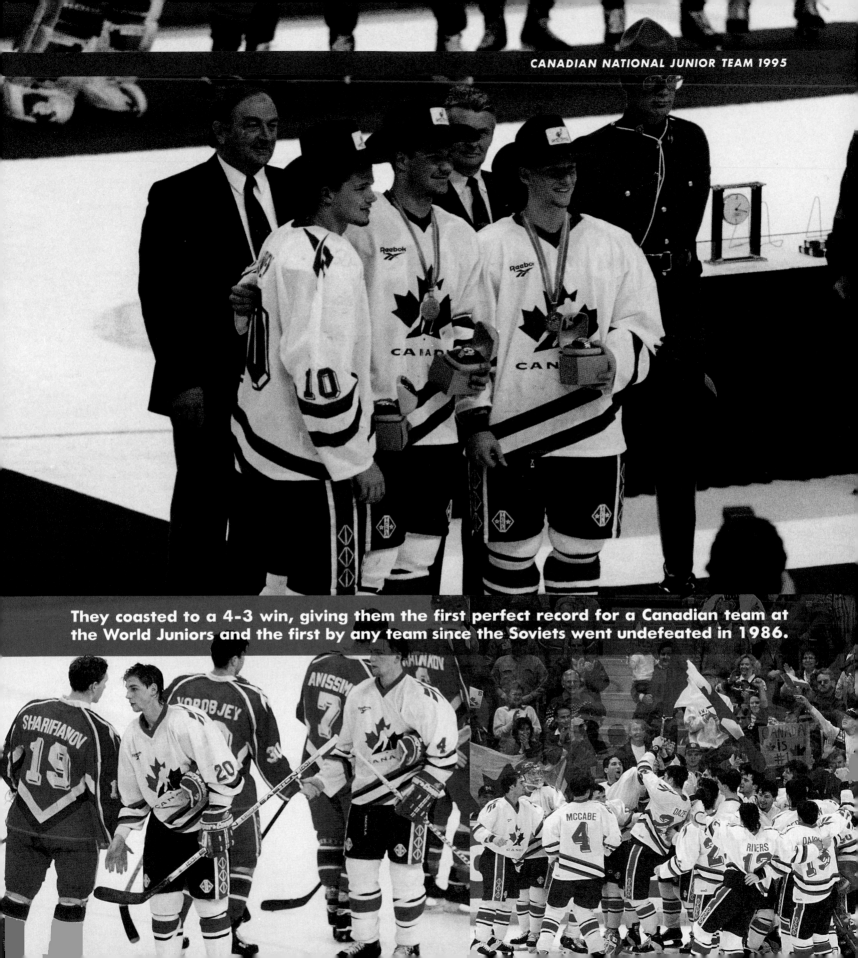

**They coasted to a 4-3 win, giving them the first perfect record for a Canadian team at the World Juniors and the first by any team since the Soviets went undefeated in 1986.**

# WORLD CUP OF WONDERS

1996 TEAM USA

The United States has never been known as a hockey power. Its three international gold medals – at the 1933 World Championships, and the 1960 and 1980 Olympics – were aberrations too separated in time to constitute a winning tradition. Thus, when Canada's Adam Foote scored at 12:50 in the third period of the deciding game of the 1996 World Cup to give his team a 2-1 lead over Team USA, another in a long line of dramatic international wins for the Red and White seemed assured: Just seven minutes to play, and all Canada had to do was play defence and the World Cup was theirs. But a strange thing happened on the way to victory. Team Canada sat on its lead, and the Americans went on the attack. At 16:42 Brett Hull tied the game by tipping in a point shot. Only 43 seconds later Tony Amonte scored the go-ahead goal. When the game was over, the Americans had exploded for a 5-2 win, not only stunning Team Canada and the hockey world but achieving their first bona fide international hockey victory. Whether this triumph marked the beginning of a new era for Americn hockey remained to be seen, but Team USA's success undoubtedly grew out of an emerging tradition of hockey excellence that helped its veteran players believe winning was possible. That belief, as much as skill, was the key to their success.

M UCH MORE THAN A COLLECTION OF NHL STARS, TEAM USA 1996 was unlike any previous team the country had sent to international competition. In terms of skill, Team USA matched up well against Canada player for player. It had a world-class goalie in Mike Richter, a solid defence corps led by Chris Chelios and brothers Derian and Kevin Hatcher, and forwards who could match Canada's scoring ability and physical play – Keith Tkachuk, John LeClair, and Doug Weight among them. Most were at the peak of their careers, with significant international as well as NHL experience under their collective belts. One of the team's elders, centre Pat LaFontaine, had begun his career at the 1984 Sarajevo Olympics as a member of the USA's "Diaper Line" alongside Ed Olczyk and David E. Jensen. Chris Chelios had not only played in the Sarajevo Olympics but in three subsequent Canada Cups. Defenceman Phil Housley was a veteran of three World Championships and two Canada Cups; Brian Leetch and Joel Otto had played in four international tournaments for the United States; goalie Mike Richter in five. Tony Amonte, an emerging NHL scoring star, had been to the World Championships in 1991 and '93. The few members of Team USA 1996 who lacked international experience made up for it with Stanley Cup success, namely forwards Adam Deadmarsh (with Colorado), Joel Otto (Calgary), Scott Young (Pittsburgh and Colorado), and John LeClair (Montreal). Guiding this team of veterans was coach Ron Wilson of the Mighty Ducks of Anaheim, who'd played in the NHL for 14 years with Winnipeg, St. Louis, and Montreal.

Those who remembered America's bitter defeat to Canada in the 1991 Canada Cup finals, when the host Canadians swept the best-of-three championships two games to none, had played for a young and talented team that was definitely on the rise. In the succeeding five years they had learned from their mistakes and developed as players. Experience and maturity were elements critical to the most important ingredient of all: confidence. Before Team USA's first practice in Providence, Rhode Island in August 1996, Mike Richter remarked, "When we play against Canada, will we honestly believe in ourselves as a unit that we can win, that we belong there? That's the hurdle we have to jump if we're going to win, and that's what this training camp will be all about." Richter's question sounded much like a challenge – to his teammates and to himself. "I think we're a pretty good team," coach Wilson opined, "It's just a matter of confidence and believing we can do it."

Team USA's confidence improved considerably after the second of two pre-tournament exhibition games against Team Canada. In the first, on August 20 in Vancouver, the Canadians, led by 35-year-old veteran Wayne Gretzky, won 3-1. But the next night in San Jose the Americans not only won by a convincing 7-5 score, they won in their heads and hearts. Toward the end of the game the teams fought twice, and twice the Americans emerged on top. They skated off the ice knowing that they could win the tournament. Bolstering their optimism was the knowledge that Canada lacked three

"I think we're a pretty good team," coach Wilson opined, "It's just a matter of confidence and believing we can do it."

of its greatest players. Mario Lemieux and Ray Bourque refused to give up their holidays to represent their country, and Paul Kariya was injured. "I remember as a player in 1981," American scout Paul Holmgren commented, "I didn't think there was any way we could beat Canada, and I think we all felt that way deep down inside. They had Ray Bourque, Larry Robinson, and all those players. There was no way to win against those guys. I don't think that kind of feeling exists with this current group of players." In 1996 the players on Team USA looked back, not to earlier defeats, but to 1980's Miracle on Ice, when the Americans beat the Soviets en route to an Olympic gold. "It had everything to do with it," Pat LaFontaine said of that historic victory. "We're the product. We were all in our teens watching that game…. Every kid in the United States wanted to play for the Olympic team after that game."

## TRUE GRIT

The setup for this first World Cup broke Canada Cup precedent, the contestants being grouped in a European Pool and a North American Pool. Finland, Germany, Sweden, and the Czech Republic were placed in the former; Canada, Russia, Slovakia, and the U.S. in the latter. European Pool games were played in Stockholm, Helsinki, and Prague; North American games in Philadelphia, Ottawa, Montreal, and New York. After a round-robin series of games in each pool, the top three teams went to a playoff elimination that yielded the two teams that would play for the World Cup in a best-of-three finals. The games were officiated by NHL referees, and NHL rules applied, which meant that fighting did not result in an automatic game misconduct.

On August 31 Team USA played its first game of the tournament, against Canada. In the opening 20 seconds at the new CoreStates Centre in Philadelphia, the Americans picked up where they'd left off from the exhibition series. Keith Tkachuk slashed Eric Lindros from behind as the Big E crossed the blue line. Canada's Scott Stevens came in to stand up for Lindros; Stevens was smacked by Bill Guerin. Everyone else on the ice quickly joined the melee. Tkachuk was given a game misconduct for his vicious slash, but so, too, was Claude Lemieux of Canada for fighting Tkachuk. The tone was set for a fierce game. "We're not here for a walk in the park," Bill Guerin said later.

The U.S. killed off the Canadian power play and then moments later John LeClair scored the first goal of the game. Parked to the side of the net, he knocked in a rebound from a

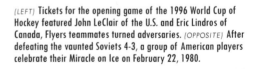

(LEFT) Tickets for the opening game of the 1996 World Cup of Hockey featured John LeClair of the U.S. and Eric Lindros of Canada, Flyers teammates turned adversaries. (OPPOSITE) After defeating the vaunted Soviets 4-3, a group of American players celebrate their Miracle on Ice on February 22, 1980.

In 1996 the players on Team USA looked back, not to earlier defeats, but to 1980's Miracle on Ice, when the Americans beat the Soviets en route to an Olympic gold. "It had everything to do with it," Pat LaFontaine said of that historic victory. "We're the product."

Brian Smolinski slapshot that goalie Martin Brodeur couldn't clear quickly enough. The two old reliables, Wayne Gretzky and Mark Messier, gave the Red and White a 2-1 lead before the end of the period, but the Americans weren't about to capitulate. Early in the second Doug Weight tipped in a point shot to tie the game, then Scott Young put the Stars 'n' Stripes up 3-2 on a low spin-around shot that beat Brodeur to the glove side. In the third, the Americans continued to take it to Canada and went on to win 5-3, their first victory in nine international "pro classics." "To gain respect, you have to beat the best," coach Wilson remarked following the game. He knew that his team had overcome an important psychological barrier, but that there was plenty more hockey still to be played

Team USA played its second game, against Russia, on Labour Day, and quickly proved that an aggressive style was not reserved strictly for its Canadian nemesis. The post-perestroika Russians certainly weren't the dominant force of days gone by, but the team still had a number of the world's best players on its roster, namely Pavel Bure, Sergei Fedorov, Viacheslav Fetisov, Alexander Mogilny, and Igor Larionov. The Russians entered the World Cup as decided underdogs, but every game between these former Cold War rivals was imbued with political significance. The game was chippy and physical, with a total of 23 minor penalties called. The Americans didn't initiate any violence, but they wouldn't brook any either. "We will not let ourselves be pushed around," Guerin said, referring as much to the psychological aspects of the game as the physical. The U.S. won 5-2. "We're starting to play as a team and getting an identity," goalie Richter said after their second impressive victory.

*Russia's Alexei Yashin, one of the world's top players, failed to raise his level of play and was shut down by the stifling defence of Team USA.*

After closing out the round robin with a hammering of Slovakia 9-3 in an inconsequential game, the Americans faced Russia in their half of the semi-finals, a game played in Ottawa on September 8. They already knew that a win would pit them against Canada in the finals. In the other semi-finals, Canada had beaten Sweden 3-2 in double overtime in Philadelphia the previous night. In Ottawa, right-winger Brett Hull played the role of hero, scoring twice and helping on two others in a 5-2 win. He and his emerging team were roundly booed by the Corel Centre fans, largely because Hull had decided never to play for Canada again after being cut at the 1987 Team Canada training camp for the Canada Cup. The booing also acknowledged an extra measure of respect for Team USA. Despite the Russian firepower, the U.S. team again produced a more potent offence backed by better goaltending. Moreover, coach Wilson had put together a better team game plan than his Soviet counterpart Igor Dmitriev. The win set up the modern-day dream finals, Canada versus the United States, a repeat of the 1991 Canada Cup.

## WE HAVE TO WIN

As he anticipated the best-of-three series, Canadian forward Rod Brind'Amour declared, "We have to win. There's no other choice." That was the pressure the Canadians always felt, a sense of obligation to continue Canadian dominance of a Canadian game. In the American dressing room the mood was no less intense, though the public pressure negligible. The Americans were playing more for themselves than for their country, but they felt a strong desire to prove to the world that they ranked among hockey's elite. And for once, they not only believed they could win but that they were the better team. "We're younger and quicker, and we can maintain a high tempo longer," Wilson said of his players. Just voicing those feelings out loud spoke volumes about the team's confidence and mental preparation.

Wilson approached this finals with strategic precision. He matched Chelios against Eric Lindros, and he had the towering Hatcher brothers on defence in all other important situations. And a coach never looked smarter than when his goalie was the team's best player. Canada's Glen Sather had put together a physical team, but Wilson had equal size in a lineup that matched the Canadians shot for shot and pound for pound.

Game one, however, started out in a dismally familiar manner for the Americans. Eric Lindros, playing in front of his Philadelphia home fans, deflected Rob Blake's slapshot past Richter to give Canada a 1-0 lead. Unfazed, the U.S. tied the score in the second period, then moved in front on the strength of two rare goals from defenceman Derian Hatcher. But a late goal by Claude Lemieux at 19:21 tied the game after 40 minutes. Midway through the third, Theoren Fleury scored to put Canada ahead 3-2 and in seeming control. Yet Canadian coach Glen Sather had his team sit on the lead rather than play with the puck, and the Americans summoned all their confidence and desire. Although Team USA kept coming and coming, Canada clung to its one-goal lead. Then with Mike Richter on the bench and just 10 seconds to play, the Americans' Joel Otto won a faceoff from Adam Graves in Canada's end. There was a mad scramble in front of the net, and John LeClair tied the score with just 6.3 seconds left on the clock. In the first 10 minutes of overtime, Steve Yzerman scored on a quick opposite-wing wrist shot on a play that was clearly offside. The goal stood, and Canada led in the series heading back to Montreal for game two. Canadian fortitude – and luck – had prevailed.

The Americans were bent, but as the next game proved they were not broken. Younger and faster, they took the play to the Canadians from the opening faceoff. Late in the second period, with the game tied 2-2, Brett Hull scored on a breakaway to put the U.S. in the lead to stay. Leading their defence was the ferocious checking of Chelios, who did a terrific job shadowing Eric Lindros. Richter held the lead in the third; Canada outshot the Americans 18-8 but couldn't score. The Americans won 5-2 to set up a deciding third game, a victory that already put them one better than at the 1991 Canada Cup when they were swept by the Canadians in two straight games.

## MAKING HISTORY

What the United States did in game three at the Molson Centre in Montreal on September 14 was more than just come out of the dressing room to play their best. They actually made history. In the first period Brett Hull scored the first goal of the game, his tournament-leading sixth of the World Cup, while in the U.S. net Mike Richter was nothing short of spectacular, conjuring up Canada Cup memories of Vladislav Tretiak, Rogie Vachon, Grant Fuhr, and Bill Ranford. In the second period, however, the Canadians took full control of the game. They outshot the U.S. 22-9, and the Americans were lucky simply to chip the puck beyond their blue line for most of the 20 minutes. It was likely the most one-sided period of hockey ever played in international competition at this level. But despite the edge in play, the Canadians didn't score for the longest time, showing a lack of touch around the ever-sensational Richter. With five seconds left in the period and with Team Canada on a power play, Eric Lindros finally put the puck past Richter – Canada's first goal of the game. The teams left the ice tied 1-1, knowing the entire series had come down to a single period of hockey.

If at the start of the tournament coach Ron Wilson had been told the World Cup would be decided in the last 20 minutes of play with his team tied against Canada, he would have been delighted. Although the Americans had already earned a huge measure of respect in pushing Canada to the limit and proving they could compete with the best, they still had one even more remarkable period of hockey left in their legs and hearts. As expected, the Canadians came out attacking in the third period, but the Americans skated just as fast, hit just as hard, and created just as many scoring chances.

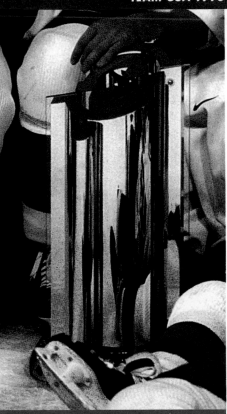

## A NEW TROPHY

Following the Summit Series of 1972, Alan Eagleson arranged the first Canada Cup, a tournament in which the finest players – amateur or pro – from a number of countries would compete. It was held during the training camp of the 1976-77 NHL season and was won on Darryl Sittler's historic overtime goal against the Czechs. The second edition, held in 1981, ended in a resounding 8-1 loss to the Soviets. But the Canadians exacted revenge in 1984 by sweeping Sweden in two straight of a best of three finals. The scheduled 1988 tournament was played in 1987 to avoid conflicting with the Summer Olympics in Korea. But following the 1991 edition, with Eagleson accused of misappropriation and misallocation of player pension funds and forced from office, the tournament and the trophy (above) were revamped. In 1996 the best players in the world competed for the World Cup of Hockey.

This battle for supremacy continued evenly matched until 12:50, when an Adam Foote point shot slipped by Richter, sending the crowd at the Molson Centre into a frenzy of celebration. With just seven minutes to go, Canada was in the lead 2-1. But instead of giving in, the Americans rallied. On the bench players were talking confidently. "We're still going to win!" LeClair hollered. "We're still in control!" Amonte added in support. Once again Canadian coach Glen Sather let his team play right into enemy hands; Canada retreated into a shell and barely tried even to shoot the puck beyond the U.S. blue line.

was allowed. The game was tied with a little more than five minutes to go. "This is what we talked about," coach Wilson reminded his players. "It's 2-2. We know what to do and the Canadians don't. They thought they'd be up 5-1 at this point."

Just 43 seconds later, Tony Amonte scored on a shot that on replays appeared to have been kicked in. The goal stood, and now, incredibly, the Canadians were trailing 3-2 with less than three minutes to play. After Wayne Gretzky missed an open net off a beautiful pass from Mark Messier, the kind of play the two had converted a hundred

Mantle could help us." Perhaps Hull's goal and Richter's goaling and the Hatcher brothers' defensive strength would become the stories that boys who watched Team USA play in 1996 would be telling each other as they took the ice in similar circumstances 20 years hence.

Winning the World Cup may have helped create a more favourable climate for the game's growth in the United States. The Americans beat the best team in the world, coming from behind to win the last game of the finals. Their goaltending was superb, as it must be any time a team wins a champi-

(ABOVE LEFT) Canada's Eric Desjardins fights for position with Keith Tkachuk. (ABOVE RIGHT) Tony Amonte (seen here moving in on Curtis Joseph) scored the winner in game three. (OPPOSITE) Doug Weight leaps into the welcoming arms of Brett Hull after Team USA defeated Canada 5-2 in the final game of the World Cup. Hull led the tournament with seven goals and 11 points in winning the first major championship of his career.

With less than four minutes to go, defenceman Brian Leetch stopped a bad clearing pass along the boards. He feathered a quick shot at the goal, and Brett Hull, with his stick well above the crossbar (legal height), deflected the puck into the net. Although the play was reviewed by the video goal judge, just like Yzerman's illegal score in game one, the goal

times before, Derian Hatcher scored an empty-netter. The U.S. went on to win the game 5-2, a score that had become emblematic of U.S. success. This was their fourth win of the seven games by a score of 5-2. The United States had won the inaugural World Cup of Hockey.

## A NEW TRADITION

"It is like a tribal storytelling," coach Wilson said of the victory. "You pass it on from generation to generation. There is nobody telling the stories about glorious victories in the past. If we could put ice in at Yankee Stadium, maybe the ghosts of Babe Ruth and Mickey

onship, but ultimately it was the players' belief in their own abilities that placed them first in their country's hockey history. In 1996 Team USA possessed an inner confidence that manifested itself in each key game it played – against Canada before the tournament began, against an underrated Russian team, and again against its greatest rival Canada when the championship was at stake. They believed and so they won; they won because they believed. "In the past, we said we could beat Canada," Doug Weight later opined. "But when we were in our hotel room, all alone, did we really believe it? Maybe not. This team believed it."

# CHAPTER 15

# BOWMAN'S INTERNATIONAL TEAM

1996-97 DETROIT RED WINGS

When Detroit coach Scotty Bowman acquired defenceman Viacheslav Fetisov from the New Jersey Devils in April 1995, many critics thought he was making a mistake. Why would the most successful coach in NHL history, with more than 1,000 wins and six Stanley Cups to his credit, want to deliberately create a team with a greater Soviet presence? True, Bowman had inherited a team clearly in need of improvement and direction, but surely after 28 years in the NHL he would see that his ever more international lineup wouldn't stand a chance against more North American-constructed teams. Kids in Canada and the United States grew up cherishing the Stanley Cup, a motivation most NHL coaches believed players from the Soviet Union lacked. As it turned out, Bowman knew exactly what he was doing. His thesis was that the Detroit roster didn't need a complete overhaul so much as fine-tuning. He didn't want to dismantle what he had inherited, just make it run better and more smoothly. In the context of the new polycultural, 26-team NHL of the 1990s, Bowman decided that he had to create a different kind of atmosphere at the Joe Louis Arena if Detroit were to challenge for the Stanley Cup any time soon. There were many styles of play being drawn on the modern chalkboard, and he opted to integrate them all, rather than rely on just one.

WHEN BOWMAN WAS ABLE TO ACQUIRE FETISOV FROM THE Devils for nothing more than a third-round draft choice, he didn't hesitate. He knew he was getting three players in one: a superb defenceman, an assistant coach for his young players, and a cultural hero for his trio of talented Soviet draft choices – Sergei Fedorov, Vladimir Konstantinov, and Vyacheslav Kozlov – who felt alienated from the North American game by their language, system of play, and citizenship. For them, Fetisov was the frontiersman who had cleared the perilous path from the land of impoverished Communist hockey to the wide-open riches of North America. He was at once their hero, mentor, and leader.

Bowman knew the impact that the legendary Fetisov would have on his Soviet players. He also believed that on a team captained by Steve Yzerman, Fetisov would be welcomed and admired for his superior on-ice ability. Like Bowman, "Stevie Y," leader of the Wings since his fourth year in the league in 1986, understood the potential advantage of the trade. The current Red Wings team was by far the best Detroit fans had seen in his 12 seasons in Motown, and Fetisov could help move it from the merely good to a Stanley Cup contender.

Fetisov had spent most of his playing career in Moscow before coming to North America in 1989, but he still had a few good years of playing left. His very presence in the NHL was culturally and politically important. For the many players skating in the Soviet Union – Communist CCCP – who aspired to NHL stardom, he was an icon. He had been drafted by Montreal in 1978, a time when no sane hockey person thought a Soviet national would ever sweat and swear on an NHL sheet of ice.

In 1983 Fetisov was redrafted by New Jersey, but continued to play for CSKA Moscow until 1989, when the Soviets falteringly began to permit a few of their aging players to come to North America. By then he was 31, had been an Iron Curtain star for 14 years, and had won a neck-load of gold medals at the World Junior Championships, World Championships, and Olympics. If he never took a single breath of rarefied NHL air, he would still have been considered the Bobby Orr of international hockey. But Fetisov had yet to prove himself in a more physically demanding league that played a schedule double the length of what he was used to. And so for him, coming to the NHL was equal parts politics and personal challenge.

Bowman, a man who always broke statistics down into ideas and plans, paired Fetisov on the blue line with young Konstantinov. He was sure the gaga-eyed "Vlad the Impaler" – a nickname earned from the sometimes vicious use of his stick – would worship every word of advice Fetisov imparted. And the two emerging Soviet forwards on the team – 26-year-old Fedorov and 23-year-old Kozlov – both played with greater confidence and motivation, not wanting to disappoint their elder statesman. Fedorov and Konstantinov had, in fact, played with Fetisov on CSKA. While the older Fetisov came to North America in 1989 with the Soviet Union's blessings, his two mates, the backbone of future national teams, had to defect to join the NHL. Of the three, Fedorov in particular embodied the next generation of Soviet player: the cocky, skilled, money-minded star. He was

## Fetisov had been drafted by Montreal in 1978, a time when no sane hockey person thought a Soviet national would ever sweat and swear on an NHL sheet of ice.

good-looking and flashy, and played in Nike-sponsored white skates. In short, the teen heartthrob was everything Fetisov wasn't allowed to be under the 1980s Soviet regime.

### BEATEN BY "THE TRAP"

Just weeks after Fetisov joined their blue line the Red Wings advanced to the 1995 Stanley Cup finals against the New Jersey Devils, a franchise whose playoff history could be encapsulated on a single strand of DNA. Detroit was irrefutably the better team; it had won seven Cups since 1926 while New Jersey hadn't been to the finals since they joined the league in 1974 as the Kansas City Scouts. Detroit's long and storied tradition of success should have intimidated the expansion Devils – but it didn't.

Ironically, the Devils were coached by Jacques Lemaire, centreman with the same Canadiens that Bowman had guided to four consecutive Stanley Cups in the 1970s. If Lemaire had become a winning coach, it was in part because he had watched and learned from Bowman for so many successful years. It was also because he deployed a system of hockey that, for a time, was unbeatable. It was called "the trap."

The trap was the anthrax of hockey, a strategy implemented by coaches of teams lacking offensive talent or imagination. It was counter-offensive, anti-entertaining un-hockey, boring not only to watch but to play. A trap team didn't give up any scoring chances, and almost never created any either. Just as Italian soccer is often called negative soccer, so too may the trap be called negative hockey.

The trap had firmly established itself in the NHL during the 1993-94 season when coach Roger Neilson of the expansion Florida Panthers used the system as a way to keep his talent-thin team competitive. Within three years, the Panthers were in the Stanley Cup finals and the trap had become the system of choice around the league. Barry Smith, Detroit's assistant coach, knew much about the trap, having coached in Italy, Norway, and Sweden. It had originated in Russia, but Swedish coach Lasse Falk perfected the technique in his country with Stockholm AIK. Both countries' national teams had won World Championships using the trap, and this was how Smith learned of the strategy.

There was really only one surefire way to beat the trap: score first and force the trapping team to go on the attack. But Detroit was able to score the first goal only once in the Stanley Cup finals against the Devils, in game two, and that lead lasted less than three minutes. They led again later in that game, 2-1 in the third, but New Jersey scored three times in the final 10 minutes to crush Detroit and take a 2-0 lead in games. The Devils were never in

(LEFT) Detroit's Steve Yzerman was without question the most popular athlete in the Motor City, as his picture on this cereal box attests. (OPPOSITE) A friendly arm wrestle provides a rare break from Soviet coach Viktor Tikhonov's austere if not altogether cruel training methods.

Fedorov in particular embodied the next generation of Soviet player; the cocky, skilled, money-minded star. He was good-looking and flashy, and played in Nike-sponsored white skates. In short, the teen heartthrob was everything Fetisov wasn't allowed to be under the 1980s Soviet regime.

trouble again. In each game the Wings faced an impenetrable wall at their own blue line – five New Jersey Devils who refused to cede centre ice. In game four Detroit was trailing just 3-2 entering the third period but managed exactly one shot in the last 20 minutes, whereas the Devils scored twice. After four games the Cup was on its way to Jersey, the Wings having been outscored in the series 16-7. The Devils didn't out-play Detroit; they de-played them.

In the Detroit dressing room after the deciding game the players were not so much upset as stupefied; not so much disappointed as confused. They couldn't believe they had generated so few scoring chances, that they were simply unable to beat the trap.

### BOWMAN'S CREATION

Just four months after the defeat that had left "Hockeytown" fans burning with indignation, Bowman acquired centre Igor Larionov from the San Jose Sharks, the first time a coach had acquired a player because of his nationality (read his natural style of play) and the logical culmination of Bowman's international strategy. Bowman's plan was brilliantly simple. By adding a fifth Soviet player to the team he could use his Russians as a single unit, as Soviet coaches had always done with their forwards and defencemen. He was the first NHL coach to attempt such a plan. He believed that their twirling, turning, ziggurat-style offence would flummox the dreaded trap, and that the chemistry between the five – their ability to read each other's moves, passes, and habits – would overcome strictly defensive teams.

Larionov's impact was felt immediately. Detroit won the first six games he played with them, including an 11-1 hammering of Montreal at the Molson Centre that was Patrick Roy's last game with les Canadiens. Then, after a single loss, the Wings won another nine in a row.

Now that his Soviet five had quickly proved their ability to skate through the trap, Bowman set out to adapt it to his own team's strategy. After all, any system that forced turnovers inside the other team's blue line couldn't be all bad. For this he relied on Barry Smith, who had been Bowman's assistant for his two Stanley Cups in Pittsburgh in 1991 and '92 and had been hired by the Wings at Bowman's insistence when Scotty came to Detroit in 1993. Bowman called his system the "left-wing lock." The difference between it and the trap wasn't much more than semantics, however. Each was designed to force turnovers and each depended primarily on the counter-attack for scoring chances. When the Wings were without the puck they'd try to contain the other team in a small area by quickly outnumbering them, forcing a bad pass. Bowman had dubbed it "left wing" because that was the side where he preferred his men to force the play.

To help defeat the trap Bowman also created the perfect offensive strategy, a sort of second breakout play to dismantle the opposition wall at the blue line when his team had possession. Typically, when a defenceman has the puck behind his own net he'll pass to a winger waiting along the boards at the faceoff circle. The winger will either skate with the puck or, if an opponent comes at him, drop it right back to the same defenceman. Instead, Bowman told his defencemen to hold onto the puck, then pass to a winger near the blue line. When the trapping players on the other team swarmed to that side of the ice to force a turnover, the winger in possession would drop the puck back to his defenceman, who would rifle a quick pass to the winger on the far side of the ice where there was nothing but open space and rinkside advertising. This play ensured that the Wings usually maintained possession and were able to dump the puck deep into the offensive zone, making the trapping team vulnerable.

With his five-man Soviet unit and his anti-trap system in place, Bowman had created a team that would play twirl-and-swirl hockey when the Soviets were on and trap hockey when the other three forward lines took the ice, a virtually foolproof strategy for winning consistently. As the 1995-96 season progressed and the Red Wings' overall lead in the standings grew ever more insurmountable, everyone

and team misfortune. He was the Wings' most experienced player, its most desperate for success, and its emotional rock.

## THE DEFINING DEFEAT

As the league became more defensive in the 1990s, coach Bowman had transformed Yzerman into a two-way player, thus subtly enhancing his on-ice role. Now Yzerman not only scored, he blocked shots, backchecked, forechecked, pokechecked, rubbed his man out along the boards, took all key faceoffs, killed penalties, and played with a two-way pride that seemed heaven-sent. His Gretzky-like intensity

which was every bit as skilled, every bit as tough, and now much fresher than the Wings.

The 1996 semi-finals between Detroit and Colorado got more bitter and ferocious with each game. In game three the Avalanche's Claude Lemieux sucker-punched Kozlov to the head and was given a game misconduct and a one-game suspension. Then, midway through the first period of the sixth game in Denver, with Detroit facing elimination, Lemieux cross-checked centre Kris Draper into the boards from behind. Draper's jaw and cheekbone smashed into the top of the dasher right at the Red Wings bench.

*(ABOVE LEFT)* A Soviet chance on the Czech goal. The Soviets' great Iron Curtain rivals were the underdog Czechs, who had beaten them in the 1972 World Championships. *(ABOVE RIGHT)* For all their pride and independence the Soviets relied on Canadian-made equipment, including their Montreal-brand sticks. (Slava Fetisov, # 2, is front and centre.)

began to believe that this was Detroit's year for the Cup. At the hub of this wheel of success was Steve Yzerman, the longest-serving captain in NHL history. He had been a 50-goal, 100-point man on terrible Red Wings teams dating back to 1983, when he had joined Detroit as an 18-year-old rookie. Over his 14 years in the NHL Yzerman had experienced the full range of playoff failure, nightly loss,

each night not only set the tone for the Cup-contending team, it inspired the players around him to play better on every shift.

By the trading deadline in mid-March 1996, with first place overall a virtual *fait accompli* for the Wings, Bowman became obsessed with breaking his own Montreal record of 60 wins in a season. He kept pushing the team when it might have been better to rest some players and save their intensity for a run at the Cup. By the time the playoffs arrived the Wings had indeed set an NHL record with 62 wins, but they were worn out from the effort. After playing tough early-round series with Winnipeg and St. Louis they weren't prepared for a team like Colorado,

Bleeding and semi-conscious, he slumped to the ice as the Detroit players rose in concern and protest. Lemieux's hit had violated the Stanley Cup code of ethics, which although demanding relentless tenacity and playing even in extreme pain beyond what the body could reasonably be expected to endure, naturally drew the line at vicious play. This hit wasn't Stanley Cup tough or playoff intense; it was below-the-belt dirty, plain and simple. The Red Wings could not retaliate for fear of a penalty that would jeopardize a game tied 1-1. (Detroit ended up losing 4-1.)

Draper was a good kid in only his third season with Detroit. He was just beginning to establish himself as a regular and had earned every minute of his ice time. Lemieux was a well-known agitator and cheap-shot pest, but this time his actions went well beyond accepted tactics. For his horrific check Lemieux received a slim two-game suspension for the ensuing Stanley Cup finals, further infuriating the Red Wings. But the Draper hit transformed the Wings from a collection of fine players into a true team, a hockey-playing family that would stick together through adversity. Not only did they now have a tenable goal for next season – the Stanley Cup – they also had a rallying point to help get them there – vindication for a vicious cheap shot. Draper required major plastic surgery over the summer to set his face straight, and wasn't fully healthy until training camp in September. The Wings might have been eliminated from the '96 playoffs, but they were a stronger and more determined team for it.

Almost every team that has won the Stanley Cup in the modern era has first suffered heart-rending defeat. Bobby Orr's Boston Bruins lost in the 1969 semifinals before winning the following year. The Philadelphia Flyers fell short in the 1973 semis before winning in '74; the Habs lost in the semis in '75 before winning in '76. While Montreal was winning four in a row they were beating the Islanders, who were learning how-to and would ultimately dethrone the Canadiens to win four of their own. In so doing the Islanders were beating the Oilers, who would form a 1980s dynasty. As one of the teams Edmonton usually beat, Calgary went on to win their own Cup in 1989. And finally, New Jersey lost in '94 before winning the next year. It seems that falling just short of the ultimate goal is essential to gaining the requisite experience and desire to win the Cup, to knowing how much controlled emotion and passion, not just skill, are needed to play under the ultimate pressure.

Detroit's Scotty Bowman, the only man to coach in five decades and win Cups with three teams.

## THE FINAL INGREDIENT

Two games into the 1996-97 season, Bowman sent Paul Coffey and Keith Primeau to Hartford for Brendan Shanahan, a power forward who could hit hard and score fast. Other than trading for goaler Mike Vernon in the summer of 1994, this was the only significant non-Soviet deal in Bowman's first four years at the Joe, and proved to be the final piece of Detroit's Stanley Cup puzzle. And while Primeau seemed destined for stardom, Bowman wanted someone who already had the gut-wrenching hunger needed to win in the playoffs.

After 10 years and four NHL teams Shanahan had been in the league long enough to know that he didn't have many chances left to win the Cup. The very model of a team player, Shanahan developed a hatred for

the Avalanche and Lemieux as soon as he put on a Red Wings sweater. He was exactly the kind of player the team could have used against Colorado the previous spring to nullify the impact of Lemieux's hit on Draper, either by delivering one of clean but equal severity or scoring a power-play goal.

Detroit's 1996-97 regular season again proved the relative unimportance of the 82-game preparation for the playoffs. The Wings won only 38 games, some 24 fewer than the previous year; finished with 94 points, 38 fewer; and were sixth overall. They were no longer Cup favourites. Bowman hadn't altered his team over the summer, and opinion around the league held that Detroit's Stanley Cup chances had come and gone the previous spring against the much younger and equally talented Avalanche. The regular season had featured only one night on the calendar worth circling – March 26, 1997 – when Colorado visited the Joe Louis Arena for the first time since the Draper incident.

Predictably, all hell broke loose. Late in the first period the Wings' Darren McCarty dropped Lemieux to the ice after holding him up with his fists for a time, and even the two goalies – Patrick Roy and Mike Vernon – took part in a brawl that engaged all 12 players on ice while Kris Draper looked on from the Detroit bench. There were nine fights all told, including one between Shanahan and Adam Foote. It was Detroit's night to exact sweet revenge, the kind of necessary retribution that only the closest of teammates would seek for one of their own.

That enmity was still front and centre a few weeks later when the Wings faced Colorado in the semifinals, yet the Detroit players harnessed their anger and played fierce but disciplined hockey while the Avs lost all control. In game four Detroit took advantage of an incredible 13 power plays and hammered Colorado 6-0 to take a 3-1 series lead. "You look at last year's conference final and it was probably a role reversal," Colorado coach Marc Crawford conceded. "We were the team winning the battles. We were the team that got to the puck quicker. We were the team that looked desperate and a team possessed to win."

In the first period of game six, with the series so close to won, Sergei Fedorov left the ice with an apparent injury to his diaphragm. Russian masseur Sergei Mnatsakanov was ministering to a prone Fedorov on the trainer's table when Fetisov burst into the dressing room. A heated conversation in Russian ensued. Fetisov asked the masseur if Fedorov were seriously hurt, and the trainer replied in the negative. Then Fetisov spoke sternly to his young, white-skated comrade: the two of them were leaving this room together, voluntarily or otherwise. Fedorov got up from the table and returned to the ice to score the game-winning, series-winning goal off a perfect Kozlov pass in the third. Appropriately, Shanahan added an empty netter, assisted by Larionov. And it was only poetic justice that Lemieux's hit, which had helped Colorado win the Stanley Cup the year before, contributed to that team's undoing in 1997.

## THE DEFINING VICTORY

The '97 Stanley Cup final between Detroit and Philadelphia looked to be a classic confrontation: Eric Lindros and his up-and-coming

Just as important, the Red Wings also got better goaltending, so often the key to playoff victory. Bowman had made 24-year-old Chris Osgood the number one goalie during the regular season, but in the playoffs it was thirtysomething Mike Vernon who played every minute for the Wings. Bowman knew he needed a money goaler, and so had acquired this Conn Smythe Trophy winner of Calgary's 1989 Cup team. Now Vernon performed to expectation. Meanwhile Philadelphia general manager Bob Clarke had gambled on veteran Ron Hextall. But when coach Terry Murray put Garth Snow in

Hakan Andersson and Tomas Storm at "the Factory," a dingy arena in Stockholm renowned for producing skilled players. And so it was that a Canadian with Swedish training playing on a team with a five-man Soviet unit won the Stanley Cup. Detroit was the first NHL champion with an undeniably international makeup.

William "Scotty" Bowman, the father of this United Nations Red Wing family, had never seemed so content or relaxed in victory as when Steve Yzerman lifted the Cup high in the Joe Louis air the night of June 7, 1997. Although this was Bowman's seventh NHL championship, his players urged him to hurry

(ABOVE LEFT) Avs goalie Patrick Roy (LEFT) and Detroit's Mike Vernon duke it out during the retributive brawl the season following Claude Lemieux's vicious hit on Kris Draper. (ABOVE RIGHT) Rod Brind'Amour (FOREGROUND) and the Flyers met their match in the Stanley Cup finals, being swept by a single-minded Red Wings team led by Steve Yzerman. (OPPOSITE) The victorious Wings hoist the Stanley Cup at the Joe Louis Arena, celebrating their first championship in 40 years.

Flyers against Steve Yzerman and his now-or-never Wings. But after eliminating Colorado it almost didn't matter who the Red Wings played; they weren't going to lose. Their experience had given them an intensity and focus that the Flyers, never having been there themselves, could neither match nor sustain.

the blue ice for game two after a shaky opening game from Hextall the Wings gained a huge psychological advantage that the Flyers never overcame.

Darren McCarty's goal midway through the third period of game four won Detroit the Stanley Cup. With the score tied 1-1 he made a highlight-reel rush in which he deked Flyers' defenceman Janne Niinimaa and goaler Ron Hextall out of their proverbial jocks. McCarty, no offensive wizard by any stretch, had been encouraged by assistant coach Barry Smith to work on his skills during the off-season. For the past two summers he had practised the fine art of stickhandling with Swedish hockey experts

to the dressing room and put on his skates for a victory lap with the Cup. While he had dreamed of winning the big prize as a teenager during his days with the Montreal Junior Canadiens, his career had been cut short by a serious head injury. Now 63 years old, he displayed an uninhibited enthusiasm with the Wings that his austere Montreal countenance would never have permitted on Forum ice 20 years earlier. The coach watched Shanahan, Draper, Fetisov, and Larionov all take victory laps, then hoisted the heavy Cup high above his head and went for a skate of his own. Only one thing was on his mind – the sheer pleasure of success.

# APPENDIX

# TEAM ROSTERS

The following rosters are in chronological and alphabetical order and include everyone who played for the team during the season or series highlighted in the book. Coaches and other key personnel are at the end of each list. In one case (the Preston Rivulettes), the roster covers a team's decade of existence.

**LEGEND**

*Elected into the Hockey Hall of Fame*
*Member of the International Ice Hockey Federation Hall of Fame*
*Still active*

### 1924 TORONTO GRANITES

Jack Cameron, Ernie Collett, Bert McCaffery, Harold McMunn, Dunc Munro *(captain)*, Beattie Ramsay, Sig Slater, Hooley Smith*, Harry Watson**, Frank Rankin*(coach)*, William Hewitt**(manager)*.

### 1930s PRESTON RIVULETTES

Marie Beilstein, Dorothy Bricker, Ruth Dargel, Eleanor Fairgrieves, Marg Gabitas, Violet Hall, Betty Hallman, Gladys Hawkins, Fay Hilborn, Norma Hipel, Marie Kurt, Sheila Lahey, Winnie Makcrow, Pat Marriott, Myrtle Parr, Gladys Pitcher, Hilda Ranscombe, Nellie Ranscombe, Marion Reid, Midge Robertson, Helen Sault, Helen Schmuck, Marm Schmuck, Toddy Webb, Alvis Williams, Herb Fach *(coach)*, Marvin Dykeman *(manager)*, Mrs. Olive Dykeman *(chaperone)*.

## 1947-48 TORONTO MAPLE LEAFS

Syl Apps*(captain), Bill Barilko, Max Bentley*, Garth Boesch, Turk Broda*, Les Costello, Bill Ezinicki, Ted Kennedy*, Joe Klukay, Vic Lynn, Howie Meeker, Don Metz, Nick Metz, Gus Mortson, Phil Samis, Sid Smith, Wally Stanowski, Jim Thomson, Harry Watson*, Happy Day*(coach), Conn Smythe*(general manager).

## 1949-50 DETROIT RED WINGS

Sid Abel* (captain), Pete Babando, Steve Black, Joe Carveth, Gerry Couture, Al Dewsbury, Lee Fogolin, George Gee, Gordie Howe*, Red Kelly*, Ted Lindsay*, Harry Lumley*, Clare Martin, Jim McFadden, Max McNab, Marty Pavelich, Jimmy Peters, Marcel Pronovost*, Leo Reise, Jack Stewart*, Johnny Wilson, Larry Wilson, Tommy Ivan* (coach), Jack Adams*(general manager).

## 1952 EDMONTON MERCURYS

George Abel, John Davies, Billy Dawe (captain), Bruce Dickson, Don Gauf, Billy Gibson, Ralph Hansch, Bob Meyers, David Miller, Eric Patterson, Tom Pollock, Al Purvis, Gordie Robertson, Louis Secco, Frank Sullivan, Robert Watt, Lou Holmes (coach), Jim Christianson (manager).

## 1959-60 MONTREAL CANADIENS

Ralph Backstrom, Jean Béliveau*, Marcel Bonin, Bernie Geoffrion*, Phil Goyette, Doug Harvey*, Bill Hicke, Charlie Hodge, Tom Johnson*, Al Langlois, Don Marshall, Ab McDonald, Dickie Moore*, Jacques Plante*, André Pronovost, Claude Provost, Henri Richard*, Maurice Richard* (captain), Jean-Guy Talbot, Bob Turner, Toe Blake*(coach), Frank Selke*(general manager).

## 1966-67 TORONTO MAPLE LEAFS

George Armstrong*(captain), Bob Baun, Johnny Bower*, Brian Conacher, Ron Ellis, Aut Erickson, Bruce Gamble, Larry Hillman, Tim Horton*, Larry Jeffrey, Red Kelly*, Dave Keon*, Frank Mahovlich*, Milan Marcetta, Jim Pappin, Marcel Pronovost*, Bob Pulford*, Terry Sawchuk*, Eddie Shack, Allan Stanley*, Pete Stemkowski, Mike Walton, Punch Imlach*(coach, general manager).

## 1969-70 BOSTON BRUINS

Don Awrey, Johnny Bucyk*, Wayne Carleton, Wayne Cashman, Gerry Cheevers*, Gary Doak, Phil Esposito*, Ted Green, Ken Hodge, Eddie Johnston, Bill Lesuk, Jim Lorentz, Don Marcotte, John McKenzie, Bobby Orr*, Derek Sanderson, Dan Schock, Dallas Smith, Rick Smith, Bill Speer, Fred Stanfield, Ed Westfall, Harry Sinden* (coach), Milt Schmidt* (general manager).

## 1972 TEAM CANADA

Don Awrey, Red Berenson, Gary Bergman, Wayne Cashman, Bobby Clarke*, Yvan Cournoyer*, Ken Dryden*, Ron Ellis, Phil Esposito*, Tony Esposito*, Rod Gilbert, Bill Goldsworthy, Vic Hadfield, Paul Henderson, Dennis Hull, Guy Lapointe*, Frank Mahovlich*, Pete Mahovlich, Stan Mikita*, J.P. Parisé, Brad Park*, Gilbert Perreault*, Jean Ratelle*, Mickey Redmond, Serge Savard*, Rod Seiling, Pat Stapleton, Bill White, Harry Sinden*(coach), John Ferguson (coach).

## 1976-77 MONTREAL CANADIENS

Pierre Bouchard, Rick Chartraw, Yvan Cournoyer*(captain), Ken Dryden*, Brian Engblom, Bob Gainey*, Rejean Houle, Doug Jarvis, Guy Lafleur*, Yvon Lambert, Guy Lapointe*, Michel Larocque, Jacques Lemaire*, Pete Mahovlich, Pierre Mondou, Bill Nyrop, Mike Polich, Doug Risebrough, Jim Roberts, Larry Robinson*, Serge Savard*, Steve Shutt, Mario Tremblay, Murray Wilson, Scotty Bowman*(coach), Sam Pollock*(general manager).

## 1987 TEAM CANADA

Glenn Anderson, Ray Bourque*, Paul Coffey*, Doug Crossman, Kevin Dineen*, Grant Fuhr, Mike Gartner, Doug Gilmour, Michel Goulet*, Wayne Gretzky**(captain), Craig Hartsburg, Dale Hawerchuk, Claude Lemieux*, Mario Lemieux*, Mark Messier*, Larry Murphy*, James Patrick*, Brian Propp, Normand Rochefort, Brent Sutter, Rick Tocchet*, Mike Keenan (coach).

## 1987-88 EDMONTON OILERS

Keith Acton, Glenn Anderson, Jeff Beukeboom, Geoff Courtnall, Grant Fuhr*, Randy Gregg, Wayne Gretzky**(captain), Dave Hannan, Charlie Huddy, Mike Krushelnyski, Jari Kurri*, Normand Lacombe, Kevin Lowe, Craig MacTavish, Kevin McClelland, Marty McSorley*, Mark Messier*, Craig Muni, Bill Ranford*, Craig Simpson, Steve Smith*, Esa Tikkanen, Glen Sather* (coach, general manager).

## 1995 CANADIAN NATIONAL JUNIOR TEAM

Chad Allan, Jason Allison*, Nolan Baumgartner*, Jason Botterill*, Dan Cloutier*, Larry Courville*, Alexandre Daigle*, Eric Daze*, Shean Donovan*, Jeff Friesen*, Todd Harvey*(captain), Ed Jovanovski*, Bryan McCabe*, Marty Murray*, Jeff O'Neill*, Denis Pederson*, Wade Redden*, Jamie Rivers*, Ryan Smyth*, Lee Sorochan*, Jamie Storr*, Darcy Tucker*, Don Hay (coach).

## 1996 TEAM USA

Tony Amonte*, Shawn Chambers*, Chris Chelios*, Adam Deadmarsh*, Bill Guerin*, Derian Hatcher*, Kevin Hatcher*, Guy Hebert*, Phil Housley*, Brett Hull*, Steve Konowalchuk*, Pat LaFontaine, John LeClair*, Brian Leetch*(captain), Shawn McEachern*, Mike Modano*, Joel Otto, Mike Richter*, Brian Rolston*, Mathieu Schneider*, Bryan Smolinski*, Gary Suter*, Keith Tkachuk*, Doug Weight*, Scott Young*, Ron Wilson (coach).

## 1996-97 DETROIT RED WINGS

Doug Brown*, Mathieu Dandenault*, Kris Draper*, Anders Eriksson*, Sergei Fedorov*, Viacheslav Fetisov, Brent Gilchrist*, Kevin Hodson*, Tomas Holmstrom*, Mike Knuble*, Joey Kocur*, Vladimir Konstantinov, Vyacheslav Kozlov*, Martin Lapointe*, Igor Larionov*, Nicklas Lidstrom*, Jamie Macoun, Kirk Maltby*, Darren McCarty*, Dmitri Mironov*, Larry Murphy*, Chris Osgood*, Bob Rouse*, Brendan Shanahan*, Aaron Ward*, Steve Yzerman*(captain), Scotty Bowman (coach), Ken Holland (general manager).

Every effort has been made to contact copyright holders. In the event of omission or error, the editor should be notified at Otherwise Inc., 356A Queen Street West, Toronto, Ontario, M5V 2A2.

Some agency and archive names have been abbreviated in this source list:

AO: Archives of Ontario
AP: AP/Wide World Photos
BBS: Bruce Bennett Studios
CEA: City of Edmonton Archives
CP: CP Archives
CSHF: Canada Sports Hall of Fame
CTA: City of Toronto Archives
HHOF: Hockey Hall of Fame
IHA: International Hockey Archives
NAC: National Archives of Canada
MTL: Metro Toronto Library

## OPENING PAGE

Sanderson: London Life-Portnoy/HHOF

## TITLE PAGE

Detroit-Leafs: Imperial Oil-Turofsky/HHOF

## COPYRIGHT PAGE

Detroit-Canadiens: HHOF

## INTRODUCTION

p. 8 Detail of team picture: HHOF; p. 10 Montreal AAA game advertisement: NAC; p. 11 Lord Stanley: HHOF.

## THE FIRST GREAT AMATEURS

p. 12 Detail of team picture: IHA; p. 14 Watson's telegram: Dave Sandford/HHOF; p. 15 (clockwise from top) Team portrait: HHOF; Preacher in cockpit: NAC PA-172550; Soldier performing ablutions: NAC PA-1193; Billy Bishop: NAC PA-1675; Lester Pearson: NAC PA-110824; p. 16 (top) "Jane Avril" print: Henri de Toulouse-Lautrec; Ship scene: Hans Fennekahl; p. 17 Opening ceremonies: HHOF; p. 18 Sonja Henie: MTL; p. 18-19 Canada-USA game action: IOC/Olympic Museum Collections.

## WOMEN'S FINEST HOUR

p. 20 Detail of team picture: HHOF; p. 22 Winnipeg-Preston game advertisement: Dave Sandford/HHOF; p. 23 Rivs ball team: Betty Barnes Collection; p. 24 (left) Hilda et al.: CTA; (right) Relay team: CSHF; p. 25 Hilda: HHOF; p. 26 Rivs on bus top: Betty Barnes Collection; p. 27 Team portrait: Betty Barnes Collection.

## THE TEAM SMYTHE BUILT

p. 28 Detail from Leaf practice: HHOF; p. 30 Leaf calendar: HHOF; p. 31 Smythe in dressing room: AO F223; p. 32 (left to right) Leaf practice: HHOF; Smythe in Caen: AO F223; Battle

for Ortona: NAC PA-124364; p. 33 (left) Hip check: AO 4844; (right) Young fans at MLG: Imperial Oil-Turofsky Collection/HHOF; pp. 34-35 Maple Leaf Gardens interior: HHOF; p. 36 (left) Cartoon: HHOF; (right) Syl Apps Beehive Card: Dave Sandford/HHOF; p. 37 (clockwise from top) Victory parade: AO 4848; Happy Day drinking from Cup: HHOF; Leafs celebrate: AO 4848.

## THE PRODUCTION LINE

p. 38 Detail of Red Wings logo: HHOF; p. 40 Detroit area map: MTL; p. 41 Celebrating Red Wings: HHOF; p. 42 Detroit-Chicago game action: HHOF; p. 43 Jack Adams: HHOF; p. 44 (top) Wings at breakfast: Detroit Free Press; (bottom) SI cover: HHOF; p. 45 Assembly line: David Peskin; p. 46 Semi-comatose Howe: Imperial Oil-Turofsky/HHOF; p. 47 Howe and Cup: HHOF.

## THE FORGOTTEN AMATEURS

p. 48 Mercs logo: CEA EA-600-3524b; p. 50 Mercs sweater: HHOF; p. 51 (top) Jim Christianson: CEA EA-600-3622b; (bottom) Car dealership: CEA EA-88-139; p. 52 Celebration dinner: CEA EA-10-2673; p. 53 Mercs sweater: HHOF; p. 54 Game action: IHA; p. 55 Gold medal celebrations: Bettman/Corbis.

## GREATEST OF THE GREATS

p. 56 Player detail: NAC PA-194044; p. 58 Hockey card: Dave Sandford/HHOF; p. 59 (clockwise from top) Forum at game time: NAC PA-194041; Toe Blake: Frank Prazak/HHOF; Rocket's line: NAC PA-194044; p. 60 Rocket and Irvin: Montreal Gazette; p. 61 Habs on Broadway: Montreal Gazette; p. 62 Plante and Hay: Montreal Gazette; p. 63 Béliveau and fans: Frank Prazak/HHOF; p. 64 Plante's mask: Doug MacLellan/HHOF; pp. 64-65 Cup presentation: NAC PA-119859.

## THE OVER-THE-HILL GANG

p. 66 Detail of Leaf sweater: Imperial Oil-Turofsky/HHOF; p. 68 Bower record: Dave Sandford/HHOF; p. 69 Sawchuk and Bower: Graphic Artists/HHOF; p. 70 Frank Mahovlich: HHOF; p. 71 Bobby Hull: NAC PA-184537; p. 72 (left to right) Horton and Bower: Frank Prazak/HHOF; Expo 67: MTL; Punch Imlach: Graphic Artists/HHOF; p. 73 Cup celebrations: HHOF.

## BOBBY ORR TAKES FLIGHT

p. 74 Cup and detail of team portrait: IHA; p. 76 Bruins pennant: Dave Sandford/HHOF; p. 77 (clockwise from top) Orr in action: Frank Prazak/HHOF; Kraut Line: IHA; Harry Sinden: IHA; p. 78 Leafs-Bruins game action: Graphic Artists/HHOF; p. 79 Alan Eagleson: HHOF; p. 80 Green-Maki incident: CP; p. 81 (left) Hodge-Espo-Cashman: O-Pee-Chee/HHOF; (right) Cheevers in action: IHA; p. 82 Rick Smith: IHA; p. 83 (clockwise from top left) Orr shoots: IHA; Orr scores: IHA; Orr flies: IHA/Ray Lussier.

## US AGAINST THEM

p. 84 Cournoyer's back: IHA; p. 86 Moscow tickets: Gary Smith Collection/HHOF; p. 87 Trudeau at opening ceremonies: NAC PA-193986; p. 88 (clockwise from top left) Espo in action: IHA; Kharlamov in action: IHA; Soviet bench: HHOF; p. 89 Espo hockey card: Dave Sandford/HHOF; p. 90 Ken and Lynda

Dryden: Brian Pickell; p. 91 Teams enter ice together in Moscow: Denis Brodeur; p. 92 School children: CP; p. 93 Henderson scores for Canada: IHA/Denis Brodeur.

## THE EXECUTIVE CLASS

p. 94 Habs logo detail: Montreal Gazette; p. 96 Béliveau on cereal box: Dave Sandford/HHOF; p. 97 (clockwise from top) Parent stops Gainey: Denis Brodeur; Habs-Flyers fight: BBS; Pollock and Ferguson: Montreal Gazette; p. 98 (left) Guy Lafleur: BBS; (right) Ken Dryden: BBS; p. 99 Scotty Bowman: IHA; p. 100 (left) Bob Gainey: IHA; The Game: Ken Dryden; p. 101 (clockwise from top) Mondou and Cheevers: IHA; On-ice Cup celebrations: Denis Brodeur; Cup parade: Frank Prazak/HHOF.

## CANADA-SOVIET DÉJÀ VU

p. 102 Logo detail: BBS; p. 104 Program: Dave Sandford/HHOF; p. 105 Wayne Gretzky: IHA; p.106 Mario Lemieux: BBS; p. 108 Banners: IHA; p. 109 (clockwise from top) Gretzky and Lemieux: BBS; Canada-Czech game action: BBS; Mark Messier: BBS.

## HOCKEY'S GREATEST FAMILY

p. 110 Detail of Oilers' crest: BBS; p. 112 Cereal box: Dave Sandford/HHOF; p. 113 (top) Glen Sather: BBS; (bottom) MacTavish and Messier: BBS; p. 114 Edmonton-Boston game action: BBS; p. 115 Denis Potvin: Montreal Gazette; p. 116 (left) Edmonton-Boston fog: BBS; Boston Garden in dark: BBS; p. 117 (clockwise from top) On-ice portrait: BBS; Gretzky with Stanley Cup: BBS; Gretzky and Krushelnyski with Cup: BBS.

## PROGRAMMED TO PERFECTION

p. 118 Sweater detail: BBS; p. 120 The Hockey News: Dave Sandford/HHOF; p. 121 Canadian Juniors during warmup: Doug MacLellan/HHOF; p. 122 (left) Canada-USA game action: BBS; Canada-Sweden game action: Doug MacLellan/HHOF; p. 123 Jamie Storr: Doug MacLellan/HHOF; p. 124 (left) Darcy Tucker: HHOF; (right) WJC Media Guide: Dave Sandford/HHOF; p. 125 (clockwise from top) Gold medal ceremonies: Doug MacLellan/HHOF; Celebrating with fans: Doug MacLellan/HHOF; Handshakes: Doug MacLellan/HHOF.

## WORLD CUP OF WONDERS

p. 126 Team USA sweater detail: IHA; p. 128 World Cup tickets: Dave Sandford/HHOF; p. 129 Miracle on Ice: IHA; p. 130 Alexei Yashin: Doug MacLellan/HHOF; p. 131 World Cup trophy: IHA; p. 132 (left) Canada-USA game action: BBS; (right) Canada-USA game action: BBS; p. 133 Hull and Weight celebrate: Doug MacLellan/HHOF.

## BOWMAN'S INTERNATIONAL TEAM

p. 134 Red Wing detail: Doug MacLellan/HHOF; p. 136 Cereal box: Dave Sandford/HHOF; p. 137 Soviets arm wrestling: Tarasov; p. 138 (left) Soviet-Czech game action: Miles Nadal/HHOF; (right) Fetisov on bench: IHA; p. 139 Scotty Bowman: IHA; p. 140 (left) Roy-Vernon fight: AP; (right) Philadelphia-Detroit game action: BBS; p. 141 Hoisting the Cup: BBS.

## APPENDIX

p. 142 Maple Leaf Gardens interior: HHOF.